THE COMPLETE IDIOT'S GUIDE® TO

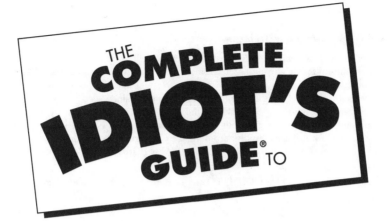

Managing Your Time

Third Edition

by Jeff Davidson, MBA, CMC

ALPHA

A Pearson Education Company

Publisher: *Marie Butler-Knight*
Product Manager: *Phil Kitchel*
Managing Editor: *Jennifer Chisholm*
Senior Acquisitions Editor: *Renee Wilmeth*
Development Editor: *Amy Gordon*
Production Editor: *Billy Fields*
Copy Editor: *Krista Hansing*
Illustrator: *Chris Eliopolous*
Cover/Book Designer: *Trina Wurst*
Indexer: *Brad Herriman*
Layout/Proofreading: *Angela Calvert, Svetlana Dominguez, Mary Hunt*

Contents at a Glance

Contents

Appendixes

Foreword

The twenty-first century, we were foretold, would be characterized by paperless offices, video telephones, and perhaps travel in hovercrafts. As late as the 1970s, some futurists proudly proclaimed that the work week would drop to 35, or even 30 hours and that too much leisure time would present a major challenge.

Few people could foresee the impact of the Internet, the "24 × 7" society, globalization, the clash of civilizations, and a variety of other developments that have had a dramatic impact on not just our culture, but cultures worldwide. As Jeff Davidson convincingly explains in the coming pages, society seems at times to be racing ahead faster than anyone's comfort level, toward ends that we can only imagine. While hundreds of books on time management, software, technological innovations, and a variety of other related tools have been created in recent years, when you consider your own career and life, and those of the people around you, it seems there is even more to do than before. Individually and collectively, we seem to be a time-challenged people with no solutions in sight.

You can fantasize about having 36- or 40-hour workweeks, but that's not going to happen. You can surmise what it would be like to be independently wealthy, to not commute to work and fight with all the other salaried drones seeking to carve out a living for themselves. Yet, even if the physical length of the day was longer and you had multimillions of dollars, you'd likely discover that the day still seemed to race by.

Jeff maintains that your life will stay the same until you recognize that the sheer number of items competing for your time and attention is increasing at an unrelenting pace. More time in the day, more wealth, or more support services wouldn't be enough for you to stem the tide of the ever-increasing array of news, information, bulletins, broadcasts, competitor products, and service information that finds its way to your mind.

Even if you knew, without question, that you would live to be 105, having 25 to 40 more years than your counterparts of yesteryear, it would be to no avail if each day raced by at the same speed or faster than it does now.

With this in mind, Jeff shows that the only sane route to managing your day, your week, your career, and your life, is to recognize that you have to make key choices—choices as to where you will focus your time and attention. You may end up ingesting less information, engaging in fewer activities, owning fewer gadgets, subscribing to fewer publications, and interacting with fewer people, but that's okay. The quality of your interactions and the quality of your choices is what counts. Less can be more. In a future in which you'll be exposed to more of everything, making critical choices can spell the difference between a hectic, frenzied, time-pressed life and one of relative grace and ease.

More than 165,000 readers have found the first two editions of *The Complete Idiot's Guide to Managing Your Time* to be valuable texts, offering insights and observations along with suggestions and recommendations to help readers stay consistently in control of their time and their lives. From college students to homemakers to business executives to heads of state, everyone these days needs a little coaching when it comes to staying in control of their time.

In this book, Jeff Davidson offers valuable services by first giving you a friendly, in-depth view of the realities that each of us faces nearly every minute of the day. He then moves on to offering highly effective solutions to time-crunching situations. Some of the solutions are ancient, while some are cutting-edge. The common denominator is that they work, and they can work for you in the various aspects of your life, whether you are at work, at home, reading, traveling, on vacation, at a conference, or anywhere else. Jeff has assembled this book so that you receive top-drawer advice offered with humor and blatant truth, in a style that keeps you glued to the page. Jeff forsakes tired clichés about time management and instead offers real-world observations, hands-on suggestions, and imminently practical advice. His mission is grand—to assist you in enhancing the quality of your life for the rest of your life. His main thesis is that a higher quality of life is obtainable for everyone, based on how they approach each day.

As with the first two editions, Jeff first discusses how leaving the workplace at the "normal" closing time is a fundamental component to getting back in control of your time. Starting with only one day per week and eventually escalating to two or three, Jeff explains that by having separate and distinct evenings, divorced from the matters of the workday, you're able to renew yourself in little ways that add up to more energy week in and week out. The chapters that follow tackle a wide range of common issues such as commuting, being more effective in the workplace, traveling, taking time for leisure, and rediscovering relaxation.

Don't be fooled by the subtlety of many of Jeff's suggestions. He has learned over years of observation and analysis that the most effective way to help people change is to offer them bite-size tasks with which they will have a high probability of success. Jeff has found that when a person tries to change too much too quickly, the change doesn't take hold.

Recognizing that your calendar is already full, that you are already balancing more than you might care to, and that you already have much competing for your time and attention, Jeff deftly offers tips and recommendations that can become part of your daily routines. While not every suggestion is right for every reader, there are enough that will be right for you—this book will be of great utility even after a second and third reading.

As with all books in *The Complete Idiot's Guide* series, you'll find a section titled "The Least You Need to Know" at the close of each chapter. This section offers quick bulleted highlights from the chapter. If you were only to read these bulleted points, you would still enjoy tremendous benefits from this book.

With *The Complete Idiot's Guide to Managing Your Time, Third Edition,* even after a cover-to-cover reading, you'll want to review the book over and over again for its treasure trove of insights and practical ideas. As months pass, if you find yourself slipping a little here and there in your quest to manage your time, crack open this book to the chapter or page that addresses the issue currently confronting you. By doing so, you will be invigorated by Jeff's profound and practical suggestions.

As tens of thousands of readers before you have found, *The Complete Idiot's Guide to Managing Your Time* is an eye-opening, mind-stirring, schedule-freeing experience. By adopting the guidelines in this book, you will be contributing to the quality of your life and perhaps even to its duration. Have a wonderful journey!

Dr. Tony Alessandra

Noted Keynote Speaker and author of *The Platinum Rule* and *Charisma*

Introduction

Get in Control of Your Time (or Someone Else Will)

The quest to win back your time is a noble pursuit, but it's a fast-paced and frenzied existence that you're enduring. With all that competes for your time and attention, how do you alter the pace of your career and life so that you are in control of your time? How can you enjoy what your career and life have to offer, and once again have time to reflect, to ponder, to muse? Keep readin'.

You're holding a book about winning back and managing your time. The chances are astronomical-to-nearly-100 percent that you lost it in the last decade. In this book, we'll stay with the tried and true. Some of the tips may seem quite innovative, but I've practiced them myself and I *know* that they work. So, it is my duty to offer them to you! Many people lay claim to being time-management or life-balance experts, including authors, speakers, and, heck, even talk show hosts. Some do quite well in making presentations or in offering the written word.

If I was a member of their audiences or a reader of their works, I would be concerned about what kind of lives they lead. For example:

What are their tangible accomplishments?

Are they healthy?

Are they overweight?

What are their relationships with their children?

Do they take trips to expand their horizons?

Do they take trips abroad?

If they are not able to devote enough time to their families, jobs, health, and continuing educations, then they don't know the true cost of obtaining life balance. They can't talk to you about what it took to get there if they are not there themselves, because they don't know the trade-offs or the sacrifices.

Too many authors or speakers who bill themselves as experts in this arena continually juggle every aspect of their lives and only fleetingly get their acts together. While they may do so sufficiently enough to convince readers or audiences that they have something important to say, they may not have the nuances or the infinitesimal edge necessary to offer long-term impact.

We will examine how to improve the quality of your life for the rest of your life—a tall order, to be sure. To achieve all this, first understand that whatever changes you make have to come without too much pain. I know that this is contrary to what you've been led to believe about change, but bear with me. If the changes needed to win back your time are too difficult—too many rules, too many things to remember or do—then you're not going to stay with them.

I've observed that simple steps—a moderate shift here, an adjustment there—works best in winning back your time. Gradual, subtle, natural changes in what you're already doing yield far greater long-term results. Changes that are radical or anxiety-provoking have much less chance of taking hold. Why? Well, if you've been alive for 25, 35, 45 years or more, it took that long to become who you are—just the way you are. You're clearly perfect at it! You're probably not going to change suddenly in 35 minutes or 35 hours, and, in many cases, not in 35 days.

Whenever you embark upon making changes that are too big of a leap from your current ways of doing things, they won't last—or be effective. Therefore, ignore anything in this book that represents too much of a stretch for you right now. Proceed with the suggestions that you can undertake most readily. As you initiate more changes, others will fall into place from the momentum of your actions. Such a deal! Gradually, with the proper perspective, a few specific techniques, and some built-in follow-up, you'll be able to naturally and easily win back your time.

This book eases you into each topic as you reclaim your time. It moves from broad-based to nitty-gritty workaday issues; in the last few chapters, it tackles personal perspectives.

Part 1, "The Big Clock Is Ticking," takes a look at why you feel mounting time pressure and gives you definitive strategies for winning back your time. It emphasizes the basic notion of departing from your workplace at a semireasonable hour and having the gall to feel good about it! You'll read about pervasive ways that your time gets used up, why many other working professionals feel almost exactly like you do, and how to assume greater control over your time, more of the time!

Part 2, "Appointing Yourself in Charge," examines how you can determine what's most important to you and what you'll realistically need to do to support your priorities, how much sleep you're getting (which is likely to be way less than your body requires!), the time-money connection, and how to keep others from encroaching on your time.

Part 3, "Taking Back Your Turf," discusses maintaining a reasonably organized office, setting up a home-based office, and managing your files. You'll be exposed to tools and technologies to help you be more efficient—if you don't take advantage of them, you'll remain in an endless well of clutter, confusion, and time pressure!

Part 4, "Connecting to Others," examines fundamental problems that people encounter when coming face to face with technology that allows them to be in touch all of the time. The trick is how to do this without diminishing other aspects of your life. We'll also efficiently tackle dealing with correspondence.

Part 5, "Thinking Your Way Out of Time Traps," discusses key areas for saving time—making decisions more quickly, honing the ability to focus on one thing at a time, treading more lightly, and constantly reducing what you hold on to (it'll keep your own systems uncomplicated).

Part 6, "Your Relationship, Your Time, and Your Sanity," highlights how to carve out time for yourself and for others in your life. After all, if managing your time applies to only the functional aspects of your work and life, your life could seem quite empty. We'll delve into higher-order notions such as undertaking a quest to live in "real time," catching up with today, and occasionally withdrawing from the maddening crowd.

Extras

Throughout the text, you'll find boxes with familiar icons and added information to help embellish what you've been absorbing, including these:

Pause!

Issues for which you need to be cautious.

The Time Master Says

Sage advice and insights from a learned master.

Coming to Terms

New words and terms that can aid your overall understanding.

Reflect and Win

New angles on familiar or unfamiliar issues that help trigger the gray matter and prompt you to take action right away, while you're thinking about it.

To start right away, flip to Chapter 1, "The Overtime Epidemic: How to Nip It in the Bud," for a look at the reality of how much time you get in this life (if you're lucky, that is!). Otherwise, let's roll some credits ….

Acknowledgments

Thanks to all the wonderful folks at Alpha Books, a division of Pearson Education, for having the profound wisdom to publish the third edition of *The Complete Idiot's Guide to Managing Your Time, Third Edition*, and for giving me the editorial support to keep it in the winner circle. Thanks to Marie Butler-Knight, publisher, and Renee Wilmeth, senior acquisitions editor, for their keen insights and guidance. Thanks to Jennifer Chisholm the managing editor, Amy Gordon, development editor, and Billy Fields, the production editor.

Thanks also to Chanel Cunningham, Emilee Martin, Jason Hand, Shawn Rue in International Sales, Debbie Parisi in Special Sales, Vickie Skelton in Public Relations, Eve Tabin in Electronic Rights Sales, Gardi Wilks in Promotion, Rachele Schifter in Subsidiary Rights, Jeannie McKay in Communications, and Dawn Werk in Marketing.

Thanks to Sharon Askew, Jessi Bromwell, and Christie Koch for their original writing and editorial assistance as well as research, reviews, and copyediting.

Thanks to Susan Davidson for word-processing assistance, and, most importantly, to Valerie Davidson, age 11, for always having time for Daddy.

Special Thanks to the Technical Reviewer

The Complete Idiot's Guide to Managing Your Time, Third Edition, was reviewed by experts who not only checked the technical accuracy of what you'll learn here, but also provided insight and guidance to help us ensure that this book gives you everything you need to know to begin making better decisions about how you spend your time. We extend our special thanks to these folks:

Claire Conway is a freelance writer who served as features editor for *Psychology Today* in New York City. Prior to that, she was managing editor of *Stanford Medicine* magazine, a publication of the Stanford University Medical School Alumni Association. Born and raised in California, she received an M.S.J. from Northwestern's Medill School of Journalism.

Carol Krucoff writes a health and fitness column for the *Washington Post*, where she was founding editor of the weekly Health Section. A freelance writer based in Chapel Hill, North Carolina, she contributes to a variety of publications, including *Reader's Digest, Self, Parents,* and *The Saturday Evening Post.* She also teaches Creative Nonfiction for Duke University's Continuing Education Department. She has two children, is married to a cardiologist, and holds a brown belt in karate.

Trademarks

All terms mentioned in this book that are known to be or are suspected of being trademarks or service marks have been appropriately capitalized. Alpha Books and Pearson Education, Inc., cannot attest to the accuracy of this information. Use of a term in this book should not be regarded as affecting the validity of any trademark or service mark.

Part 1

The Big Clock Is Ticking

For all that has been written about life, it is still finite. Your life, in particular, had a distinct beginning and will have a distinct ending—at least the part that occurs on Earth—unless, of course, you believe that you're coming back as someone else or in some other form.

Back in the here-and-now, I'll gingerly present several hard-hitting chapters that explore mysteries of the ages. Among these revelations: why staying at work longer can be self-defeating, what really happens to your time, quality (versus quantity) of life, whose fault the present mess isn't, how your house got so crowded, and slowing down to take a breath. You know, the basics ....

The Overtime Epidemic: How to Nip It in the Bud

In This Chapter

- ◆ You're already successful
- ◆ Working too long takes its toll
- ◆ The workplace is often competitive and demanding
- ◆ To leave work on time, start with a small step

When you look at the big picture of your life and career and where you've progressed thus far, you have to concede that, despite the feelings of stress, the frenzy, and the hurriedness, you've done a pretty good job of managing your time. Your challenge becomes that of drawing on three things:

1. Your experience
2. The principles that you have developed along the way
3. The time-management tools and resources that you can identify

Your quest is to give yourself the opportunity to be at your best day in and day out. You've got a long way to go in your career, and, wherever you're heading, you want to arrive there in style, rested and relaxed, energized and invigorated. Prudent use of your time, perpetually, will get you there.

Following the terrorist attacks on America, many people report that they immediately shifted priorities, perhaps working fewer hours and spending more time with family and community. Only time will tell if this is a permanent shift. Nevertheless, for many professionals working long hours remains the norm.

One of the most insidious time traps that you can fall prey to is believing that by working a little longer (or taking work home on the weekend) you can finally "catch up." This is a fallacy that will keep you chasing the clock for at least the rest of your career—and maybe the rest of your life.

I can sympathize with you if you've found yourself staying at the office later or toting a bulging briefcase home with you. At face value, these maneuvers probably seem to be the logical response to the pressures you face. For too many people, however, they are also a trap.

Staying Longer: Not the Answer

The Time Master Says

Occasionally it makes sense to take work home from the office. All career achievers do. During specific campaigns (such as the launch of a new business, product, or service), when you change jobs, or when you're approaching a significant event, it makes sense to bone up and spend a few extra hours at work. But this should be the exception, not the rule.

Once you begin perpetually taking work home or working a little longer at the office, putting in overtime becomes the norm. Soon you're taking another 30 or 40 pages of reading material home at night, as if this habit was necessary.

What happens, however, when you consistently work longer hours or take work home from the office? You begin to forget what it's like to have a free weeknight—and eventually a free weekend! I've observed the working styles of some of the most successful people in many countries: multimillionaires, best-selling authors, high-powered corporate executives, association leaders, top-level government officials, educators, people from all walks of life. The most successful people in any endeavor maintain a healthy balance between their work and nonwork lives.

A Time-Pressured Decade

Based on survey information from the U.S. Census Bureau, it's easy to understand why more people in society are feeling more time pressure. Consider the following:

♦ The median mortgage was $737 in 1990, but it climbed to $1,307 by 2000. The median rent in 1990 was $447, but it climbed to $612 10 years later. The median household income in 1990 was $30,056, stepping up to $41,343 in 2000. So, while people earned more, the cost of housing, particularly for mortgages, rose even faster.

- In 1990, the average commute was 22.4 minutes, but it climbed to 24.3 minutes by 2000. That's not quite a two-minute increase, but spread it across a 160-million-person workforce, and you begin to realize this increase within a single decade represents monumental change.

- In 1990, 86.5 percent of the workforce drove cars, trucks, or vans; that climbed to 87.5 percent by 2000. Use of public transport dropped off a bit, moving from 5.3 percent of the workforce to 5.2 percent. Hence, cars predominate and, for the foreseeable future, will continue to do so.

- Whereas 3.9 percent of the workforce walked to work in 1990, only 2.7 percent did so in 2000. This statistic is consistent with Americans' dramatic weight gain during the 1990s.

Telecommuting Doesn't Take Off

What about the potential for telecommuting—working at home? In the last decade, many homes became connected to the their offices and to the Internet in ways that were simply not available in the 1980s. Yet, 3 percent of the workforce worked at home in 1990, rising to only 3.2 percent by 2000. In a *Wall Street Journal* article, Nicholas Kulich wrote, "For all the talk of telecommuting and the virtual office, the fraction of Americans breaking free from offices and cubicles stayed about the same." This is still likely to be the case even with all the talk about rethinking the commute to high-rise office buildings and densely packed urban areas.

The bottom line: People are still trudging into work. It is taking them longer to do so, they are getting less exercise, and they are returning at the end of the day to a home that costs more to live in, is filled with more gadgets, and supports a sedentary lifestyle.

Source: 2000 Figures from the U.S. Census Bureau's Test Survey.
1990 Figures from the U.S. Census Bureau's long form data.

Not Everyone Is in the Marathon

Americans, in particular, are working too much—far more, in fact, than any other nation. According to The United Nations' International Labor Organization (ILO), "workers in the United States are putting in more hours than anyone else in the industrialized world."

The ILO team, led by Lawrence Jeff Johnson, produced its new "Key Indicators of the Labor Market 2001–2002" study. Although it did show that American workers are productive, it also proved that we're not nearly as efficient as those in other countries. Could it be the cell phones and pagers, surfing the Web, and all the other potential distractions the Americans are subject to are having an impact? My guess is yes. According to

Johnson, Americans are actually increasing the hours they work each week, while citizens in other countries decrease theirs.

The study shows that Americans worked 1,978 hours last year, which is up from 1,942 in 1990. "The increase in the number of hours worked within the United States runs counter to the trend in other industrialized nations," Johnson says. "(In other nations,) we're seeing a declining number of hours worked annually."

The average Australian, Canadian, Japanese, or Mexican worker was on the job about 100 hours less than the average American worker in a year, according to the ILO. Brazilians and British employees worked some 250 hours—or more than 5 weeks—less than Americans. Germans worked roughly 500 hours, or 12 and a half weeks, less.

Pause! _____

According to Oxford Health Plans, 18 percent of professionals in the United States don't use up their vacation days.

There are only a few countries, like South Korea and the Czech Republic, whose workers put in longer hours than Americans. Europeans often take four- to six-week vacations from the job. These breaks, according to Johnson, may reduce their stress and generate greater efficiency.

High Demands Take a Toll

Americans, in general, also are sleeping less (the subject of Chapter 10, "Becoming a Snooze-Savvy Sleeper"), which significantly affects work performance. In fact, all aspects of life are becoming more complex. As a result, you may be enjoying your life a bit less these days. (Chapter 3, "Time Flies Whether You Want It to or Not," discusses five megarealities that may tell you why.)

People aren't just working more because they feel like it—our society as a whole has become more competitive and demanding. Employers require more. Kids seem to have to be part of more activities, filling up the week with music lessons, sports practice, and play dates. Such items fill the gaps with noise and stimulation, rather than peace and quiet.

Pause! _____

U.S. Department of Labor statistics reveal that in the past quarter century, the amount of time that Americans have spent at their jobs has risen steadily.

People are insistent upon staying busy, even if it's by entertaining themselves. There are kabillions of entertainment options, and the forms of entertainment are proliferating. The video games get wilder and more complex. Instant messaging, cyberdating, chat rooms, and all the myriad ways that you can be seated at your desk and still have the hours fly by may be entertaining, but at what cost? We work more hours, seek to entertain ourselves, try to keep up, quietly go nuts, and consider it normal.

Part-Timers, Students, and Homemakers Are Not Exempt

Nearly all the time-pressure problems that plague the denizens of the full-time working world will visit others as well. While you may have extra moments to yourself here and there, everyone who holds any position of responsibility today—and those responsibilities include studying, managing a home, caring for others, and nearly any other pursuit you can think of—faces pressures unknown to previous generations (as you'll learn in Chapter 3).

Your key to reducing the time pressure that you feel is not to stay longer at work. Indeed, to reclaim your day, you cannot stay longer. This will become clear shortly.

Reflect and Win

Your quest becomes accomplishing that which you seek to accomplish within your eight- or nine-hour workday.

Day Is Done

Based on a survey by Integra Realty Resources, 52 percent of Americans report that they sometimes have to work more than 12 hours a day to get their jobs done. This confession is undesirable but understandable for interim short-run challenges. Suppose that you're among those whose workday is 8:00 A.M. to 5:00 P.M., with an hour for lunch, yielding a total working time of eight hours. Studies show that most people are working only about 60 percent of those eight hours for which they were hired. Even in a tough economy, most people spend 3 hours and 12 minutes daily not focusing on the tasks, assignments, and activities for which they were hired. Could those who report working 12 hours actually be including all kinds of other activities within that estimate?

You could make a strong case!

Many people don't work a full day, regardless of the number of hours on the job. Suppose that someone is on the job eight hours a day. Is it eight dedicated hours? Unlikely! A study by the Angus Reid Group, for example, revealed that 46 percent of American workers who surf the Net use it on the job for personal reasons!

Many people don't work a full eight hours a day, though they spend eight hours on the job, as these charts illustrate.

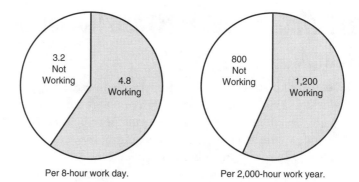

Per 8-hour work day.

Per 2,000-hour work year.

Note: Exceptions include the self-employed and the professionally driven.

When asked to estimate how much time they waste during a day, most workers are forthright, if widely mistaken, in admitting that it is something above 20 percent. If we use the 20 percent figure, which is extremely conservative, that still means, within a given 8-hour day, that 1 hour and 36 minutes is wasted.

Using the 20 percent estimate, if there are 20 people in your department or division, that means that you lose 16 hours a day and 76,800 hours in a year consisting of 240 working days. Counting salaries, taxes, insurance, and benefits, the typical work hour costs the company $25 to $30; that means that the 76,800 hours lost in a year add up to nearly $200,000.

So maybe you're not among those who dawdle—and you certainly don't goof off for 20 to 40 percent of your day. Still, it's unlikely that you're working the full eight hours.

Among the many factors that inhibit your inclination to work a solid eight hours every day are these:

- ◆ **Too many domestic tasks**—See Chapter 9, "Buying Yourself Some Time," to learn how easy it is to believe that if you spend a few minutes here and there taking care of domestic tasks yourself, you can stay on top of it all, save a little money, and cruise into work in high gear.

- ◆ **Not getting enough sleep**—Zzzz. See Chapter 19, "An Internet You Can Live With," which discusses why you're probably not getting enough sleep and how this leads to lack of efficiency and effectiveness.

- ◆ **Overcommitting**—See Chapter 11, "Loaning Yourself Out Less and Being Happier Because of It," to learn about how widely available technology gives managers and businesses the opportunity to get more done—and also to expect more from their employees. Much more.

- ◆ **Not being sufficiently organized**—See Chapter 12, "The Efficiently Organized Office," which explains that a desk is not a filing cabinet and that windowsills and the corners of your room are not permanent storage locations. You can rule an empire from a desk if you know how to do it correctly.

◆ **Lacking effective tools**—See Chapter 15, "Top Time-Management Tools Revealed," on how you can put new technology to work for you—and how to avoid being overwhelmed by what you acquire.

Beyond these factors, oversocializing is another culprit in many offices. Also, some professionals develop elaborate rituals, such as sharpening three pencils, refilling the coffee cup, making a personal call, or waiting until the clock on the wall is at the top of the hour before they get down to work. (I know, that's not something that you would ever do, but it happens.)

What a Difference 2,000 Hours Can Make

Eight-hour workdays, of which you have about 250 a year, yield a work year of 2,000 hours. Can you get done in 2,000 hours that which you want to do (or for which you were hired)? Yes—2,000 hours, 200 hours, 8 hours, or even 1 hour can be a great deal of time if you have the mind-set, the quiet environment, and the tools that you need to be productive.

Leave Now, Feel Good All Evening

To sustain the habit of leaving work on time, start with a small step. For example, decide that on every Tuesday, you will stop working on time and take no extra work home with you. After freeing up Tuesdays for an entire month, perhaps add Thursdays. In another month, add Mondays; in the fourth month, add Wednesdays. I'm assuming that there's no way you work late on Friday! (Or do you? If you do, then start with Fridays!)

What transpires in the first month when you've decided that each Tuesday will be a normal eight- or nine-hour workday and nothing more? Automatically, you begin to be more focused about what you want to get done on Tuesdays. Almost imperceptibly, you begin to parcel out your time during the day more judiciously.

By midday, stop and assess what you've done and what else you'd like to get done. Near the end of the day, assess what more you can (realistically) get done and what's best to leave for tomorrow.

> **CAUTION**
>
> **Pause!**
>
> If you deplete yourself of crucial elements to high productivity by coming to work feeling exhausted or mentally unprepared—or if you keep getting interrupted—1 hour, 8 hours, 200 hours, 2,000 hours, or more won't be sufficient for you to do your work. (See Chapter 18, "Mastering Email So That It Doesn't Master You," for a simple system to minimize interruptions.)

The Time Master Says

For some reason that only the gods of Mount Olympus can explain, once you've solidly made the decision to leave on time on Tuesdays, every cell in your body works in unison to help you accomplish your goal.

You begin to set a natural, internal alignment in motion. (Sounds exciting, doesn't it?) Your internal cylinders fire in harmony to give you a vibrant, productive workday on Tuesday so you can leave on time.

Expect the Unexpected

Okay, so these resolutions look good on paper, but what about when the boss comes in and hands you a four-inch stack of reports at 3:45 in the afternoon? Or what about when you get a fax, an email message, or a memo that upsets the applecart? These things do happen—and not just to you!

Take a practical approach to your time, your life, and what you're likely to face during the typical workday. Consider how to approach the predictable impediments to leaving on time on Tuesday.

Rather than treat an unexpected project that gets dumped in your lap late in the day as an intrusion, stretch a tad to view it as something else: You got the project because you were trusted, accomplished, or, in some cases, simply there.

Many government workers have no trouble establishing their time boundaries at work. They leave on time because that's what their government policy manual says, right there in clause 92-513-ak7-1, subclause 8-PD 601-00 07, paragraph 6.12, line 8—no overtime, pal. If you're in the private sector, however, you may not have such regulations on your side. (See Chapter 9 for some options that you do have.)

More Hours, More Mistakes

First the data! Professor Carey Cooper, an American at Manchester University in England, is one of Europe's foremost stress specialists. He has found that performance declines by 25 percent after a 60-hour workweek. He also calculated that the annual cost of stress-related illnesses attributed to overwork topped $80 billion in the United States—more than $1,600 a year for every other worker in America. Other studies show that work output is growing faster in Germany than in the United States—even though (as you've seen) Germans work fewer hours than Americans.

Stated bluntly, excess work hours put in by already overtaxed employees are of negative value to an organization when viewed in the context of overall work performance, direct healthcare costs, and productivity lost to absenteeism and general lethargy on the job.

The Least You Need to Know

◆ In the past quarter century, the amount of time that Americans have spent at their jobs has risen steadily.

◆ When you consistently work longer hours, you begin to forget what it's like to have a free weeknight.

◆ When you decide that, say, each Tuesday will be a normal workday, automatically you begin to be more focused about what you want to get done that day.

◆ Excess work hours put in by already overtaxed employees actually are of negative value to their employers.

Chapter 2

Strategies for Survival

In This Chapter

♦ Leave work at a reasonable hour
♦ Create a strategy that coincides with your type of organization
♦ Strike a dynamic bargain with yourself
♦ Realize that you are not rooted to your desk

Now that you know the downside of overwork, as if you weren't already experiencing it, let's focus on the strategies for avoiding it. Begin by taking a small step—stop working one evening per week at a reasonable hour.

If this represents an impossible task for you, either stop reading this book and continue suffering the way you have been, or change jobs and try to find a more enlightened employer. Otherwise, begin to plot your strategy now: It's your job, and it's your life.

Your Plan and Welcome to It

For now, I'm discussing ending work at a sane hour only *one* night a week. Here are eight steps to get you going:

1. Let it be known that you maintain a home office where you devote untold hours to the organization after 5:00 each evening. Then take most evenings off.

2. Invite bosses and coworkers to your home for some other reason, and conveniently give them a tour of your command-center-away-from-the-office.

3. When you discuss your work, focus on your results (as opposed to the hours that you log after 5:00). It's difficult for anyone to argue with results.

4. Find role models—outstanding achievers within your organization who leave at (close to) normal closing time at least a few nights a week—and drop hints about those role models' working styles in conversation with others in your organization.

5. Acquire whatever high-tech tools (see Chapter 15, "Top Time-Management Tools Revealed") you can find that will help you be more productive. If your organization won't foot the bill, do it yourself. Often your long-term output and advancement will more than offset the up-front cost.

6. On those evenings that you do work late at the office, be conspicuous. Make the rounds; be seen! After all, if you've got to stay late, at least make sure that it's noticed.

7. On those evenings when you take work home, use oversize containers or boxes to transport your projects. You may choose to bring boxes back and forth to the office even when you have no intention of doing any work at home (this makes you look productive).

8. If zipping out at 5:00 carries a particular stigma in your office, leave earlier. Huh? Yes, schedule an appointment across town for 3:30 P.M., and when it's completed, don't head back to the office. Work for the last 30 or 45 minutes (or however much time may be left to complete a normal workday) at home.

A Smashing Idea

Mr. David Cohn of Surrey, British Columbia, wrote me after reading the second edition of this book and suggested an ideal way to ensure that you leave work on time. "If you join or organize a reliable, prompt, effective carpool," he says, "you have an irreproachable reason to leave work on time." A tip of the hat to David—this is a master stroke of getting out of the office.

Bring on Da Crunch Time

When developing Microsoft Windows XP and getting it out the door on time, the elite Seattle corps found themselves working progressively longer hours each day. For some, it became unbearable. Some went into a robot phase (you know, work, work, work, work). Some quit. Some will be added to the ranks of the millionaires. All got the opportunity to chill out afterward. Yes, there are exceedingly tough campaigns, but they are always of finite duration.

If you saw the 1985 movie *Broadcast News* with Holly Hunter and William Hurt, recall the scene in which a party is disrupted so that the staff can return to the studio to cover late-breaking news. Hunter's character, Jane Craig, takes on the role of a change manager in a crunch-time situation.

She starts directing virtually everyone in the newsroom so that the station is able to present a timely, professional, and insightful news alert to its viewers. Later, because of her take-charge capability, Craig is promoted to the position of broadcast manager. It's a valuable skill to be able to handle a crunch-time situation. Fortunately, unavoidable crunch times tend to come and go.

Pause!

When you treat every workday as crunch time, you start to do foolish things—like throwing more and more of your time at challenges instead of devising less time-consuming ways to handle them—and that means not leaving work on time tonight, tomorrow, or any other night in the foreseeable future.

Cut a Deal with Yourself

A master stroke for winning back your time at any point in your day—Tuesdays or any other day—is to continually strike a *dynamic bargain* with yourself. It's a self-reinforcing tool for achieving a desired outcome that you've identified within a certain time frame, as in the end of the day! Here's the magic phrase that you should begin using:

> What would it take for me to feel good about ending work on time today?

Coming to Terms

A **dynamic bargain** is an agreement that you make with yourself to assess what you've accomplished (and what more you want to accomplish) from time to time throughout the day, adjusting to new conditions as they emerge.

This is what I mean when I talk about a dynamic bargain. I have this powerful question posted on my wall in my office. It can give you the freedom to feel good about leaving the office on time because, when you answer it each morning, you're making that bargain with yourself—you're stating exactly what you'll need to accomplish to feel good about leaving on time that day.

Suppose that today your answer to the question is to finish three particular items on your desk. Now suppose that the boss drops a bomb on your desk late in the day. You automatically get to strike a new dynamic bargain with yourself, given the prevailing circumstances. Your new bargain may include simply making sufficient headway on the project that has been dropped in your lap, or accomplishing two of your previous three tasks and x percent of this new project.

TGIF? You Bet!

The same principle holds true for leaving the office on Friday: feeling good about what you accomplished during the workweek. Here is the question to ask yourself (usually sometime around midday on Friday, but even as early as Thursday):

> By the end of work on Friday, what do I want to have accomplished so that I can feel good about the week?

By employing such questions and striking these dynamic bargains with yourself, you get to avoid what too many professionals in society still confront: leaving, on most workdays, not feeling good about what they've accomplished, not having a sense of completion, and bringing work home. If you're like most of these people, you want to be more productive. You want to get raises and promotions, but you don't want to have a lousy life in the process!

Rather than striking dynamic bargains with themselves, most people frequently do the opposite. They'll have several things that they wanted to accomplish that day, and they'll actually manage to accomplish some of them, crossing them off the list. However, rather than feeling good about their accomplishments and accepting the reward of the freedom to leave on time, they add several more items to the list—a great way to guarantee that they'll still leave their offices feeling beleaguered. Here you have the perfect prescription for leaving the workplace every day not feeling good about what you've accomplished. If you always have a lengthy, running list of "stuff" that you have to do, you never get a sense of getting things done, and you never get any sense of being in control of your time.

Reflect and Win

Regardless of projects, email, faxes, phone calls, or other intrusions into your perfect world, continually strike a dynamic bargain with yourself so that you leave the workplace on time, feeling good about what you accomplished.

Reinforce Yourself

When you've made the conscious decision to leave on time on Tuesday and you strike the dynamic bargain with yourself, almost magically the small issues drop off your list of things to do. You focus on bigger, more crucial tasks or responsibilities. On the first Tuesday—and certainly by the second or third—you begin to benefit from a *system of self-reinforcement*, whereby the rewards that you enjoy (such as leaving the office on time and actually having an evening free of work-related thoughts) are so enticing that you structure your workday so as to achieve your rewards.

Eventually, when you add Thursdays, then Mondays, and then Wednesdays to the roster of days that you leave work on time, you begin to reclaim your entire work week. A marvelous cycle is initiated. You actually …

- Leave the workplace with more zest.
- Have more energy to pursue your non-work life.
- Sleep better.
- Arrive at work more rested.
- Are more productive on the job.

And as you increase the probability of leaving another workday on time, you perpetuate the cycle and its benefits.

Coming to Terms

A **system of self-reinforcement** is a series of rewards that you enjoy as a natural outcome of particular behaviors.

Now It's Time to Say Goodnight

How do you get this ball rolling? Declare that next Tuesday will be an eight- or nine-hour workday and nothing more. Leave on time that day feeling good about what you've completed. That's it—no grandiose plan, no long-term commitment, no radical change, and 'nary any anxiety.

If you're having trouble giving yourself permission for this one-day, no-overtime treat, recall how long you've been in your profession, and remember that you're in your present position for a lengthy run. On no particular day and at no particular hour are you truly rooted to your desk. After all, you're a professional. You've gotten the job done before; you'll get it done now as well. Feel free to trust your own judgment about when it's okay for you to go home.

On a given day when you've decided that you're going to leave on time, something may happen to upset your workload so that you have more to do than you can get done that day (and when won't that happen?). The temptation will be to stay late and deal with the new task. Resist it! Instead, map out exactly what you're going to begin on the next morning to handle this addition to your workload. Preparing a plan for tomorrow will reduce any anxiety or guilt that you feel about leaving on time today. Ultimately, you'll have little anxiety or guilt. After all, you have a right to a personal life, don't you?

Let everyone in your office know that you're leaving at 5:00, or whatever closing time is for you. Announce to people, "I've got to be outta here at five today," or whatever it takes. People tend to support another's goal when that goal has been announced. Some people may resent you for leaving on time; fortunately, most will not. You have to decide whether to let the resentful attitudes of a few control your actions.

If you must have a list of "steps," here's what you can do on that first Tuesday, or any other day, to leave on time when you choose to:

1. Get a good night's rest the night before so that you'll feel up for the effort of fulfilling your dynamic bargain with yourself.

2. Strike a dynamic bargain with yourself at the start of the day, in late morning, in early afternoon, and in late afternoon. (Remember, it's okay to modify the bargain to accommodate a changing situation.)

3. Mark on your calendar that you'll be leaving at five.

4. Announce to everyone that you have a personal commitment at 5:30 that evening. If you have a child, you could say that your child is in need of your assistance.

5. Eat a light lunch; it keeps you from being sluggish in the afternoon.

6. Regard any intrusion or upset as merely part of the workday, deal with it as you can, and plan tomorrow's strategy for coping. Do not let it change your plans about leaving on time.

7. After striking the dynamic bargain with yourself, don't be tempted to add more items to your list at the last minute.

8. Envision how you'll feel when you leave right at closing time (but there is no reason for you to be staring at the clock for the last 45 minutes).

9. If you want support, ask a coworker to walk you out the door at closing time.

Reflect and Win

Silently repeat to yourself, "I choose to easily leave at closing time today and feel good about it." Never mind if at first you think that this mantra doesn't have any power. Do it. You'll find yourself easily leaving on time more often.

The Time Master Says

This chapter is intentionally simple: The more you have to do and remember, the less you'll do and remember. Your only assignment, boiled down to four words: Leave work on time.

Ensuring that you leave the workplace on time may seem too involved to accomplish. If you engage in only two or three of these steps, however, you'll still get the reinforcement that you need.

The Least You Need to Know

- ◆ Depending on your organization's culture, you may have to use one or more of the strategies discussed in this chapter to leave on time.

- ◆ The changes that you need to make have to be easy to follow. If they're too difficult, they won't hold. Winning back your time requires only small steps, but you'll need a progression of them.

- ◆ To leave on time, start with one day per week (such as Tuesday) and strive to leave on time every Tuesday for an entire month.

- ◆ You can strike a dynamic bargain with yourself to feel good about what you've done, choose what else you want to accomplish, and feel good about leaving.

- ◆ As you develop the habit of leaving on time, you develop a positive cycle of high productivity, even while leaving on time more often.

Chapter 3

Time Flies Whether You Want It to or Not

In This Chapter

- ◆ A cheerful subject: how much longer you're likely to be on the planet
- ◆ The number-1 activity that sucks the time out of your life
- ◆ Spending time daily on what you don't enjoy doing
- ◆ Simplifying things is vital

Have you ever considered how much time you have in your whole life and how much time you've spent on various activities? Suppose that you graduated from college at the age of 22, and in the course of your life expect to work about 48 years, bringing you to age 70. Over those 48 years, how much time would you suppose you spend on routine activities such as working, sleeping, watching television, recreating, eating, and commuting?

In 24 × 7 terms, here's the typical breakdown, based on various demographic studies and my own calculations:

Working	16 years
Sleeping	15 years
Viewing TV	5–7 years

Recreation	2–4 years
Eating	3 years
Commuting	2 years

To a Long and Healthy Life

It's amazing when you look at the cumulative total of the time you'll spend engaged in these activities during your productive work life, isn't it? Suppose that you're already 30-something and, on average, will live another 45 years. Thus, you have about 30 waking years left, and about 15 years to accomplish whatever you're seeking to accomplish. That realization alone may help you focus your time.

If you're thinking, "Hey, I'm 35 now, but I don't expect to reach age 80," think again. The Society of Actuaries estimates that if you're female and you're 40 years old, your life expectancy exceeds age 85—for males, age 80.

Data from the National Center for Health Statistics shows that every 25 years since 1900, the life expectancy of both men and women has increased by about 5 to 7 years. The increase in life expectancy for people born between 1975 and the year 2000 was nearly 10 years (see the following table).

CAUTION

Pause!

Based on data from the research firm Veronis Suhler, the average American will spend 3,571 hours in the course of a year watching television, listening to the radio, reading newspapers, or being online. Since there are only 365 days in the typical year, that means that these activities consume a little less than 10 hours per day!

Life Expectancy of Americans (from Birth, by 25-Year Intervals)

Year Born	Female Expected Life (Years)	Year Born	Male Expected Life (Years)
1900	48.3	1900	46.3
1925	57.6	1925	55.6
1950	71.1	1950	65.6
1975	76.5	1975	68.7
2000	85	2000	79

Even when a nation is at war, on average, most people are likely to live longer than they think they will. If you think that you're going to reach 75, you may well reach 85. If you think that you'll reach 85, you may hit 95!

The realization that you may live much longer than you think necessitates developing some longer-term perspectives about how you want to spend your life. (This is covered in the last few chapters of the book.)

When Limits Help

With decades to go, it's easy to get caught in the trap of delaying the activities and events that you promised yourself you'd undertake. Whether life seems short and merry or long and boring, there's only so much of it. Architect Frank Lloyd Wright once observed that people build "most nobly when limitations are at their greatest." You can use the limits on your time or resources to achieve your most desired accomplishments.

Consider how productive you are, for example, before you leave for a vacation, or consider how well you do on a task when a deadline's been imposed (even though you might not enjoy having the deadline or like the person who imposed it). As the author of many

books, I can testify about deadlines. Each time I signed a book contract, I had to deliver a specified number of manuscript pages in coherent order and accomplish what I said I would do by a certain date. These contracts with their deadlines imposed limits that actually helped me be productive.

CAUTION **Pause!**

Whether you have 30 or 60 years left, it will be to no avail if your days race by; you wake up thinking, "I'm already behind"; you stay late at work night after night; or you let stuff pile up and then feel exhausted because you can't get to it.

These limits may not always appear helpful or supportive, yet you undoubtedly have many of them confronting you. Here are some examples of limits you may be facing right now:

- ♦ You have to pick your kids up by 5:30 P.M. each weekday.
- ♦ You have to turn in a work log on Fridays.
- ♦ The author of this book suggested leaving the office most days by 5:00 P.M.
- ♦ You can work about nine hours daily before your mind turns to mush.
- ♦ Your hard drive is almost full, and you won't spring for a larger one.
- ♦ Your contract is ending in 11 weeks.
- ♦ You have only 24 minutes left on your lunch break.
- ♦ The oil in your car needs changing after another 300 miles.
- ♦ A loved one is nearing the end of his life.
- ♦ You get paid every two weeks.

What limits do you face in your career or personal life that you could employ to propel yourself to higher productivity? When you learn to harness these for the benefit that they provide, you begin to reclaim your time. I suggest that your daily, primary limit be finishing your day so that you leave work at the normal closing hour.

The Time-Theft Culprit

After examining the problem for many years, sifting through extensive research, interviewing dozens of people, collecting articles, and tapping the minds of many learned people, I found that the number-1 element that robs people of their time can be boiled down to a single word. (Be seated in a chair that can support your full weight in case you slump over when the answer is revealed to you.)

Okay, if you're ready, take a deep breath, because here's the revelation of the ages. The number 1 activity in society, in your life, that steals your time is (here it is—I hope you're ready for this): television.

> **CAUTION**
>
> **Pause!** _____
>
> Staying up all hours leads to mental dullness during the day: the essence of poor time management.

People are flipping on the television the first moment they wake up. They get dressed to it. They drink coffee to it. They eat breakfast to it. They shave or put on makeup while watching television. Then they trot off to work only to return and, before doing nearly anything else, flip their television back on. Unfortunately, this has become the norm.

Is there anything I can say in a couple of pages that will help you reduce the amount of TV you watch? Consider the findings of TV-Free America, a public service organization in Washington, D.C., that has compiled some rather startling data about television viewers in America.

The average American watches more than four hours of TV each day, equal to two months of nonstop TV watching per year, and equal to more than 12 solid years of nonstop TV watching in the life of a person who lives to age 72. African Americans, on average watch 50 percent more TV than that. (You, of course, don't fall under any of these statistics, right? ... or so everyone proclaims!)

Consider these numbers:

- ◆ 66% of Americans regularly watch TV while eating dinner.
- ◆ 49% of Americans say that they watch too much television.
- ◆ 19% of Americans say that they'd like to read or visit friends but have no time!

The Time Master Says

More than 90 million adults watch television at least two hours on any Monday and Tuesday nights—that's at least 360 million viewer-hours. These viewer-hours, if applied elsewhere, could transform the nation. Ah, but you can turn off the TV whenever you want, can't you? Or can you? Television is a drug, with many of the same side effects as other drugs. And as the Internet becomes an even more dominating aspect of more people's lives, it will compete (or merge!) with TV to claim your time.

Oblivion Starts Here

In his book *Amusing Ourselves to Death*, Dr. Neil Postman says that entertainment is the dominant force in public discourse in society, affecting the arts, sciences, politics, religion, and education. Certainly, entertainment has a necessary function in your life: It stimulates thinking. It can be liberating to your soul. It can give you a break from the monotony of daily living. Of note, entertainment can free you to explore new ways of thinking, new ideas, and new possibilities.

The harm in being overentertained—which everyone faces—is that your daily life seems to pale by comparison to what you view on the screen. What is the true cost of entertainment? Certainly, your time, and usually your money. You're willing to trade these because entertainment expressly is not reality. It's designed to be "superior" to reality—it's more titillating and more engaging.

Fantasy sells almost as much stuff on TV as sports, and a lot more stuff than reality ever could. In a 1978 lecture at Indiana University, the late Gene Roddenberry, creator of *Star Trek*, boldly stated: "TV does not exist to entertain you. TV exists to sell you things."

When compared to what you see on the screen, your own life may seem dull and plastic. Instead, it is real and holds great potential. Ultimately, the quality of your life and your memories will depend on what you actively did, not what you passively ingested (such as seeing *Titanic* for the fourth time). What will you do in the next month to enrich your life—actually enrich it? Who will you meet? What will you risk?

Consider how much time and energy you're willing to spend with your favorite TV personalities. Now compare that figure with how much time you actually spend with any of your neighbors.

Reflect and Win

Don't make the erroneous assumption that watching brain-drain TV or listening to shock-talkers on the radio has no impact on your time. They vacuum up time that you could have used doing something worthwhile. Turn 'em off.

Neighbors. You know, those near-strangers next door. Do you even care about their lives? They are, in fact, flesh-and-blood people with real strengths, real weaknesses, and real lives. They could even become your lifelong friends. Do they offer as much pleasure to you, however, as the so-called heroes on *Survivor*, Matt Damon in his latest role, or Elle McPherson simply posing in garments that you'll never own? You might have a reason to like your neighbors: Consider all the expensive stuff that they're not trying to sell you.

"I Tune In Only to Stay Informed"

I'm not saying that you shouldn't watch any news. Rather, you need to understand the context in which news is presented. News shows are designed to attract viewers so that sponsors can sell things, the same as with any other show; they heighten the emphasis on some stories and completely ignore others.

As long as you understand the limitations of TV news, watch away! Don't turn off your brain when the news comes on.

Telekiddies

Maybe you didn't watch as much television when you were young as today's kids are watching, but you probably watched a lot, and the habit is ingrained. Kids today, however, are going to set some all-time records. Here's what TV-Free America found out about children's television viewing:

- The number of minutes per week that parents spend in meaningful conversation with their children is 38.5.
- The number of minutes per week that the average child watches television is 1,680.
- 50% of children ages 6–17 have television sets in their bedrooms.
- 70% of day-care centers use TV sets during a typical day.
- 73% of parents would like to limit their children's TV viewing (but apparently they don't or they can't).

> **Pause!**
>
> Dr. James Twitchell, author of *The Carnival Culture*, notes that most American children begin watching television before they can talk. A child by age six will have invested more hours watching television than in speaking with his father over an entire lifetime.
>
> So sad.

As if you're not watching enough television, what are the chances that you're turning on the radio, cluttering up your mind with that source as well? I know, I know, if you listen to the radio on the way to work, how can that possibly be stealing your time? Well, it is. Consider a friend of mine who liked to listen to a West Coast shock-jock in the morning. Year after year, my friend Bill was titillated on his way to work by the shock-talk.

In essence, he settled for an electronic fix that briefly took him out of his own life and into some form of contemptuous humor that got him through the next 10 minutes (or however long) on his way to work. After all the years of listening, my friend is not empowered, energized, or any better able to face his day. More important, he may be worse off: cynical, apathetic, or lethargic. In any case, he's devoted dozens of hours of his life to a medium that provides him with an arguably poor payoff for the time invested. Bill isn't alone; this particular shock-jock has become a multimillion-dollar media franchise and has had strong ratings for more than a decade.

If you listen closely to the shock-jocks of the world, you can sometimes detect that they are angry people. They vent their anger through a form of broadcast that has (for whatever reason) become a socially tolerated route to riches.

Question: How many shock-jocks does it take to change a light bulb? Answer: Three— one to throw the bulb away, one to stick his finger in the socket, and one to scream about it on the air.

New Routines for New Perspectives

Instead of listening to the radio on his drive to work, Bill could contemplate what he'd like to achieve for that day. If he has meetings, he could consider some of the points he would like to make. He might visualize having a pleasant lunch with a coworker. He might put on some classical music to ease his mind as he makes his way through the otherwise-unforgiving rush-hour traffic.

If he consciously chooses to play the radio, maybe he'll switch to a provocative news magazine–type show in which issues are covered with some depth and perspective. Perhaps he'll tune into something that truly stimulates his intellect.

Of course, he has the option of playing CDs or cassettes. He can listen to famous speeches, motivational programs, or entire books on cassette. He can play cassettes of famous old-time radio programs or listen to the Bible on cassette. By applying a modicum of creativity, he can turn his commuting time into something special. In the same manner, he can turn his use of the television into something special.

My friend has many different pockets of time available. He also has many options to determine how he spends them. So do you.

Jeff Davidson's Ten Steps to Kick Electronic Addiction

"But I'm not giving up television. There are some worthwhile things on TV, and I can turn it off whenever I want." If that's so, then fine. If you're hooked and you can't admit it to me, however, perhaps you can admit it to yourself. Here are 10 techniques that you can use to get yourself unplugged:

- ◆ Go a whole weekend without turning on a radio or television.

- ◆ Call your friends (both local and out-of-town) one evening per week instead of watching any television.

- ◆ Return to hobbies such as stamp collecting, playing a musical instrument, gardening, or playing word games one other weeknight instead of watching TV.

- ◆ Allow yourself to selectively watch two hours of programming each Saturday and Sunday for one month.

- ◆ Permit yourself one high-quality video per weekend during another month. The video has to inspire, inform, reflect history, be biographical, or be otherwise socially redeeming. Stop watching shoot-'em-ups, chase scenes, and films that titillate but add little to your life.

- ◆ If you walk or jog with a Walkman, undertake these exercises three times in a row without such a device so that you can experience another way to jog: naturally taking in what you pass.

- ◆ Look for others seeking to wean themselves from electronics. Is there a book discussion group? How about a bowling league, outing club, or biking group?

- ◆ Attend sporting events rather than viewing the same type of event on television. Watching a good high school baseball team or women's collegiate tennis match can be as rewarding as watching major-league baseball or Wimbledon. And you visibly support the athletes by being there.

- ◆ Recognize that the number of videos, CDs, computer games, and other electronic items competing for your attention exceeds the time you have in life to pay homage to them.

- ◆ Recognize that, rightly or wrongly, you've been programmed since birth to tune in to electronic media for news, information, entertainment, and diversion. It's by no means your only option.

Easy Math for Reclaiming Your Time

While the cumulative impact of being hooked on electronic media is considerable, the cumulative impact of doing what you don't like to do, such as household tasks, is equally insidious.

Recall the example of your 48-year career—graduating college at age 22 and working until age 70. Here's a quick way to see that you need to delegate or cast off those things that you don't like to do. Any activity in which you engage for only 30 minutes a day in the course of your 48-year productive work life will take one solid year of your life! Any activity in which you engage for only 60 minutes a day will take 2 solid years of your 48 years. How can this be so?

Think of it as a mini-math lesson that most of us never had in school: "Numbers That Really Mean Something." One half-hour is to 24 hours as 1 hour is to 48 hours. That's true by the good old commutative principle of arithmetic. Likewise, 1 hour is to 48 hours as 1 year is to 48 years.

Reflect and Win

Identify those activities that you currently handle yourself that could be handled some other way.

For you math buffs, here it is in equation form:

$\frac{1}{2}$ hour is to 24 hours as 1 hour is to 48 hours, or $\frac{.5}{24} = \frac{1}{48}$

1 hour is to 48 hours as 1 year is to 48 years, or $\frac{1}{48} = \frac{1}{48}$

When you consume $\frac{1}{48}$ of your day (only 30 minutes out of 24 hours), the cumulative effect over 48 years is to consume 1 year of your 48 years. There's no way around it. If you clean your house, on average, for 30 minutes a day, then, in the course of 48 years, you've spent the equivalent of 1 solid year, nonstop, cleaning your house.

If you don't relish cleaning your house (or something else you don't like) for an average of 30 minutes a day, stop doing it. Don't let your house get filthy; hire somebody to clean your house, clean it yourself less often, or find some other alternative. Why? Because the time in your life is being drained; the cumulative impact of doing what you don't like to do, as illustrated above, is that your precious years are being consumed. This is time that you simply cannot reclaim under any scenario.

"Well," you say, "that's fine to pay somebody to clean the house, but ultimately I'll be paying people for all kinds of things that I don't like to do, just so I can have more time." Yes! Exactly. In Chapter 7, "What Matters Most to You?" I'll get into this in spades.

What things do you know you need to stop doing because they are taking up valuable time in your life? For openers, here are some suggestions:

◆ Cleaning the house.

◆ Reading the newspaper every day. If it makes you late for work or prevents you from handling higher-priority activities, do it only now and then.

◆ Cutting the grass, or doing any other yard work. (See Chapter 9, "Buying Yourself Some Time," about when it makes sense to pay others to do it.)

- Fixing your car.
- Cooking.
- Reading junk mail because it's addressed to you. (Don't laugh. I know many people who feel compelled to read their junk mail: "Gee, somebody took the time to send me this.")
- Reading every godforsaken e-mail message zapped over to you.
- Answering the phone.

Confusion Contusion

If you enjoy some of these activities, by all means keep doing them. Perhaps you can do them a little less; perhaps there's another way to proceed. Your goal is to delegate or eliminate those tasks or activities that you can't stand doing. One author advises, "Don't manage something if you can eliminate it altogether." Not bad advice.

What have you been putting off that you could handle right now, knowing that you would simplify your life? I won't be offended if you stop reading for a moment, close the book, and give this question the full consideration that it merits unless, of course, a *Sopranos* rerun is coming on.

The Least You Need to Know

- You're probably going to live longer than you think, but it will be to no avail if your days continue to race by full of frustration and the same old stuff.
- To the extent that you can reduce your television viewing, you'll experience an abundance of extra time in your life.
- The cumulative impact of doing what you don't like to do is profound. A 30-minute, 20-minute, or even 10-minute savings per day is significant and increases the amount of discretionary time you have in your life.
- If drudgery sticks you up for either your life's time or your money, which would you rather hand over?
- Don't manage what you can eliminate altogether; simplify what you can't eliminate.

Chapter 4

Time-Binding Dilemmas That Can't Be Ignored

In This Chapter

◆ Why the time pressure you face is not a personal shortcoming

◆ Other people's time-pressure problems

◆ Five converging factors that conspire to consume your time

◆ More choices than you ever imagined

Suppose that all of society was in a hurry (which at most times seems to be the case). People are having to do more all the time, in less time. Sound familiar?

The emergence of the "24 × 7" society is troubling for many reasons, the least of which is that no one can be up for 24 hours—and no one needs to be. So you can order pizza at 3 A.M., go shopping after midnight, and be on the Internet all night long. Big deal. The key question is, can you physiologically afford to engage in such activities? And even if you could, why would you want to? As you'll see in Part 2, "Appointing Yourself in Charge," your body needs sleep and regular routines—in a word, predictability. You do have decades to go—don't play beat the clock.

Nearly Everyone Is Feeling Time-Pressure

Let's consider the two major principles you've been exposed to thus far. From Chapter 1, "The Overtime Epidemic: How to Nip It in the Bud," and Chapter 2, "Strategies for Survival," you learned that the key to winning back your time is to redevelop the habit of getting your work done within the course of a normal eight- or nine-hour workday. In Chapter 3, "Time Flies Whether You Want It to or Not," you saw that even small segments of time each day have a dramatic impact on the amount of time in your life over which you have control. The dilemma of this entire culture, however, is that everybody is feeling time-pressed—and feeling as if they are poor time managers, as if somehow they are at fault. (Can you relate?)

It may not be your fault, and you're not alone. The problem you face is a wide-sweeping phenomenon more than a personal one. Fortunately, there are measures you can take in your career and life to win back more of your time. First, however, you have to understand the true nature of the situation.

Does Retirement Bring Salvation?

Some people think that once they retire, they will have all the time in the world. Well, you get a little more time, but many retirees will tell you that the days fill up just as quickly. You're managing your investments and your garden; you're seeing doctors and your grandchildren; you're keeping up with the news—the day still flies by.

> **CAUTION**
>
> **Pause!**
>
> For the balance of this book, let's face an ever-present reality: It doesn't matter what your stage or position in life is— old or young, rich or poor, with children or childless. There is more than enough competing for your time and attention.

Even those not in the work force who volunteer for various causes find that the day gets taken up rather quickly. You have to volunteer for only a few groups a couple times a week, and, soon enough, you find yourself getting roped in. More projects, more causes, more interaction with more people, and, in the end, more to keep up with.

A Rare Commodity

The evidence is mounting that time has become the most valuable commodity in society. A study titled "Time Pressure in the 1990s," conducted by Hilton Time Value Surveys, found that folks feel just plain rushed:

◆ 77% of people surveyed selected "spending time with family and friends" as their top goal in the 1990s.

◆ 66% said they would put more emphasis on "having free time."

♦ 38% report cutting back on sleep to make more time.

♦ 33% said they seldom can make time for their ideal weekend.

♦ 33% said they don't accomplish what they set out to do each day.

♦ 31% worry that they spend too little time with their families and friends.

♦ 29% constantly feel under stress.

♦ 21% said they don't have time for fun anymore.

♦ 20% reported calling in sick to work at least once in the past year when they simply needed time to relax.

 Pause!

Simply being born into this culture at this time all but guarantees that much of your day will be consumed, if you're not careful.

We Want Our Time Back!

Before widespread use of the Internet, aspiring professionals traditionally faced steep challenges in keeping pace with the developments in their industries. Now the situation seems overwhelming. You can plan your day with the skill and precision of a surgeon. However, at some point in the day, mail, an email, a website, or a phone call will serve as the tipping point, throwing you off schedule. You have new decisions to make about how to incorporate the new information and handle your time.

Each new intrusion can take anywhere from a few minutes to several hours. Added to everything else you are balancing, even small amounts of information can bring on feelings of frustration and anxiety.

Rolling Rock Forever

The evil Greek King, Sisyphus, was condemned for all eternity to roll a rock up a never-ending hill. Most adults in society also feel as if they are facing a never-ending task. As they get close to putting their desks and files in order, feeling as if they have mastered the body of information that they need to grasp, they get hit by more, and more, and more.

Your email inbox provides the perfect analogy. You can read your incoming mail and then respond, delete, file, or delegate the messages. However, the task inevitably seems to grow longer and longer each day. The moment when you feel that you have everything under control, you log on and become freshly inundated.

Staggering numbers of emails are merely a highly visible symptom of a society awash in communication and information overload. The next day, the cycle starts again.

The Shower That Won't Turn Off

If you're like the typical working professional, your day begins with the latest news, weather, and traffic reports blaring from your bedside clock radio. You turn on the TV while dressing, and you scan the front page of the newspaper while gobbling down break-fast. Then you commute to work, alternately talking on the cell phone and listening to news, music, or audiotapes as you drive.

You arrive at work and open your email to see how many new unread messages have stacked up in your inbox. You open the first message, hoping that you can get through most of the new ones before you have to run off to your first meeting. You temporarily ignore the old messages still awaiting your attention. Your day has just begun, but your constant struggle to manage information overload is well under way.

Who isn't overwhelmed today by information competing for one's time and attention? People are constantly wading through masses of facts from TV, radio, newspapers, books, magazines, and the Internet.

In my book *Breathing Space: Living and Working at a Comfortable Pace in a Sped-Up Society*, I identify five megarealities that have an unconditional impact on everybody all the time. The factors include the following:

- An expanding volume of knowledge
- Mass-media growth and electronic addiction
- The paper-trail culture
- An overabundance of choices
- Population growth

Does it seem as if these factors are ganging up on you? If so, it's time to divide and con-quer: Let's examine them one by one.

Knowledge by the Ton

While information has become easier to find, access, store, and share, concurrently it becomes more difficult to keep up with, massage, and apply in meaningful ways to your career and life.

There is always far more that competes for your attention than you can ever handle. The volume of available information keeps increasing, while the time you have available to absorb it is limited. Few career professionals today have any sense of mastery when it comes to keeping pace with the information with which they feel they "ought" to keep up. The flood of yet more information arriving like unrelenting waves wreaks havoc on your ability to engage in quiet contemplation—how to apply what you have learned.

A Flood Without End

Some people have devised routines to help them make it through the information flood. Many people leave their offices in search of a quiet place where they can sit and reflect. Many carve out times during the day in which they exclusively open the mail, return phone calls, sift through the email glut, and so on.

Just when you get everything in order, the flood of information continues, and you feel overwhelmed even by midweek. You have chapters of books, magazines, mail, and other stuff piling up that you look at with disdain. So you start again.

Regardless of the ritual, one salient fact remains clear: The amount of information that you are subjected to today is only the tip of the iceberg compared to what is coming. All the management systems, rituals, disciplines, and superhuman efforts to keep up eventually fall to the ever-present reality: There is no keeping up. You must make tough choices as to what merits your time and attention, and you must have the mental and emotional strength to let go of the vast majority of information that you encounter.

Pause!

Here's the impasse of this overinformation era: The time necessary to learn all the rules for effective living now exceeds your life expectancy.

Power to Spare?

Knowledge is power, or so they say, but how many people feel powerful? Do you? Many people fear that they are underinformed. The volume of new knowledge broadcast and published in every field is enormous; it exceeds anyone's ability to keep pace. All told, more words are published or broadcast in an hour than you could comfortably ingest in the rest of your life. By far, America leads the world in the sheer volume of information generated and disseminated.

This is why so many books designed to help readers be more effective in managing their time fall wide of the mark. They list dozens, if not hundreds, of rules. You already have more "rules for being effective" to follow in your career and life, however, than you can comfortably handle. I doubt that feels effective.

The Time Master Says

The key to winning back your time is to be more effective at *being* rather than *doing*. If this sounds like mumbo-jumbo, let me say it another way: Winning back your time ultimately means having less to do, not more. Doing the "less" that I'm talking about means carefully identifying what's vitally important to you, which is the subject of Chapter 8, "Sustaining Your Priorities for Fun and Profit."

The Hierarchy of Input

We have to recognize that less is more—that we can take in, retain, and use only so much information. Here is a classification system that can help you keep it all in perspective.

Itty Bitty Bits

The lowest level of input is bits, single packets of information that essentially say "yes" or "no," "left" or "right," "on" or "off." In combination, bits add up to data.

Data, Data, Everywhere

Data represents raw numbers in chart form, equations, lists, and so on; ideally, it is objective, readily observable, and readily understandable.

Information Abounds

One step up from data is information. This stage represents the manipulation of data, analysis, interpretation, and reporting. Most articles that you come across in magazines and newspapers represent information. The author has drawn upon some data or observable phenomena, made some conclusions, and offered commentary.

Knowledge Knocking

When information is added to experience and viewed with reflection, depending upon whose brain is in the driver's seat, it can yield knowledge. Think of knowledge as the culmination of information that somebody gathered, thought about, and started to draw conclusions from.

The most knowledgeable people in your profession, not by coincidence, tend to read considerably, develop original thoughts, and then postulate (and draw conclusions) from what they have taken in.

Comparing knowledge with others makes a person valuable both within an organization and with clients and customers. The most knowledgeable salespeople, all other things being equal, have the best chance of achieving greater results. When new knowledge is gathered and added to on one's existing knowledge, wisdom becomes possible. This is as true for societies as it is for individuals.

Wisdom Happens

Wisdom often comes slowly, only after years and years of accumulated knowledge. At one time, women could not vote in elections. Ultimately, wisdom prevailed; now it's absurd to think that women should be denied the right to vote.

In your career, it's easy to get caught up in the overglut of data and information. It may be temporarily satisfying to maintain an unrelenting pace of reading everything that crosses your desk, downloading files, subscribing to publications, and so on. Indeed, much new knowledge can be generated from such efforts.

Wisdom, in an age in which far too much information confronts each of us, often comes in the form of the ability to recognize broad-based patterns and long-term trends instead of being caught up in short-term phenomena and, worse, fads.

Drawing Upon Accumulated Knowledge and Wisdom

As you begin to draw upon your own accumulated knowledge and the wisdom that you develop, you'll be able to free yourself from ever-accelerating flows of information.

If everyone is constantly besieged by information, the most prosperous among us will be those who are able to discern the direction in which society and markets are heading.

The Mass Media That Ate Society

As discussed in Chapter 3 (and probably from personal experience), the negative effect of the mass media on people's lives continues unchecked. With its sensationalized trivia, the mass media overglut often obscures fundamental issues that do merit concern, such as preserving the environment or feeding the starving. In America, more than five out of six households own VCRs. In 1972, three major television networks dominated television: ABC, NBC, and CBS. Now there are more than 500 full-power independent television stations. Many cable TV subscribers receive up to 140 channels that offer more than 72,000 shows per month. Bruce Springsteen once understated it best: "Fifty-seven channels and nothin' on." It may soon be 5,700 channels. The problem now is that there *always is something on that's worthwhile*, if not five or six programs! Alas, you've got only one life, you can live it only one day at a time, and you can absorb only so much.

> **CAUTION**
>
> **Pause!**
> You cannot read, learn, or absorb information fast enough to keep up. It's humanly impossible.

Paper Party

Dr. Keith Davidson, president of XPLOR International (and no relation to me), says:

> Paper-based documents, which accounted for 90 percent of document production in 1995, will only account for 30 percent in 2005. In the meantime, digital technologies will dramatically increase access to information and drive up the number of documents used by companies. The end result will be an overall increase in printed documents—the number practically doubling from 1995 to 2005.

So while the percentage of paper documents within your office is declining, the overall number of sheets of paper that you will be confronted by is only going to climb. Consider these statistics:

- ◆ Based on data from CAP Ventures of Norwell Massachusetts, the typical U.S. office is increasing its paper consumption by 6 percent each year.

- ◆ *CEO Magazine* reports that five billion photocopies are made each year in the United States. With a workforce of about 167 million people, that means about 3,000 sheets per person per year, breaking down to about 12 sheets per workday.

- ◆ Price Waterhouse Cooper's Technology Forecasts reveal that for each $100 million increase in sales experienced by a company, 8.8 million sheets of paper are consumed.

- ◆ The typical executive receives more than 225 pieces of unsolicited mail each month, or about 12 pieces daily.

- ◆ Annually, the average family receives more than 200 catalogs that it did not request—add to those the ones it did request, with an onslaught arriving between late August and Christmas.

It's like being a computer overloaded with data or a detective swamped with too many eyewitness reports. Having too much paper to deal with makes you feel overwhelmed and overworked.

Behind the statistics loom two basic reasons why American society in particular spews so much paper: We have very low postal rates, and we have the most equipment that can generate paper!

Choices Beyond Counting

Choice is the blessing of a free market economy. Like too much of everything else, however, having too many choices is, well, overwhelming. Currently, more than 1,350 varieties of shampoo are on the market. More than 2,000 skin care products are currently selling. Some 100 different types of exercise shoes are now available, each with scores of variations in style, functions, and features. Every choice demands time; increased time expenditure means mounting exhaustion.

The Weight of the World

World population grows unabated. More people, everywhere, inevitably means more lines, more delays, and slower progress when it comes to many daily activities.

In the Philippines, the Manila Hotel now provides five-minute helicopter rides for guests between the hotel and the downtown business district. Otherwise, the rush-hour trip would take an hour and a half by car.

60 Minutes reporter Morley Safer narrated a segment on the show that discussed how mass tourism is "turning the world's places of beauty into swarming ant hills and rancid junk heaps." Among the worldwide treasures being laid to waste are these:

- Venice is sinking more rapidly than it would be otherwise because of the extreme number of pedestrian tourists.
- The Great Wall of China is crumbling under the weight of increasing numbers of tourists.
- The face of the Parthenon is slowly but surely being scratched to oblivion.

Coming to Terms

In *Future Shock* (1970), Alvin Toffler used the term **overchoice** to describe the stress that comes from too many options, especially the so-what variety. In paperback, the book itself was a classic example: You could buy it with a blue, orange, or hot-pink cover.

Reflect and Win

If you feel better about your own life, it's easier to empathize and take action on behalf of those who need help. For one thing, you have a little more time to do so.

Cheaper by the Billions

Not only are you not alone, but you're also less alone all the time. From the dawn of creation to C.E. 1850, the world population grew to one billion. It grew to two billion by 1930, three billion by 1960, four billion by 1979, five billion by 1987, and six billion by 1996, with seven billion en route. Every 33 months, the current population of America is added to the planet.

Each day, the world population (births minus deaths) increases by more than 275,000 people. Geometric growth in human population permeates and dominates every aspect of the planet: its resources, the environment, and all living things.

One could argue that having all these new people around makes the world more hectic, its people more competitive for fewer economic niches, and employers more apt to see the labor force as a cheap commodity whose personal time they can claim willy-nilly. Regardless, the increasing effects of population pressure have a profound impact upon the reality of current human existence. I don't see how you can ignore it.

The megarealities are not likely to diminish, but, by understanding them, you're in a far better position to take effective action. Read on!

The Least You Need to Know

- ◆ Physiologically, you can't afford to engage in activities on a 24×7 basis.
- ◆ It doesn't matter what your stage or position in life is—there is more than enough competing for your time and attention.
- ◆ Time has become the most valuable commodity in society.
- ◆ The volume of new knowledge in every field is enormous and exceeds anyone's ability to keep pace.
- ◆ Choice is the blessing of a free market economy, but, like too much of anything, having too many choices is overwhelming.

Chapter 5

A Crowded House

In This Chapter

- A larger population results in more gridlock in every aspect of life
- No clear solutions for decades; so now what?
- Increased waiting time is now a part of everyone's life
- Patience is a seemingly vanishing virtue

The rapid increase in population alone has a dramatic impact on the pace of society and your life. The more densely packed an urban area is, the more likelihood there is of gridlock—traffic jams of cars, buses, subways, and planes. Ultimately, that takes time away from you.

It is taking you longer to drive merely a few blocks; it's not the day of the week or the season, and it's not going to subside soon. Our population and road use grow faster than the government's ability to repair highways, bridges, and vital urban arteries.

People, Roads, and Gridlock

The roads aren't going to clear up soon; it would cost more than $2 trillion over the next 30 years to repair and maintain the nation's pipes, tunnels, cables, and roads. More than half of the heavily traveled roads in America that link urban and suburban areas are in fair to poor condition. Is it any wonder that you lose a large chunk of your time getting to work and back?

Commuting snarls are increasing. City planners report that there will be no clear solution to gridlock for decades, and population studies reveal that the nation's metropolitan areas will become home to an even greater percentage of the population.

Coming to Terms

What the words **grid-lock, airlock, camplock, and shoplock** tell you is that it pays to be a contrarian, a word I like that means somebody too stubbornly individual to do what everybody else is trying to do at once.

Crowding makes urban spaces harder to traverse, which eats up more time; hence, the less space there is, the less time there is. Even suburban areas will face unending traffic dilemmas. If only the gridlock was confined to commuter arteries. Not so. Shoppers, air travelers, vacationers, even campers—everyone in motion—is (or will be) feeling its effects. We'll get to counteracting them in a minute; for now, consider some of these "locks" on your time.

Airlock

As a result of the terrorist attacks, fewer people may be flying, at least temporarily. However, the delays will be just as long as before; as a result of heightened security, it may actually take longer to board planes.

Overall, airline passenger traffic has more than tripled since 1980. Airport expansion trails the increased passenger loads. Worse, all airlines pad their scheduled departure and arrival times—extended more than 50 percent since 1980—to appear as if they're not late, while actual air time remains about the same. When you're scheduled to board at 10:10 A.M., that is simply when you're supposed to be seated in the plane. Rollout from the gate is always later. Consequently, the airlines are as slow and late as ever, but now they're within the promised limits.

If you're not already doing it, bring plenty of work (or another diversion) with you so that you can remain productive (or at least calm) despite flight delays.

Camplock

On an average summer day, Yellowstone Park has more visitors than the population of Houston. Other national parks across the country are faced with swarms of visitors; campsites are in high demand. While the federal government is making good progress restoring the parks, vacationers have to contend with traffic, lines for concessions, and waiting lists for campsites in the meantime.

Hereafter, it may make sense to do your camping Tuesday through Thursday—whenever the masses are not there—or find "undiscovered" parks closer to home.

Shoplock

There is more retail space in America today than ever. For an indication of how much we are all bombarded by choices and information, consider this. Use of the Internet grew dramatically between 1994 and 1999. More people began using the Internet for gathering information, shopping, and entertainment than anyone could have predicated a decade ago. Yet, from 1986 to 1999, shopping center square footage per U.S. resident climbed from 14.7 square feet to 20 square feet! Since 1991, it has climbed from 18.1 square feet to 20 square feet.

We have far more shopping center square footage in this country than ever before. While the Montgomery Ward, Bradley's, Sears, and JC Penney were closing stores—or in the case of the first two, going out of business—other chains such as The Dollar Tree, Target, Best Buy, and Barnes & Noble were expanding markedly.

Despite the dramatic increase in Internet, catalog, and TV shopping, shopping malls still always appear crowded. Waiting for a parking space can take 10 minutes, unless you're willing to park in the far reaches of some lots. Once inside, you have to jostle through crowds to get to shops, movie theaters, and restaurants—and that's on slow days. This effect is tripled during the holidays.

Cyberlock

Millions of people are getting online every day and every evening. As broadband capabilities such as DSL, cable, and satellite transmission become widespread, the ability to get online in a hurry and download information at frightening speeds only gets easier. Yet the Internet both gives and takes away.

How much time do you want to be seated in the evening after being seated all day at work? Considering how much time some people spend in front of their computers, they might as well be strapped to their seats. Locked in. And the results are that friendships erode. Hobbies are forgotten. The parts of themselves that make them unique are lost.

Reflect and Win

To avoid the "locks" that so many others encounter, commute early or late in the day, fly during the week, camp at less populated sites, and so on.

Having to Wait

Any way you slice it, waiting is going to be a part of your life. Some varieties of waiting are not so bad. Waiting at your desk for your computer to boot up is only nominally frustrating because you're relatively in control—plus, you have things with which to occupy yourself. Similarly, waiting at either your home or your office for someone to arrive affords you the opportunity to take care of other tasks, although you still may feel slightly imposed upon.

Delays Away from Your Turf

Experiencing a delay away from your own turf potentially has a different impact. For example, here's a synopsis of three delays most frequently occurring outside of your immediate environment and how they are commonly perceived:

- **Waiting to see a service professional.** Delays incurred by waiting to see a doctor or a lawyer, as long as the length of the wait remains within acceptable limits, usually don't throw people off stride.

- **Waiting for an appointment to arrive.** Beyond a reasonable threshold, waiting for a service provider or anyone else to come to you begins to feel like an imposition, and each passing minute can seem like two or three times what it actually is. Some people construe being late for an appointment as an overt or a covert lack of respect. A person might feel that whoever keeps him waiting is being careless with his time.

- **Unforeseen delays.** These can easily be the most frustrating kinds of delays. For instance, you expected to simply dash in and out of the convenience store; however, you experience a seven-minute delay. Those seven minutes seem infinitely longer than other seven-minute segments in your life. And a series of unrelated delays can make each successive delay more untenable!

Some factors make people less prone to delays, which impacts the way an occasional delay is experienced. For example, the more privileged you are, the less likely you are to experience delays, and perhaps the less adept you are at dealing with them.

Delay-Lengthening Culprits

A delay will seem longer when you feel it's unjustified. Take the case of a hotel clerk answering the phone before tending to you. Why would somebody calling be more important than someone who is standing at the hotel registration desk?

A wait under less than favorable circumstances such as in humid weather, amid disruptive noise, or in an inhospitable setting will always seem to last longer. If you are anxious or under stress, any delay can and will seem excessive.

What? Me Have Down Time?

Personal technologies have greatly affected people's inability to wait. When you can change channels or Web sites with a single click, why would you want to spend an extra minute in a supermarket checkout line? Patience is seemingly a virtue.

Much of the fascination and overuse of cell phones undoubtedly stems from users' inability to incur any down time, let alone delays or waiting time. Yet, by reflexively stuffing all spare moments with filler phone calls, the "race-through-the-day" mind-set takes holds, becomes seemingly irreplaceable, and then further exacerbates one's upset at having to wait for anything.

Time-Shifting 101

When you find yourself waiting in lines, practice appropriate time-shifting to avoid crowds. Consider these suggestions:

◆ Buy your movie tickets early, take a walk, and then return three minutes before the picture starts (after everyone has already filed into the theater). There are always available seats, even for twosomes; theater management knows exactly how many tickets they're selling for each show.

◆ Take a different approach to movies: Go to the theater early for the first showing, buy your tickets, go in and take a seat, and, for the next 20 minutes or so, listen to your favorite music with a Walkman headset.

◆ If you commute, rather than going earlier or later, explore not going in at all—by telecommuting. (I'll discuss this in detail in Chapter 8, "Sustaining Your Priorities for Fun and Profit.")

◆ To avoid airlock, fly in the day before and fly out after everyone else has. Schedule vacation travel time, particularly around Thanksgiving and Christmas, as much as six months in advance. You might stay home during those times and travel when everyone else isn't—namely, the week after the holidays. More on this in Chapter 23, "Treading Lightly—And Loving It."

◆ To avoid camplock, patronize some of the less-traveled national and state parks. There are more than 200 national parks and thousands of state parks; most do not experience hordes of visitors.

◆ To avoid shoplock, make more purchases by catalog—but be careful of how and when you give out your name. Otherwise, you'll be inundated by dozens of other catalog vendors. You probably have a fax machine at work, and you may even have one at home. Shopping by fax has never been easier. It's actually a great time-saver because your name, address, phone, and fax number are accurately submitted to vendors, along with your order, order number, and the price.

Coming to Terms

Telecommuting is working outside the office (that is, away from your employer's base of operations) and staying in touch with coworkers via electronics, such as a computer, a fax, a pager, and a phone. It can be done from your home, a hotel, a satellite office, or even your car.

Transmuting Commuting

As metro areas keep expanding, and as daily commuting becomes more trying, some people, but not a significant number, telecommute (see Chapter 1, "The Overtime Epidemic: How to Nip It in the Bud"). Telecommuters complete much of their work back in the traditional office.

The benefits to you include decreased commuting time; reduced personal cost for travel, clothing, and food; flexible working hours; more time for dependents; and potentially greater autonomy.

You can rack up significant time savings by *telecommuting*, as detailed in the following table.

How Commuting Adds Up to Lost Time

Round-Trip Minutes/Day	Hours/Year	Equivalent Number of Forty-Hour Weeks
40	160	4
60	240	6
80	320	8
100	400	10

Believe it or not, the federal government is on your side when it comes to telecommuting! In 1990, the Clean Air Act mandated that all businesses employing more than 100 people in a single location reduce their employees' commute time by 25 percent. Employers could encourage the use of public transportation, car-pooling, condensed work weeks, or telecommuting. The act has since been implemented, primarily in the states with the worst pollution.

Perhaps you can sell your employers on this trend. The benefits to them include potentially higher productivity, reduced office or plant costs, the ability to accommodate physically challenged employees, and the ability to motivate new employees with an attractive stay-at-home-and-get-paid option.

Stockbrokers, consultants, writers, and some top-level executives are finding that telecommuting enables them to maintain—and even increase—their overall productivity. Jobs such as computer programming, translating, software engineering, sales, and system analysis are well suited for telecommuting. Other professions, such as word processing, book publishing, telemarketing, research, and architecture, also lend themselves to effective telecommuting.

Still, despite all the technological breakthroughs, telecommuting has been employed only marginally. Some employees have been directed to telecommute; others have requested the option. Yet, in business and government, most employees don't telecommute, even periodically.

Even on a limited basis, telecommuting can provide you with many benefits beyond the time saved. These include cost savings, as well as the freedom to focus on projects, initiate conceptual thinking, and exercise more control over your environment. Check it out!

Shopping Secrets of the Unfrazzled

"Shop 'til you drop" is often too true for too many people. Why do it? The list in this section contains a host of tips that you can use to budget your time more effectively and feel less stressed when shopping (in general and during the holidays):

♦ Don't wait until the last days or hours before picking up a crucial item.

♦ Avoid going to huge shopping malls if you can. Use the 1-800-numbers found in catalogs or go online. Ask that your name be kept off the vendors' direct-mail lists. Receiving dozens of unwanted catalogs throughout the year diminishes your breathing space and contributes to landfills.

♦ Spend a few minutes at home or work contemplating what you are going to buy and for whom. Then draw up a list and bring it with you—this will help keep you focused and less prone to becoming overwhelmed once you're inside the stores.

♦ If you choose to go to a super regional mall because of the wide selections available, arrive near the opening or closing. Don't compete with the mad rush of shoppers during peak hours.

♦ Find a mall entrance that is less popular than the others. You're likely to find a parking space more easily.

♦ Reduce the strain of carrying large bundles by choosing smaller-size gifts, such as jewelry, compact discs, cassettes, gloves, sunglasses, and so forth.

◆ Shop on Monday, Tuesday, or Wednesday evenings. Avoid weekend shopping!

◆ Give yourself frequent breaks while shopping. It's not a marathon event. There is no reason to make shopping for friends and loved ones anything but a joyful experience. Lighten up!

◆ Patronize establishments that have one long line, now used in banks or airports, where the person at the front of the line goes to the next available service attendant. Avoid stores that have parallel lines that prompt shoppers to guess which line will be the fastest.

◆ If you find a gift that would please many of those on your gift list, such as chocolates or a book, buy multiple quantities in one transaction to reduce overall shopping time.

◆ When buying holiday gifts and cards, make your shopping count three and four times. Think: Is there someone having a wedding, birthday, or baby shower soon? It may mean doing a little more shopping now, but you'll avoid many more trips in the throes of January, February, and March.

CAUTION

Pause!

Don't patronize stores that have one line for purchases and another line for pickup. You'll easily double your time in line. Such an arrangement is highly beneficial for the store, but not for you.

The Time Master Says

From now on, you're likely to experience other forms of "lock" in whatever career or personal endeavors you undertake. Engaging in activities at times when other than those of the masses has never been a more useful option. Become a contrarian!

◆ If you anticipate a long line, bring something that will help to make the time pass by more easily. This could be a bit of reading material, something to eat, a hand-gripper, or even a handheld game.

◆ Vote with your feet. If a store consistently causes you to wait and has not figured out how to handle varying streams of customers throughout the day and week (because they've never plotted their own internal rush hours), take your business elsewhere.

◆ Once you get packages home, take them to your table, desk, or wherever you're going to complete the shopping trip—you still have to remove tags and stickers, file the invoices, wrap items, mail some of them, and store others.

◆ Designate one evening for greeting cards—if you send out cards, send them all out the same evening; then they're out of the way and en route.

The simple reality of today and of your life (not to mention everyone else's) is that society will grow more complex every day for the rest of your life. (Wow, what an existence.) Who gets the blame? As we'll see in the next chapter, nobody.

The Least You Need to Know

♦ Being born into this society, in this era, nearly guarantees that increasingly you will feel pressed for time. The time pressure that you feel is largely not your fault.

♦ More choices mean more time spent choosing.

♦ Shop, travel, camp, and drive when others are not. Time-shift to avoid crowds whenever you can.

♦ Telecommuting, though underused, offers incredible benefits.

♦ Use store services when shopping, such as catalog ordering, delivery, and gift-wrapping.

Chapter 6

Slowing the Pace of the Rat Race

In This Chapter

- ◆ Social complexity happens!
- ◆ Follow the basics
- ◆ Convert your challenge into a question
- ◆ Time and money are inextricably linked
- ◆ Relinquishing low-level choices

I often give speeches at annual conventions and conferences. No longer am I amazed at the ever-growing variety of professional associations that have not only been established but that actually have thousands of members. For example, there is (whether you believe it or not) a National Association of Sewer Service Companies, a Cranial Academy, a Medieval Academy of America, a Society of Certified Kitchen and Bathroom Designers, a Society of Wine Educators, and even an International Concatenated Order of Hoo-Hoo. Ho-ho.

More people, more groups, more information generated. Where's it all leading? One result is that the amount of information that competes for your time on a daily basis is on the rise—and taking a staggering toll. You may have an M.B.A. degree, you may have 10 years of management experience under your belt, and you may have read every book on time management in creation. Nevertheless, you can't keep up. You are not alone—and you are probably not to blame.

CAUTION

Pause!

The impact that over information has on your own sense of adequacy is rarely acknowledged. More and more professionals feel inadequate, as if somehow they're supposed to be on top of it all.

Your Self-Esteem Is Beside the Point

Feeling time-pressed today is not connected to how you were raised; it's not a question of where you went to school, where you live, what your profession is, or who you married. Even individuals who display high self-worth and high self-esteem often have too many concerns competing for their time and attention; they feel extreme time pressure. What's more, people who set goals—and do it well—frequently feel overwhelmed.

If you can accept the notion that the dissipation of your career and personal time is probably not your fault, you're well on the road to winning back your time.

Rain Barrels Keep Falling on My Head

Suppose that you were extremely parched and the only source of water was a huge, heavy rain barrel. One way to quench your thirst would be to lift it up and try to gulp a few sips at a time. This feat would require impressive strength and balance, but why waste so much effort on such a difficult way to drink? If you stuck a small cup in the rain barrel and extracted a couple of ounces at a time, you could far more easily quench your thirst. Now consider the daily information deluge. When you attempt to take in everything that's flung your way, the predictable response is that you drown in information (and still don't quench your thirst).

Tackling new information—such as navigating the Internet, integrating another technology into your work routine, or assimilating other changes—is smoother when you employ the basics.

What are the basics? It's simple:

1. Follow directions.
2. Take one step at a time.
3. Assess where you are every couple of steps.
4. After each assessment, having determined that you are on the right path, continue.

Information comes to you at a breakneck pace, and that pace will accelerate day after day for the rest of your life. How can you avoid being overwhelmed? Don't bite off more than you can chew; sometimes simply slowing down is the best response to "too much of too much" competing for your time and attention. Slow down so that you can figure out the best way to proceed.

Sit and Ponder

Hereafter, begin practicing a new response when too much is thrown at you: Take a momentary pause. Slowing down has its virtues!

I saw a clever phrase that sums up the philosophy here: "Don't just do something, sit there." Too often, the reflex to take action only exacerbates your time-pressure problems. I'll tackle this issue head-on in Part 6, "Your Relationship, Your Time, and Your Sanity."

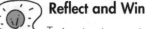

Reflect and Win

Trying to stay on top of it all only ensures monumental frustration. Nobody today can remain on top of everything, nor is the attempt worthwhile. What you can do—and this is quite a lot— is make choices about where (and to what) you'll direct your time and attention.

A Formula for Slowing Down

Over-Achievers Anonymous, an actual group of go-getters, annually bestows the America's *Most Overworked Person Award*. One winner was described as the most extreme example of someone in the position of power who has the ability to choose if and how he is going to take care of himself, and yet challenges the limits of human endurance.

When interviewed by a major newspaper, the award winner said that he wasn't proud of the title, and he knows that he needs to make some changes but doesn't know where to begin.

The solution to many dilemmas lies in taking the reverse of your situation and making a question out of it. Suppose that you don't know how to slow down. Then ask yourself, "What would someone who evenly paces himself do in my situation?" If you're honest with yourself, by merely posing the question, you open yourself up to a world of insights. I suggest writing it at the top of a blank piece of paper so that you will have plenty of room for all the self-generated solutions that you record. Or, type it at the top of your PC screen.

Even if you've been in overdrive for months, posing the question "What would a calm person do?" to yourself opens you up to intriguing insights. Answers could include these:

- Do stretches in the morning.
- Allocate more tasks to staff.

- Brainstorm with staff.
- Always have lunch with a friend.
- Concentrate on the most profitable activities.
- Take more frequent walks throughout the day.
- See a therapist.
- Schedule more vacation time.

Deficit Spending Is a No-No

Many people feel overwhelmed in handling debts and other financial obligations. The bills arrive, and they need to be paid. Staying in a positive cash-flow position can start to feel like a full-time job in itself. Running a deficit budget, if you're stuck there, is a full-scale time thief.

Chances are, you have some financial deficits (lucky guess?). For decades, millions of Americans have accumulated personal debt via credit cards, loans, and other forms of financing. In fact, personal and credit card debt are now at all-time highs. People are consistently spending money beyond their means.

Rapid Erosion

Sustained deficit spending eventually erodes your ability to prepare for the future—and, worse, to capitalize on current opportunities. What's this got to do with winning back your time? Well, it's an exercise in fiendishly simple logic: The more you owe, the more squelched you are! "I owe, I owe, it's off to work I go."

You may have learned to consume way past your needs. I have found (and you may have hit upon a similar insight) that the more material possessions I own, the less I feel in control of my time. (Not that there aren't some really neat things to buy.) For example, during my college days and early 20s, when I had little, I felt the freest—freest from worry and freest from the time-consuming task of juggling my bills.

How would it feel if all your credit cards were paid off? How would it feel if you paid your monthly rent or mortgage several months in advance? How would it feel if your car loan was paid off? How would it feel if you were actually able to pay some of your utility bills for months down the road? For most people, it would feel wonderful. You'd feel in control of your time. I've experienced this firsthand, because I do it. More to the point, the time spent worrying is reduced to zip.

I've heard the argument against paying bills in advance: that I lose the (scant) interest that I could have earned on the money if I had left it in my account. Ah, but wait. A month after I've paid my electric bill three months in advance, I get the next month's bill. Guess what? It shows that I have a huge credit and that nothing is due. I smile when I see bills like these. So will you. This approach frees you twice: The bill is already paid (which robs the bill of its wet-blanket effect), *and* you've freed yourself from having to fight the reluctance to sit down and pay it now.

A Moratorium on Spending

To reduce your personal financial deficits, I suggest placing a moratorium on spending—regardless of what items entice you—until your credit cards are paid off. Now, please, let's not confuse issues. In Chapter 3, "Time Flies Whether You Want It to or Not," I discuss briefly the value of paying others to do those things that you don't like to do—it's a way of investing in your freedom. This is a theme that I'll return to in detail in Chapter 9, "Buying Yourself Some Time." But that's not what I'm talking about here. Learning to control your tendency for overspending is different from buying back the time that you would otherwise have to spend on unnecessary chores that you actively dislike.

Here are some useful exercises for controlling your checkbook, simplifying your financial life, and winning back more of your time:

> **The Time Master Says**
>
> Paying for something that frees up your time is a life benefit. Paying for material things that you don't need (and that certainly don't save you time) may be satisfying but ultimately can be draining.

1. Write checks to pay bills in advance of their due dates. Then keep an advance file with a folder for each day of the month. Place the check in a sealed, addressed, stamped envelope. Then put the envelope in the folder of the day that it's to be mailed. This way, the money is allocated in advance in your checkbook, and your bills are paid on time. If your checking account pays interest (for you "interest" buffs), it also means that you don't lose interest.

2. Occasionally overpay the balance due on your continuing accounts, or pay early. This provides you the aforementioned psychological boost when you see a credit on your next statement, and it gives you a good reputation with your creditors—which could come in handy in the future.

3. Keep a stick-on note in your checkbook that lists what's coming in this month and what needs to go out. This provides you with a running mini cash-flow list that you can refer to any time. Update it every couple of weeks—or days, if necessary.

4. Look back through your old checks and carefully see what you paid to whom for what. Do the same thing with your monthly credit card statements. Put a red mark next to all those expenditures that, in retrospect, you could have done without.

5. Now, considering expenditures on the horizon, which ones can you cut?

6. Pay bills online when possible. It saves time, and you don't have to pay for a stamp.

As author Roger Dawson says, it doesn't matter how much money you're making; if you're spending more than you take in each month, you're headed for trouble.

Choices Beyond Practicality

One fundamental reason that you might not be enjoying this time of your life as much as you did a year (or five years) ago is the number of choices you continually confront (one of the "megarealities"). While flying from Denver to San Francisco and flipping through one of the airline magazines, I came upon an ad for jelly beans. You remember jelly beans, little bundles of mouth-size fun? When people in my age group were growing up, how many different colors of jelly beans where there? Six, maybe eight? Let's see: green, black, pink, red, yellow, blue, and orange.

The ad that I saw had names and pictures—if you can believe this—of 48 types of jelly beans. Banana mint swirl. Peppermint polka-dot patty. Lazy lime sublime. What's a kid to do? (I have tasted some of that company's product, including jalapeno. Weird, but fun. Of course, if you're going to habituate kids to overchoose, you've gotta start 'em early.)

It's not merely in the candy world that choices have proliferated. Go into an athletic shoe store today, and the clerk will ask you, "What'll it be—air up, air out, pump up, pump down?" Go into a bike store, and the clerk will ask you, "10-speed, 15-speed, 21-speed, men's, women's, mountain bike, trail bike, or racing bike?" The same phenomenon occurs when you go to buy a tennis racquet, an exercise machine, a whirlpool bath, or even a birdbath. (No kidding, you have to shop for a birdbath to appreciate the overabundance of choices that can suddenly confront you. I wonder if all this choice matters to the birds.)

The New York Times ran a major feature saying that people are experiencing stress and anxiety today when shopping for (excuse me?) leisure goods. There are so many choices! Weighing such choices takes up your time. And the problem is worse in the workplace.

> **Reflect and Win**
>
> At all times, your goal is to scoop out information in amounts that you can digest and to tackle activities in amounts that you can handle.

> **Pause!**
>
> At first blush, it wouldn't seem as if a plethora of choices is such a bad thing. After all, what can be the harm in having a wide variety of options available? The answer is that there is great harm in filling precious time with nagging-but-trivial decisions.

Choices over the Top

Consider all the vendor product catalogs that you're retaining. How about all the flyers for management-training seminars? And magazine and newsletter subscription offers at incredible savings? Everywhere you turn, you see, you're confronted with more choices than you can comfortably respond to.

Every moment adds up. If you spend a lot of them contemplating which product or service to choose from among dozens or hundreds, you are consuming considerable amounts of your time to little or no good effect. Even when you choose, however wisely, it isn't once and for all. Next week, next month, next year, a new, better, faster, sleeker, less expensive, more powerful version of your product or service will be available. It will be that way for the rest of your life. (And these choices are only some of the small stuff. In Chapter 21, "Decide or Let It Ride," I'll discuss making big decisions in record time.)

Your unrelenting responsibility to keep choosing is another one of those mostly unacknowledged aspects of being born into this culture at this time. And, once again, its cumulative effect is to rob you of your time.

As often as possible, avoid making such low-level choices. If the same yardstick is available in red, blue, yellow, or white, and it's all the same to you, grab the one that's closest—or take the one that the clerk hands you.

Whenever you find yourself facing a low-level decision, consider this: Does this make a difference? Get in the habit of making only a few decisions a day: the ones that count. For the low-level stuff, reclaim your right to say, "Who cares?" or "It doesn't matter."

Your Time, Your Decision

Many people proceed through their days and their lives as if others were in control of their time. Do you fall into this category? Right now, look at this list and put a check mark next to any party on the list that you believe is in control of your time.

❏ Parents	❏ Spouse
❏ Children	❏ Neighbors
❏ Community	❏ Landlord or mortgagor
❏ The company president	❏ The boss
❏ Coworkers	❏ Peers
❏ Your industry	❏ Opinion leaders
❏ The government	❏ Friends
❏ The president	❏ PC
❏ The governor, mayor	❏ The press
❏ Television, radio	❏ Unknown forces

When I ask people in seminars to complete this checklist, most catch on quickly and leave all the boxes unchecked. The one box that does get checked, if any, is "The boss." There are bad bosses, unreasonable bosses, workaholic bosses, and even psychotic bosses. I've had them all! (See the section "Teach Your Boss" in Chapter 11, "Loaning Yourself Out Less and Being Happier Because of It.") Your boss may pile on the assignments, but you're the one who determines how, largely when, and often with whom you'll tackle them.

> **CAUTION**
>
> **Pause!** _____
>
> Family and friends are important, of course, but their expectations should not dictate how you spend your time. "Being there" for them is not the same thing as being at their beck and call.

The degree to which you believe that your boss or anyone else controls your time is the degree to which you'll have to struggle to win back your time. Denis Waitely, author of *Timing Is Everything*, says that you are in the control booth of your life (unless, of course, you relinquished control—or, worse, forgot that you ever were in control).

Be Your Own Consultant

Perhaps you have no problem acknowledging intellectually that you are, in fact, in control of your time. Putting that knowledge into practice may be a bit more difficult. An article that I once read taught me a technique for proceeding when confronted with too much stuff competing for my time and attention. It originated with none other than Richard Nixon, America's thirty-seventh president. Nixon practiced the notion of becoming a consultant to himself.

When you're faced with many choices (what decision to make, which road to take, which dish to bake), pretend that you are a highly paid consultant—to yourself. If your last name is Smith, your internal dialogue would begin as follows: "What does Smith need to do next?" You proceed as if you are able to separate yourself from your physical shell, moving to a corner of the room and observing yourself from the vantage point of an objective third party.

Instant Objectivity

By referring to yourself in the third person ("What does Smith need to do next?"), you derive different answers from those you'd get if you simply thought, "What should I do next?"

How so? A semantic shift occurs when you refer to yourself as if you were an observer. A channel of discovery opens that's not readily available to you otherwise. (Maybe it has to do with whether you're seeing the forest or the trees.)

When can you use this technique? When can't you use it? Becoming a consultant to yourself works as well in crunch times as it does in milder times. A variation on this theme is to pretend that a real-life trusted advisor or mentor is there with you. Ask yourself how he would advise you.

Tackle Number 1

If you have six tasks facing you—or any number, for that matter—there really is no faster or more efficient way than identifying the most important one, tackling it, and then going on to number 2. In the long run, any other method for proceeding through the day, however psychologically satisfying, simply cannot compete with tackling the tasks in order of the importance that you've assigned them.

Exhibiting Your Inner Wisdom

Whether it's becoming a contrarian, taking one step at a time, spending less and keeping your debts to zero, being more prudent about the information that you ingest, remembering who's in control, avoiding low-level choices when possible, or becoming a consultant to yourself, you can always turn to yourself for the important task of safeguarding your time.

> **The Time Master Says**
>
> You are more resourceful than you often acknowledge, and you always have more options than you know of.

The Least You Need to Know

♦ Social complexity will continue, and it will make you feel less in control—it has that effect on everybody; your ability to manage your affairs is not a self-worth or self-esteem issue.

♦ The health of your cash flow influences the control that you have over your time. Spend more, work longer, and watch your control disappear.

♦ You'll face a mind-boggling array of choices competing for your time and attention; avoid low-level decision making, if possible.

♦ Take one step at a time. Don't be afraid to slow down temporarily.

♦ You, not your boss or anyone else, get to decide where you spend time. Become a consultant to yourself when you need third-party objectivity.

Part 2

Appointing Yourself in Charge

Armed with all the great stuff that you learned in Part 1, "The Big Clock is Ticking," it's time to appoint yourself as the head honcho in charge of winning back your time. This involves identifying and going after your priorities, getting real, and getting what you want. Then we'll move to other neat stuff, like why time and money are not the same thing. You'll get an eye-opening look at why you're hardly able to stay awake days and (too often) you find yourself up all night. Undoubtedly you're now ready to kick some derriere and stand up for yourself—first by lying down longer and more often, as in sleep. You're not sleeping enough.

When you're well rested, you can better handle everything that everyone is asking you to do. Not just your boss, but also your family, friends, and neighbors may tend to ask more of you simply because you can do it. So, you need some carefully considered strategies.

Chapter 7

What Matters Most to You?

In This Chapter

- ◆ Why it's crucial to choose and support a handful of priorities
- ◆ Health, wealth, and wisdom all accumulate gradually
- ◆ How to reinforce your priorities and support your goals

It seems to be getting harder and harder to know what we truly want for ourselves. The powers that be on Madison Avenue and in Hollywood have gotten so adept at manipulating us all that the wants and needs that we genuinely believe were self-generated, for the most part, come from carefully crafted campaigns that command our attention, stoke our emotions, and stimulate the deep well of desire within each of us. Although the terrorist attacks on America have prompted many to shift their priorities, one has to wonder how long that will last, especially given the profound impact of orchestrated cultural influences.

Corporate Creations

In his book *Culture Jam: How to Reverse America's Suicidal Consumer Binge-And Why We Must*, author Kalle Lasn says, "American culture is no longer created by the people. Our stories, once passed from one generation to the next by parents, neighbors, and teachers, are now told by distant corporations with 'something to sell as well as to tell.'"

Reflect and Win _____

In *Flow: The Psychology of Optimal Experience,* Mihaly Csikszentmihalyi says, "There is no inherent problem in our desire to escalate our goals, as long as we enjoy the struggle along the way."

The Time Master Says _____

If you don't know where you're going, any road will take you there.

If you don't—or can't—decide what's important to you, almost anything can (and will!) compete for your time and attention—and thereby dissipate your day, your week, your year, your career, and your life. Once you decide what's important to you, you can then become a consultant to yourself to determine what it actually takes to maintain or achieve what you've designated as important. (If it seems that the pieces are starting to fit together, read on. If not, read on anyway; they will.)

Getting real about what you want means being honest with yourself. It also means taking the time and effort to compose a list of priorities, and it means reviewing your list often until your priorities sink in. (I know that you've encountered this type of advice before, but if you had followed it well, you probably wouldn't have bought this book! Call it a hunch.)

The List of Life

The great paradox about priorities is that if you have too many of them, then, by definition, they can't all be priorities. Do you have 15 or 18 things that you list as top priorities in your life? If so, you'd better look again because no one has time to pay homage to 15 to 18 top priorities. Life doesn't work that way.

To help you identify what your priorities are, let's look at the concerns that traditionally have served as top priorities for many people. I'm not saying that your list has to match this one—it probably won't—but this is a starting point:

- Family
- Society
- Health and well-being
- Wealth
- Career growth
- Intellectual growth
- Spiritual growth

Let's tackle each of these (suggested) priority areas one by one, with some concrete examples. Keep in mind that you may have others not listed here that are appropriate for you.

Addams Family Values

For most people, the family has been and remains Numero Uno. If you're married and you love your spouse, being with your spouse is easily a top priority. If you have children and you love them, same situation. If you're single, your priority may be to find a spouse and to raise a family someday, or to treat the people closest to you like a chosen family. If you're in school, your priority may be to spend time with your nuclear family: your mom and dad and your brothers and sisters.

If family is a top priority, then one of your goals may be to earnestly listen to your spouse for at least 35 minutes three times per week. (Won't he or she be pleased as punch if you listen at all— never mind three times a week!)

Reflect and Win

As with all the priorities to be discussed, you want to attach goals—specific, action-oriented steps with timelines—to your priorities to reinforce them. Write them down.

Likewise, there are a variety of other goals that you can choose to support this priority. Here is a quick list of other possible goals related to family:

- Take the children for a day trip once every two weeks.
- Have a photo of the family taken every other December; as a shared family project every year, put some old photos in a family chronicle.
- Have or adopt one or more children within seven years. (There are a lot of kids already out there who need good homes.)
- Send flowers to your spouse, unannounced, once a month.
- Buy life insurance to ensure your family's prosperity in the event of your death. (Maybe you'd better not announce this one.)

Many of the goals that support your family priority are related to other priorities, such as wealth, intellectual growth, and so forth. Actually, that's understandable; it's wonderfully efficient when you set goals that address more than one priority.

Get Involved

If you want to do something about society's woes (besides yelling at your TV set), participate in your community—help it be the best it can be. You might get involved with religious, social, fraternal, or community groups. You might choose to run for local office—not for purposes of ego gratification, but to give something of value back to the community. Here are some possible goals that may support your social priorities:

- Volunteer to serve on the Welcome Wagon Committee for new residents.
- Contribute to the XYZ campaign in the forthcoming election.
- Begin an environmental-awareness movement in your town by the first day of spring.
- Recycle your paper, plastic, glass, and other recyclable materials every week hereafter.
- Run for town council for the next term.
- By the end of this summer, write an article on the importance of nurturing America's youth.
- Be the host to a foreign exchange student during the next academic year.
- Chair this season's March of Dimes campaign in your region, or volunteer on a Habitat for Humanity project.
- Coach a community-league sports team.
- Volunteer every two weeks at a local homeless shelter or kitchen.
- Tutor a student from your local elementary or high school.
- Participate in a community theater or choral production.

The Time Master Says

The few things that you'll do in support of your priorities will take far less time than all the things that you do now in support of who-knows-what. And they'll have the added benefit of moving you closer to your goals. That's time well spent!

You may have surmised that it takes time and energy to support your priorities. Hold that thought. If your goal is to win back your time, why would you want suggestions for new stuff that you're not currently undertaking? The answer: Tasks in support of your priorities do indeed help you win back your time. It's less of a mystery than it might seem.

When you have 15 to 18 "priorities," you're involved in many tasks, some personally rewarding and some not. There is an inherent efficiency in identifying your priorities and establishing some goals to support those priorities.

To Your Health

Some people think that they can shortchange sleep, nutrition, or some other vital component and still be at their best. In the short term, anyone can find himself in a crunch period and sometimes can proceed with less than the best rest, nutrition, and so on.

If this becomes a long-term phenomenon, however, you are doing a disservice to yourself, your employer, and probably your family and friends. Carve out 15 or 20 minutes on some Saturday or Sunday morning to take stock of your life and the fundamental resources that you need to be at your best.

- ◆ Do you need more sleep? Probably so.
- ◆ Do you need to take a multivitamin? For most people, the answer is yes.
- ◆ Do you need to see a masseuse? Ah, the wonders!
- ◆ Do you need to join a health club?

While I am a staunch opponent of multitasking, I do believe in achieving two-for-one payoffs when it is possible. If you attempt to carve out time for exercise and time to, say, watch TV with your kids, you may find that you are stretched to the limits. You can't make it work. A better alternative would be to engage in exercise with your kids. Take a soccer ball out to the field, get on your bikes, swim together, or do anything that helps condition your heart and lungs while being together. Having a meal together is certainly also worthwhile, but, these days, many American families rarely do.

Nine times out of ten, your best bet is engaging in a group exercise. It could be as simple as walking together to the store, taking a hike along a trail, or simply walking to a neighbor's house. If you live in a house with a yard, turn yard work into fun.

Maybe you have a favorite game or two that you haven't played in a while. Engage in some activity that enables you to match wits with one another. Those are the ones that tend to be the most challenging and the most fun.

Get Fit, Stay Fit

If you think that you don't have time to work out, think again. In many respects, the time that you invest in exercising more than pays off in mental alertness, creativity, and old-fashioned higher productivity. Suppose that you used to work out for 30 minutes every second or third day.

You might think that those 90 minutes every week is time that you can't afford to spend. Yet, if you let day after day and week after week go by without working out, you are not as sharp at work, you tend to be a little drowsy, you tend to drag, and your productivity can definitely suffer. You and I both know people who barely make it to

Pause!

Watching television together can be okay if you discuss what you are watching during or after the program. In general, however, watching television is simply being alone together.

Reflect and Win

Energy begets energy. Get up and walk. You've got a long journey in terms of both your career and your life. With decades to go, you don't want to let yourself become a potato puff.

the end of the day, watching the clock for the last hour or so. At home, they engage in only more energy-draining activities such as sitting in a chair with a remote control or a mouse.

Obesity is on the rise. This doesn't have to be your fate. You have the ability to work out on a regular basis, and hence be at your best more of the time.

Here are several possible goals that you could have in support of your health and well-being priority:

Pause!

Check with your doctor before you start any exercise or diet program—especially if you haven't been exerting yourself much. You'll get valuable (maybe life-saving) guidance and a kick out of the look on the doctor's face.

♦ Join a health club within a month, and set a goal of working out four times per week for at least 30 minutes.

♦ Buy five healthy foods that you've never tried.

♦ Take two health-and-fitness books out of the library, read them cover to cover, and gain at least five new ideas that you'll put into practice within one month.

♦ Become a member of a local bicycle club, walking club, or exercise group.

♦ Begin going on walking and hiking dates rather than going to restaurants and movies.

♦ Hire a fitness trainer in February.

♦ Have an annual check-up every January (especially important if you live alone and don't cook).

♦ Visit a dietitian this month to determine your nutritional needs.

♦ Take daily vitamin supplements that meet your needs, as determined by a dietitian.

♦ Imbibe 50 percent less alcohol per week, starting this week.

♦ Make a weekend hike of at least 6 miles every weekend.

Having well-being as a priority gives you a license to behave in new ways. Picking up a piece of litter in a neighbor's yard, for example, is good for you, the neighbor, and the community. I know a man who tucks a $5 bill into the last 50 pages of classic novels on the shelves at the local library. He wants to anonymously reward people, albeit in a small way, who read such books. If you're thinking, "Yeah right, five bucks down the drain," perhaps you're not ready for this level of well-being.

Money Matters

Accumulating wealth is not evil. The Bible says that "the love of money is the root of all evil." It doesn't say that money, per se, is the root of all evil. You can accumulate buckets of money, as long as you don't love your money more than you love people, God, or yourself.

There are all kinds of wealth: intellectual wealth, spiritual wealth, and so forth. These are about to be covered in subsequent pages, so let's confine the focus here to economic wealth. Here are examples of goals that you could choose in support of this priority:

◆ I will call a certified financial planner this month and pay him to advise me about how to invest for the future.

◆ I will start an IRA by this Friday and contribute X amount of dollars each month until I reach the maximum contribution level.

◆ This week, I will redirect my employer to automatically invest X amount from my paycheck in a 401(k), mutual fund account, or other investment.

◆ By next quarter, I will lower the number of deductions on my paycheck so that I get a larger refund from the IRS after filing taxes at the end of this year.

◆ I will join an investment club this month, meet with the members monthly, learn about investment opportunities, and participate in intelligently selected group investments.

◆ (For sales professionals) I will earn X in commissions for the fourth quarter of 200X.

◆ By September 30, 200X, I will launch the business venture of my dreams.

◆ This month, I will trim monthly expenditures by $400.

◆ Within six months, I will live within my means.

◆ I will open a retirement account with my credit union next week.

◆ I will bring my lunch to work at least three times per week.

◆ I will choose an automobile that gets better gas mileage.

For most people, amassing wealth is a long-term affair. Only a teeny, weeny fraction of the population ever wins the lottery. (You stand a better chance of getting struck by lightning.)

You add to your net worth a little at a time. Gradually, inexorably, the wealth begins to build. *Fortune* and *Forbes* articles on wealthy Americans reveal that the majority got wealthy slowly. The

The Time Master Says

Wealth, like happiness and fitness, is a habit. You get wealthy by developing habits of wealth. If you're on your way to wealth, it's probably those darn habits of yours.

book *The Millionaire Next Door* confirms that wealthy people developed a habit, early on, of living within their means—and one day found their nest egg had grown to a sizable sum. Wow, what a country! What a way to win back your time—by developing habits of wealth, breaking the cycle of deficit spending, and amassing a sum that lets you do what you want in life!

Your Brilliant Career

Beyond what has already been discussed, the pursuit of career growth, per se, likely is one of your priorities. If you've invested years in getting to be where you are, and if you like what you do, you may naturally look forward to rising within your industry or profession.

Independent of the monetary rewards, there's a high level of inner satisfaction among those who are highly learned and well respected in their chosen fields. For goals that you can choose in support of your career-growth priority, try these on for size:

- Read one new book a month by the top authors writing in your field.
- Subscribe to (or start reading in your company library) two important industry publications that you don't currently receive.
- Form a monthly study group so that you all encourage each other in learning more about your chosen fields.
- Register to attend a conference this week (or submit a proposal to make a presentation of your own).
- Return to school to get a graduate degree in your field.
- Undertake original research over the next six months, put your findings into article form, and pursue getting it published in a prominent industry journal.
- Complete the certification process in your industry by December 31, 200X.
- Volunteer for that special task force forming in April.
- Join your professional association, or (if you're already a member) run for office in it.

As society grows more complex (and, by now, you know that it will), it will benefit you to become more of a specialist in your chosen field. A typical business manager reads books, magazines, documents, reports, the Internet, email, and so on as much as four hours a day. The trick for most professionals when it comes to career-related reading is to get even more focused than ever.

One caveat: It pays to specialize only if you know that your specialty is marketable and has long-term prospects (as some of my friends know from bitter academic experience).

If you're worried that becoming too specialized will restrict your intellectual diversity, fear not. Once you decide on pursuing a highly narrow field and concentration, it actually expands. Often, you begin to see things within your narrow focus that you couldn't have seen before making the choice.

Reflect and Win

The more specialized you become, the more potentially valuable you become to those who need your expertise.

Thinking Is the Best Way to Travel

When Supreme Court Justice Oliver Wendell Holmes was in his 80s (quite aged for his day), he was asked why he was reading the voluminous book *Plutarch's Lives.* He responded, "To improve my mind." Rumor has it that the pursuit of intellectual growth—independent of career growth—is a worthy priority. Certainly, education and intellectual development—for its own sake, and for that of your children—rank at the top of any list of priorities you may devise. In support of this priority, here's a smorgasbord of possible goals:

- Read one new book every two weeks that is not in your field and not connected to what you do for a living.
- Spend time with your children playing games such as Scrabble to help develop their vocabulary and love of words.
- Enroll in that local community college course you've been wanting to take.
- Send away for a books-on-tape catalog so that you can listen to the classics rather than having to read them (because you already read way more than you want to).
- Take at least one international trip per year to a destination completely foreign to you so that you can learn firsthand about other cultures.
- Sign up for the lecture series sponsored by the local Chamber of Commerce so that you can hear from visiting authorities on contemporary issues.
- Drop your subscription to, say, *People* magazine (sorry, *People!*), and replace it with, for example, a subscription to *Smithsonian* magazine.
- Watch at least one program per week on The Learning Channel or PBS.
- Rent a documentary rather than a feature film.
- Read a historical account instead of a mystery.

Pause!

As with life priorities, you need some parameters before sitting down and simply surfing the Net. Otherwise, rather than winning back your time, you'll watch it dissipate among an infinite number of seemingly intellectual pursuits.

There are far more worthy and stimulating issues competing for your time and attention than you will ever be able to pursue. It takes strength to stay within the confines of a few pre-identified focus areas—while, of course, occasionally allowing yourself to freewheel all over creation. (You are, after all, only human, aren't you?)

The Great Spirit Within

I've known lots of folks who are sensitive about religion, sometimes taking offense where none was intended. I'm not assuming that your spiritual tradition is the same as mine, nor am I prescribing my own practices. Spirituality is a wellspring of the quality in life. The time that makes up an enjoyable and worthwhile life is well worth winning back.

Spiritual growth doesn't mean going to church every Sunday, although it certainly can. Your spiritual growth can occur anywhere at any time. If you choose to seek active spiritual growth as a priority, goals like these can support your choice:

- Take weekly walks in natural settings and appreciate your surroundings.
- Actually read the holy book for your religion during the next calendar year, or listen to it on cassette.
- Begin to live as if you recognize that every creature on earth is a divine creation. You can start this anytime, and it never ends.
- Practice the art of forgiveness by making three calls this week to people you need to forgive. ("Do I have to do this?" Yes, if you're serious about your well-being.)
- Give thanks each morning or evening for all that you have been given in life.
- Decide to regularly attend weekly religious services.
- Donate your time and energy once a month to a food service for the homeless, starting in May.
- Scour your home this week to find everything that you can donate to the less fortunate.
- Listen to inspirational music.
- Pray for yourself and others.

Okay, you already know many possible starting points.

That's seven possible priority areas we've looked at so far—and even they're not the be-all and end-all. You may have some that don't fit within these categories at all. That's fine, as long as you recognize what they are and choose goals that involve specific action steps and time lines in support of your priorities.

Actions Speak Louder Than Words

To support the priorities that you choose, here are some basic action steps:

◆ Write down everything that's important to you or that you want to accomplish in your life. A long list is okay.

◆ Several days later, re-examine the list. Cross out anything that no longer strikes your fancy. Feel free to add a few things, if they come up.

◆ In another day or so, review your list and see whether any items can be grouped together. Then reword or relabel those choices. Feel free to drop an item if you think it's "iffy."

◆ Put your list away for yet another day. (Yup—this is going to take a week or more!) Then review it again.

◆ Once more, combine, regroup, or delete things on the list as appears appropriate to you.

◆ Prepare the final draft of your list, recognizing that, in time, it may change. For now, these are what you've identified as your priorities.

Minimize for Maximum Value

If you're doing your list on your computer, print it out in a reduced point size (or simply hand-print it in miniature) so that it's small enough to carry in your wallet or purse. Then review your list of priorities at least once a day. With so many other things competing for your time and attention, it's easy to lose sight of your priorities by 10:00 in the morning. It's not excessive to read your priority list several times a day.

The Time Master Says

Some of the most accomplished people, who routinely appear to be in great control of their time, review their priority lists often.

The Least You Need to Know

◆ Once you've identified your priorities, you're far more likely to make incremental progress toward them.

◆ Too many priorities, by definition, can't all be priorities.

◆ The top priorities for many people have been family, society, health and well-being, wealth, career growth, intellectual growth, and spiritual growth.

♦ To establish your priorities, write down everything that's important to you, re-examine the list; cross out anything that no longer strikes your fancy; add a few things, if they come up; group similar items; reword or relabel any of your choices; and prepare the final list.

♦ Print your list in a reduced point size so that it's small enough to carry in your wallet or purse; review it often.

Chapter 8

Sustaining Your Priorities for Fun and Profit

In This Chapter

- ◆ Your unspoken commitments
- ◆ Supporting your priorities with goals that you'll follow through with
- ◆ The telltale signs that you're heading off course
- ◆ Managing your to-do list and balancing short-term and long-term tasks

In the mid-1950s song "Is That All There Is?" singer Peggy Lee rhetorically asked about life. Quite often, we may feel the same way—life doesn't meet our expectations. Some people don't want to honor their priorities and pursue supporting goals because they are afraid that their desired accomplishment will be unfulfilling.

As a struggling young actor, Clint Eastwood worked hard to become successful. When he became an international box office star and experienced worldwide adulation, he told a reporter how he was surprised that he didn't feel overjoyed and satisfied with his success. Like Eastwood, many people are let down when results don't match their expectations.

Wanting What You Have

Some people fear the consequences of success, *á la* "Be careful of what you wish for because you might get it, and if you get it, then what would you do?" It is vital to ask yourself, "Do I really want this? Do I want it so badly that I will accept the repercussions along with all the benefits?" In other words, pretend that you've already realized your pursuit. Put yourself into that space mentally. Then ask yourself, "Am I where I want to be?"

Some people maintain unspoken commitments, such as those listed here—behaviors and activities that predominate even over carefully chosen priorities.

What are your unspoken commitments?

- To be needed or accepted?
- To overfile or overcollect?
- To wait for permission?
- To hold back?
- To repeatedly push yourself to your productive limit?
- To withhold your emotions?
- To be easily intimidated by the experience or status of others?
- To spend money as soon as it comes in?

Sticking to the Path

Suppose that you identify your priorities and establish some goals in support of them. What will it take to *ensure* that you stay on your chosen path? Desire and focus. If you know what you truly want but can't maintain a clear focus, your probability of being successful diminishes markedly. Alas, focus seems to be such a rare commodity these days.

It's easy to stray—agreed? If you had a nickel for every time that you heard somebody decide to do something and then you watched him over time do little or nothing in support of the decision, well, by golly, you'd probably be rich! In this chapter, you'll learn how to reinforce your commitment to your newly established priorities, discover ways to recognize when you've derailed your progress toward achieving them, and learn one particularly useful way to make sure that your work priorities don't undermine the ones that you've set for your personal life.

Building in Positive Reinforcements

Staying on track with your priorities means staying focused. You can make it easier for yourself to keep that focus if you build some positive reinforcements into your day-to-day life. Here are reinforcement techniques to use in support of the priorities you've chosen:

1. Join others who have priorities and goals similar to yours—and those who are supporting them. Perhaps there is a professional or social organization in your town that fits the bill.

2. Surround yourself with reinforcing statements, reminders, and post-on notes so that you don't lose sight of what you have already deemed important.

3. Create a cassette tape of your priorities and supporting goals in the form of affirmations: "I choose to visit the health club four times per week for a minimum workout of 30 minutes."

4. Prepare a budget to help determine exactly what it will cost to honor your priorities and the goals that you've chosen to support them.

5. Develop rituals that support your quest. For example, if your goal is to lose six pounds by the end of June, begin taking the stairs instead of the elevator whenever you're heading down for lunch or to your car at the end of the day.

6. Keep your action steps bite-size. There's no value in choosing goals that are so difficult to achieve that you're not honoring the associated priority at all.

7. Report to someone. Have some significant other serving as a coach or watchdog to ensure that you do what you said you were going to do. (Don't be lulled into thinking that this ploy is only for the weak-willed. High achievers do this!)

8. Visualize the goal every day. Olympic athletes en route to their next meet, can actually improve their performance once they land if they visualize their events during the commute.

9. Set up a series of small rewards so that you're naturally reinforcing the behavior in which you've chosen to engage.

10. Contract with yourself. Author Dennis Hensley, based in Fort Wayne, Indiana, describes advancement by contract: "A contract takes precedence over everything else. For example, you make your monthly house payment rather than using the money for a vacation because you have to make that payment: The contract allows the bank to repossess your home if you do not fulfill your obligation."

    He suggests carefully selecting three to five major goals (in support of your priorities) and then signing a contract that aids you in reaching them. "Once under contract, you would have to succeed by a selected date or else face the consequences of defaulting on the contract," says Hensley. (It's worth remembering that, in the business world, people who default can be sued or go unpaid for the work done to date.) Make three copies of your contract (this chapter includes an example). Keep the original. Give one copy each to your spouse, a trusted coworker, and a friend.

SELF-INITIATED CONTRACT

I, _____, agree to accomplish each of the following items on or before _____ and hereby do formally contract myself to these purposes.

These goals are challenging but reasonable, and I accept them willingly.

A. _____

B. _____

C. _____

Signature: _____   Date: _____

Review your contract when you find yourself becoming distracted by small details or if you think that you are not moving in the right direction.

The Time Master Says

Give yourself flexibility; build in some downtime, vacation time, and so forth. Devise a realistic plan to accomplish your goal by the time you said you would.

11. Plot your campaign on the calendar. Start from the ending date (the deadline for completing your goal) and work back to the present, plotting the subtasks and activities that you'll need to undertake.

Proceeding in reverse through the monthly calendar helps you establish realistic interim dates that reflect not only your available resources, but also vacations, holidays, weekends, other off-duty hours, and reasonable output levels. A sample calendar block follows.

Start with a major deadline, and then work backward to set realistic interim dates for achieving what you want.

CALENDAR BLOCK BACK

MONTH ___ MARCH ___   YEAR _____

SUNDAY	MONDAY	TUESDAY	WEDNESDAY	THURSDAY	FRIDAY	SATURDAY
	1 Submitted Feb. 24	2 Deliver draft workshop planning report	3	4	5	6
7	8	9 Submitted to typing	10	11	12	13
14	15 Assessment of conf. capabilities Deliver profile revisions	16	17	18	19 Assessment of target audience, 52 pages Deliver	20
21	22	23	24	25	26	27
28	29	30	31 Deliver final workshop planning report			

Straying or Staying on Course?

On more than one occasion (I'm being kind here) you're bound to get off course. When you do, revisit the list just given and initiate a new strategy in place of—or, better yet, in addition to—the ones you're using. Here are some warning signs that you're off the path that you chose:

- ◆ **You've talked a good game.** You said that this undertaking was important to you, but you haven't scheduled any time on your calendar or budgeted any funds.

- ◆ **You're not committed.** You said that working out four times a week was important; by the third week, you're making excuses to yourself about why you're not doing this.

- ◆ **You've let piles of paper stack up.** Although you've chosen only a handful of priorities, you find yourself wading through stuff that's interesting and not important.

- ◆ **Your goals missed the mark.** Despite the toil, time, and thought that you put into establishing your goals, it's apparent that they're not supporting your priorities.

Long-Term Versus Short-Term Tasks

Whether you've identified your priorities (and some well-chosen goals to support them) or are still stuck in old habits, you likely face an age-old dilemma: staying on top of all the things that you need or want to get done.

People are always asking me about to-do lists. Do they need to maintain them? How can they go about fixing them? Everyone I know in the workaday world uses some kind of list as a tool for getting things done. I'm neither for nor opposed to any particular system that you might use to stay efficient; judge by your results. (Chapter 15, "Top Time-Management Tools Revealed," explores some time-management tools and technologies.) If you maintain some type of to-do list, you can use it to support your priorities by lengthening it for strategic reasons, without overloading yourself. Read on.

> **Reflect and Win**
>
> If you haven't yet considered using the superlong to-do strategy, give it a try. Your first superlong list will probably fill two to five pages—it should be easy to move items up to the front as needed. You'll have a clear idea of what you face when it's all on one big roster, and you'll keep your priorities sharp for years to come.

The Long and the Short of It

The primary dilemma that you're most likely to face is balancing short-term against long-term tasks and activities. For years, I maintained a 10-page to-do list! I had hundreds of things on my list, arranged by major life priorities. How did I keep from going crazy? Most of what was on the list were medium- to long-range activities.

The first page of my list represented only the short-term activities—those that I had chosen to do immediately or within a week. I drew continually from the 10-page list, moving items to the top as it became desirable (or necessary) to tackle them.

In essence, I maintained a dynamic to-do list; it contained everything that I wanted to get done, but always with only one page that I needed to look at: the top page. Yes, I am forever updating the list and printing out new versions, but there are so many advantages that I wouldn't think of doing it any other way.

I review the entire list periodically, always moving items from, say, page seven up to the front page. Thus, any anxiety stays at a rather low level.

Managing Long-Term or Repeated Tasks

Maintaining a long to-do list has helped me become more proficient in managing long-term or repeated tasks. If I am working on a long-term project, I can continually draw from it those portions that can be handled in the short-term; I move them up to the front page. Likewise, if a task is a repeat or cyclical project—something that I have to do every month or every year—I can choose a portion to get done and move into the short term (up to the front page).

End-Running Your To-Do List

On occasion, you can short-circuit the to-do list and get stuff done without even entering it on your list. Most people who encounter information worth retaining make a note or add it to a list; it may stay there for days or months. To deal with it faster, remember that useful information usually involves calling or writing to someone else. Rather than adding it to your to-do list, try a fast-action option:

♦ Pick up a pocket dictator and fire off a letter, or do the same with voice-recognition software.

♦ Dictate or type a message on your computer for immediate transmission by fax, email, or Internet message.

When I switch to voice-recognition software, I can continue to bypass the to-do list.

Goals: Setting Them and Reaching Them

All goals can be broken down into smaller chunks, and each can be assigned a time frame. Software to help you stay on track and in control of your time has improved markedly over the last several years. While there is specific project-management software enabling you to chart out every task, subtask, and so on by hour, day, week, month, and so on, many of the time-management software programs available already contain a project-management component as well. Here is a summary of two such programs.

Master List Software

The Master List provides you with software to track and manage assignments, deadlines, critical dates, and your daily, weekly, monthly, and yearly calendar.

Originally conceived as a relational database program for attorneys, the Master List can benefit almost any career-oriented professional who faces several assignments or projects:

◆ If you're working alone, the software enables you to track assignments, maintain schedules, and focus on deadlines.

◆ If you work with a staff, you can better organize, integrate, and maintain assignments, responsibilities, and due dates of each team member. You also can share schedules, data input, notepad ideas, and project tracking across networks.

Easy to Access Options

When you open the software, you encounter the main menu screen which lists all of your projects as well as the option Quick Hit. This selection supplies reports labeled My Day, My Week, Team Day, Team Week, Action Tracker, and My Calendar. You also have the option of accessing the case Master List, a notepad outline, a calendar day view, a notepad call log, a calendar week view, and a history screen.

The notepad call log screen enables you to create hundreds or even thousands of notes, each linked to an action item, memo, or agenda. The notepads can be displayed alongside your current project, providing detail on any particular task or project. Each notepad screen can be modified using word-processing commands. You can make outlines, reports, and bulleted lists to be saved in the same way that traditional word processors save files.

The Hit Parade

Here is a brief summary of the Master List features.

Notepad Call Log Screen

You can create a call log screen in your notepad that offers a chronological account of your call progress with a particular individual or on a particular project.

Calendar Day and Calendar Week View

This feature enables you to review your daily schedule broken down by half-hour segments. You can also review the schedule for any previous or forthcoming day. The calendar week view enables you to review your appointments over any seven-day period, from Sunday to Saturday. Any of these screens can be modified and updated on the fly and can be easily saved.

The Time Master Says

The beauty of the Master List system is that it separates tasks or projects into small, manageable packets that can readily be created, edited, shared, modified, or passed across a network.

History Screen and CaseMaster List

The history screen allows you to store records that reflect the project-by-project trail of what you have accomplished and review your entire list of projects in a browser. The CaseMaster List screen enables you to access each of the projects listed on the history screen and thereby review a project's history, the content of any notepad memos, or call log screens.

The KMCS Daily Planner

The Daily Planner, by KMCS, is a less involved and less expensive software program for managing your workload, tasks, and time. The Daily Planner gives you snapshot views of each day's activities. You can set it up to offer yourself reminders at critical times throughout the day, to take action at just the right time. In essence, you're letting your computer remember things for you. Many people like the daily planner for its simplicity while providing a viable option for staying in control of projects and tasks.

The Daily Planner is dispensed as shareware—you get up to 30 days free to determine whether the software meets your needs. If you decide to become a registered user, you pay only a nominal fee.

Reflect and Win

You are the driving force that spells the difference between whether these tools will have high utility for you or whether they merely become another daily burden.

Caveats with All Scheduling Tools

With the Master Lists system, the KMCS Daily Planner, or scheduling and time-management software and tools, the ever-present caveat is that the software can be only as good as your last update. If you don't maintain the system by consistently logging in your latest appointment, your project notes, and any other updates or modifications to the tasks and activities before you, then the software will not serve you.

System Limitations

Until such systems encompass artificial intelligence that includes a camera or seeing eye, an optical scanner, voice-recognition capabilities, and a mechanical arm that literally moves items about on your desk, you will have to do the work of keeping your data up to date.

Perhaps in a few years, we can all don head-bands that capture our brain waves and transmit the signals to the software. On that hallowed day, you can simply "direct your thoughts" into your computer, which will file, maintain, and update your data and offer your notes, reminders, report forms, logs, and schedules when you "mentally" request them. Until then, choose your software carefully.

CAUTION

Pause!

Remember, all time-management tools, be they software, pocket organizers, or hard-copy systems, will let you down the moment you don't keep them up. None of them operates by magic. They all require your continual and vital input.

Try It, You'll Like It

Go ahead and acquire scheduling, time-management, or project-management software if this supports the way you work. Many popular programs are available, and the learning curve is such that you can master most components of them within a day or two. Chances are, you'll become a fairly proficient user within a matter of weeks.

Whether you use software or simply plot out your progress on a wall chart, the way in which you proceed is relatively the same. You identify what needs to be done first, second, and so on; post it; proceed toward its accomplishment; plot your progress; and constantly review where you are and where you're heading. You revise your chart as necessary and remember to reward yourself along the way when you have accomplished something.

Updating Pays Off

When you update a time-management software program (scheduling appointments, putting in key phone numbers, and so forth), or when you update contact-management software (putting in the phone number, fax number, email address, and website of key contacts), magic begins to happen. As you have fewer scraps of paper in and around your desk competing for your attention, you also begin to have a clearer focus, more direction, and sometimes even more energy to face the day.

The Time Master Says

When you're using such software programs properly, they take care of things for you. The scheduler function lets you know when it's time to make a call. The various ID status components enable you to file away contacts by industry, geography, or whatever. You can easily retrieve vital information with a few key strokes because the programs are designed to be user-friendly. Therefore, take full advantage of them.

If you did nothing over the next couple of days but study the instructions and guides that come with your software, becoming a master in using such programs, you would probably enhance your use of time far more than you would by engaging in a variety of other tasks. Yet, when is the last time that you took several days or even several hours to give such powerful programs your full and undivided attention?

Reflect and Win

Even if you think that you have too much to do, clear away time to better learn to use tools that will greatly enhance your use of time in the long run so that you won't be caught in a Catch-22 to begin with.

Break out of the box now, and, whether it's consuming one Saturday morning or staying at work late one Wednesday evening, focus intently on software programs that you already have in place. Investigate palm-top, hard-wired units that are designed to serve you in ways that you haven't considered.

Old Standbys: Paper and Pencil

If you already suffer from too much technology, there's a simple system that will keep you on top of the goals that support your priorities. It works surprisingly well: Simply go to your nearest office-supply store, and buy one of those washable wall charts or an oversize set of monthly calendars in cardboard stock or paper.

Mount your calendars on the wall and use magic markers, washable felt-tip pens, sticky-note pads, gold stars, red seals, or what have you to represent what you want to accomplish by when. This isn't news to you if you work in an office where any number of people, vehicles, or goods need to be scheduled for optimum efficiency. On a personal basis, such calendar plotting works well; you're the boss of the calendar. Moving self-stick notes around is a one-second maneuver. High-tech or low-tech, do what works.

At all times, use the tools that comfort you. Watch out that you don't reclutter your immediate environment. In other words, use only the paper tools and supplies that support your efforts. Don't turn your working environment into a danger zone, with so many pieces of paper and notes competing for your attention that you don't know which way to turn.

The Least You Need to Know

- Everyone needs reinforcement. Join others who have priorities and goals similar to yours.
- Develop supportive rituals, report to someone, visualize your success, and set up a series of small rewards.
- Many effective software programs can assist you in managing your time; use them only if you intend to keep them current.
- Create a superlong to-do list, and split it into short- and long-term tasks.
- A low-tech approach to managing your time has its charms. Calendar wall charts are easy to use and reuse.

Chapter 9

Buying Yourself Some Time

In This Chapter

- ◆ Doing too many things yourself is not a good idea
- ◆ You can always make more money; you can't make more time
- ◆ Trade your money for more time; splurge for services on occasion
- ◆ Get a helper who can handle many things for you

Some time-management gurus suggest that you record how you spend each hour of the day for one week or one month. Then, like preparing a budget, you see the number of hours that you've wasted, and, like money wasted, you wish that you had those hours back. Make a time diary, if you wish, but I don't think that it's necessary. Human nature being what it is, you're going to continue to hang on to some tasks, even those that you know in your heart of hearts ought to be delegated to others or dropped altogether. Relax—it's not a death knell to hang on to some things.

Are you a strong proponent of rugged individualism, typified by John Wayne's movie roles? He took care of everything himself. Unfortunately, life is not a movie.

In the workaday world, you frequently see middle managers who attempt to leapfrog over several positions in the company by taking on more tasks and responsibilities, although they're already working beyond optimal capacity.

Reflect and Win

Start delegating, casting off, or otherwise eliminating such items from your to-do list altogether. Each time you remove some unnecessary task from your schedule, you free up your time to tackle what's more important, and you will yield far greater results.

Pause!

Watch out if you start believing that you alone are the only one who can handle things. Many organizations tend to seek out people with such urges. Only superheroes need apply.

Among entrepreneurs, you may encounter someone trying to crack a new market—even while juggling several other balls, short-changing his health to keep that circus going.

Danger Ahead

What are some of the danger signs that you believe you have to do it all yourself? Consider these symptoms: You think that you'll be able to overcome obstacles by working longer; you tell yourself (or worse, your boss) that you "appreciate the challenge." If the people around you think that it can't be accomplished, all the better; you'll wow 'em by doing the impossible, right?

You might become a little overbearing, but, hey, you're in pursuit of an important goal, and that's what counts. Besides, you're the "only one who can do the job."

Working hard, per se, is not a problem unless you maintain preposterous ambitions or let force of habit push you beyond the point of diminishing returns. If you're willing to stay late, work on weekends, and minimize your vacation time, you could very well be your organization's star performer. It's not a fair trade-off. Nevertheless, too many career achievers fall into an endless cycle. These people feel that their accomplishments are too small or too few; they experience disappointment, frustration, and health-threatening stress. To relieve these feelings, they work harder in the hope that they'll accomplish more and that a golden rainbow will appear.

"Doing It All" Is Costly

The notion that you must take care of everything is, in a word, erroneous. If you think that working too hard is the way to gain the respect of others—or self-respect—it's time to rethink your whole approach.

Some do-it-all people have the ill-advised notion that the only way to exhibit competence is by constantly proving it to everyone else. Worse, if they never quite prove it to themselves, they live in dread of being found imperfect.

◆ Rather than focus on your weaknesses, accentuate the positive! Develop your strengths. Also give yourself realistic time frames for ambitious goals.

♦ Divide and conquer. Take smaller steps when setting larger goals so that you don't burst a spleen along the way. When progress is slow, try an alternative route, a new door, or a different mind-set—anything but plodding along the same as always.

Especially when it comes to domestic tasks, do you get stuck in a miserly mode? Do you think that if you spend a few minutes here and there taking care of this and that, you can handle all you seek to keep up with—and avoid shelling out the money to have others do it? Many people do.

Each time you avoid getting a service profes-sional, helper, or part-timer—when such parties could aid you considerably—you ensure that you won't win back your time. Each time you mow the grass, for example, when you don't enjoy doing it, you add to the cumulative total of undesirable tasks in your life. Besides, you're incurring all that unnecessary tissue-and-decongestant expense during hay fever season!

Reflect and Win

Contemplate using help for selected segments of your life. Admit to yourself that you can't do everything; acknowledge that trying harder in some instances may not be worth it.

Time Is Short; Money Is Replenishable

In speeches, when I explain the value of shelling out a few dollars to preserve one's time, invariably someone asks, "What do I do if money is tight?" I don't presume that you have trunk loads of cash stashed away somewhere. (Remember, most people spend more than they have.) And the thought of parting with some of your money to hire people to do what you've traditionally done yourself may seem like heresy at first. What is the time value, however, of the money that you might part with to get a mundane chore com-pleted? Should you trade a few dollars to have tasks accomplished and free up some of your time? (Hint: The answer is three letters long.)

Consider the act of hiring others from the van-tage point of your life's big picture. You have things to accomplish that can perhaps make you much more money than the $15 that you pay somebody each time he or she mows the lawn or trims the hedges.

If you're an entrepreneur or you're self-employed, it pays to rely on outside services so that you can

The Time Master Says

It makes perfect sense to pay a high-school student $15 to mow the lawn if you can't stand doing so. In the long run, you won't miss the money, and you'll be glad that you're no longer mowing the lawn.

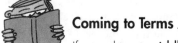

Coming to Terms

If something is **piddling,** it is paltry, trivial, or inconsequential.

focus on what you do best and make the overall business prosper. If you work for an organization, there are still countless opportunities for relief; you can rely on others (at work and away from work) to alleviate the *piddling* tasks that you don't enjoy doing. Thus, you can be at your best, get noticed by superiors, and stand a better chance of getting those raises and promotions.

When Not Doing It All Works Wonders

It's surprising how common the do-it-all urge is. Nanci Hellmich, a reporter for *USA Today,* uncovered this trend when she interviewed me for two articles. The first was a brief, two-column article; in it, Nanci invited readers to write to *USA Today* and discuss their time-pressure problems. Several lucky readers would benefit from my counsel (aw, shucks). The second article would include the results of my counseling.

Over several weeks, Nanci received hundreds of letters; she selected respondents for me to call. I had involved conversations with a female attorney and a graduate student, among others.

The attorney was constantly racing the clock, getting her daughters to school in the morning, seeing her husband off on his (frequently long) business trips, plying her trade as a partner in a successful law firm, picking up the children, driving them to various after-school activities, making dinner for them, reading to them, and putting them to bed.

After listening to her story, I asked her why she didn't treat herself to ordering dinner a couple of times a week rather than making it all the time. She said that she'd never thought about it, and it seemed a little extravagant. I asked her how much she earned. It was considerable. I asked her how much her husband earned. It was more than considerable.

"Okay," I replied, "between the two of you, you're clearing nearly a quarter million per year. Suppose that you had Chinese food or pizza or chicken delivered to your home now and then—and you didn't cook at all on those nights. How much would it cost you, once a week, to have dinner delivered?" She thought about it and said, "Maybe an average of $16 a week, so that's $800 a year."

I said, "Would it be worth $800 a year if once a week, particularly during hectic work weeks, you had dinner delivered instead of making it yourself? Would that free up some of your time? Would you enjoy it? Are you worth it?" She agreed on all counts. It's food for thought.

Be Kind to Yourself

The graduate student with whom I spoke also had a hectic schedule. Besides taking several courses, she worked in the afternoons and was a volunteer for a service organization two nights a week. Frequently, she found herself getting up in the morning barely in time to catch the bus. This kind of pressure had become routine, yet it was no way to start her day.

I listened closely to her story and asked, "How much is the bus ride to school?" She said that it was $1.75. I said, "How much would a taxi ride cost?" She was aghast. "I couldn't take a taxi!" I said, "Wait a second. How much would a taxi ride be?" She didn't know, so we paused our conversation. She called the closest taxi company and asked about the charges from her apartment to her class in the morning. At that time, the cost was approximately $4.50.

When she called back, I asked: "How upsetting would it be to your budget if, occasionally, when you're running late, you permit yourself to hail a taxi and pay $4.50 instead of paying $1.75 for the bus?" She thought about it and said, "Well, I suppose that occasionally it wouldn't hurt."

I said, "You're right. You could hail a taxi as often as once a week, and in the course of a 15-week semester, you're paying only an extra $67.50 for the luxury of not being enslaved to the bus schedule. We all easily blow at least $67.50 all the time. Why not be gentle with yourself? Acknowledge that you're handling a lot in life right now and that occasionally you deserve to take a taxi ride to school." She relented.

Make Mine Manhattan

If you're a big-city career type, the same principle applies. If you're up on East 76th Street in Manhattan and you have to get down to 44th in a hurry, once every week or so, it won't put a significant dent in your pocketbook to take a taxi rather than the subway or the bus. Suppose that it costs you $8 more per week. In the course of a year, you're paying an extra $400. How many times have you shelled out $400 in ways that were far less beneficial to your overall health and well-being?

Reflect and Win

How often do you get stuck in a miserly mode, pinching pennies here and there, while blowing triple or quadruple digits on items of marginal value?

Great Time/Money Trades

What time/money trade-offs might make good sense in your situation? Consider a few:

- **Grocery delivery**—Many supermarkets and grocery stores will deliver for a nominal fee. Some offer hard-copy or online catalogs from which you can order by phone, fax, email, or the Internet. For routine items, you can establish a standing order whereby every week the market delivers eggs, milk, or whatever. You can still shop for new or specialty food items now and then, lugging all those bags home so that you remember what it's like. It will reinforce your inclination to use grocery delivery services.

- **Office supplies by phone and fax**—Those giant superstores splashed across the terrain—you know their names—have delivery services and publish large supply catalogs (with 1-800 numbers so that you can reach semiknowledgeable attendants). The catalogs also contain 1-800 fax numbers; you can fax in your order without even talking to anybody. Or, you can order via email or the Internet, where special bargains may await. Most vendors deliver at no extra charge if your order is above $50. The orders usually are delivered the next day. It's fast, accurate, and relatively painless.

- **Gift-wrap it, please**—If you're buying presents and the store offers a wrapping service, pay the extra few dollars and have them wrap it. Do you particularly want to fiddle with wrapping paper, tape, scissors, string, bows, and all that stuff? If you do, fine; that's your option. For another dollar or so (or whatever it takes), however, isn't it worth it to have that chore completed?

- **Pick-up-and-delivery services**—Use vendors and suppliers who come right to your door. The major express package delivery services will both pick up and deliver for home as well as office locations. You can start your own account even if you send only a few packages monthly.

- **Shopping services**—There are people who can go shopping for you to buy gifts, shoes, or nearly anything. If you dislike shopping (or aren't too good at it) and someone you trust does it well, this could make sense. The professional shopper can actually save you money because he knows where to get the best buys. Often the overall cost of the item, plus the hourly fee, is less than you would have paid (especially if you often hunt for items in five or six stores and end up paying full retail price).

Maid for You

Hiring a maid can be quite beneficial, especially if you're an entrepreneur seeking local service providers. One cleaning service that I retained, for example, offered a unique approach to speedy office and house cleaning. It sent six or eight people at once who finished the job within 45 minutes!

Here are other types of services that probably exist in your community (they'll be called something else in your city, of course).

♦ Gutters-R-Us (service that clears your gutters and saves you from roof duty)

♦ Jumpin' Jack Flash (pick-up and delivery service)

♦ The Butler Did It (catering service)

♦ Everything But Windows (housecleaning service)

♦ Rent a Dad (house repair service for the terminally unhandy)

♦ The Tree Doctor (tree- and hedge-trimming service)

♦ Walkin' the Dog (service that cares for Pooch when you're gone—or when you're not)

♦ Shake a Leg (airport shuttle service)

All kinds of part-time workers are ready to help you as well; some may be more suitable to your needs than others. These include part-time regular employees, retirees, temporaries, and students (high school, college, intern, foreign-exchange, grad school, and so on).

You probably can find a bright, motivated student to help you. Schools are brimming with intelligent, perceptive young men and women, many of whom are seeking an opportunity to gain some real-world experience. Their part-time status doesn't mean that they're less intelligent or effective. Many can take a "divisible" unit of work and do a bang-up job on it.

What could helpers do for you? Fair question. Take a look:

♦ Serve routine customer needs

♦ Make deliveries and pick-ups

♦ Route/sort the mail

♦ Answer requests for information

♦ Send out mailings of any sort

♦ Make first-round or lead calls to prospective customers

♦ Search for a product or service that you need

♦ Catalog new information or products

♦ Proofread or double-check anything written

♦ Survey customers and their needs

Reflect and Win

Most communities have high-school juniors and seniors who'd be thrilled to work for 50¢ an hour above minimum wage. This might not seem like a lot of money to you, but it may to them.

◆ Keep track of necessary data and news sources

◆ Type mailing lists

◆ Type anything, for that matter

◆ Keep things tidy, clean, and in good repair

◆ Study competitors, their literature, and their products

◆ Track inventory or arrange displays

◆ Do anything that a less-essential part-time employee could do without excessive guidance

> **The Time Master Says**
>
> Every time you successfully use one of your many helpers, you're preserving your time!

> **Coming to Terms**
>
> **Seed work** is the sort of task that you can easily assign to someone else because the downside risk if they botch the task is negligible.

Your newfound mission: Identify all those nonessential-but-bothersome tasks that you've been putting off that a part-timer can handle.

Seed work functions best when it's a distinct unit of work—easily assigned to someone else. For example, suppose that you want information on the eight other local companies in your field. A high-school student can easily open the phone book or a local trade publication, visit the sites, write for the brochures (using his home address), and summarize the information gathered. A more experienced employee could spot trends or innovations from this data, all with a minimum of your time spent on instruction.

Your Service System in Ten Easy Steps

Whether you live in a community of 38,000 or 1,038,000 people, many service providers can help you with domestic as well as business tasks to free you for whatever makes the most money for you.

Perhaps you now are mildly enthusiastic to downright excited about the prospects of bringing such providers into your life. I knew you'd step aboard. If you start using such helpers in a systematic way, you'll be far along the road to winning back your time.

Here are 10 suggestions for putting your service system in place:

1. Identify all the tasks that you don't like to do. Make this list as long as possible. Be honest with yourself. Separate the list into domestic and career-related tasks.

2. On two separate pages (one for domestic and one for career-related tasks), create a matrix, listing these tasks down the left side of each page. (There's an example task matrix lurking nearby in this chapter.) Across the top of each page, leave room for three columns; label them Option 1 through Option 3.

	Option 1	Option 2	Option 3
Task A	_____	_____	_____
Task B	_____	_____	_____
Task C	_____	_____	_____
Task D	_____	_____	_____
Task E	_____	_____	_____

3. If you list five tasks down the left side of the page for your domestic sheet, with three option boxes across the top of the page, potentially you have 15 cells to fill. Fill even half of them, and you'll be in great shape.

4. Within the blank cells, list every alternative that you can imagine for not doing tasks that you don't enjoy. You may find yourself writing down such options as delegating the tasks to your kids, your neighbors' kids, or someone you found in a shopper's guide or the Yellow Pages.

5. Review your grid. If you don't have good options for some of the tasks, it's time for some fieldwork. Go to your local library, supermarket, or community center and read the bulletin boards. Often you'll find business cards or small ads posted by local entrepreneurial talents. Start collecting these leads.

6. Speak to your local librarian. Talk to the job placement officer at your local high school, community college, or university. Ask around. You're likely to get many names of people who can help you.

7. Run your own advertisement. A small classified ad in a suburban shoppers' newspaper will probably cost you less than $10. Go ahead—splurge!

8. Call potential helpers (or, better yet, get your seventh-grader to make exploratory calls for about $3 an hour; you won't miss the money).

9. Interview, interview, interview. Over the phone is fine; in person is better. Map out what you want done; break in your helpers gently, but systematically.

10. Start a file of the literature or information that you've collected on all the different types of helpers you've been seeking and talking to.

Once you have a file of helpers, keep adding to it, keep it current, and use it. You have only your time and life to win back!

The Least You Need to Know

◆ Among the best time/money trade-offs are occasional taxi rides; delivery of dinner, groceries, and supplies; and any other vendors who pick up and drop off.

◆ Service providers can help you abound. They advertise in suburban "shopper" newspapers, on the web, and at odd places around town.

◆ High-school and college students can help you enormously, part-time. Many are ready, willing, and able; they learn fast, overcoming the lack of experience.

◆ Create a grid of all domestic tasks—and then all career-related tasks—that you'd rather not be handling. Then identify three options for each task.

◆ Populate your life with people who can free up your time. You're worth it.

Chapter 10

Becoming a Snooze-Savvy Sleeper

In This Chapter

◆ You're probably not getting enough sleep

◆ Can you really catch up on your zzzzs?

◆ Too little sleep hampers your effectiveness

◆ How to get more rest throughout the day

You're not getting enough sleep. How do I know? It's not a lucky guess; study after study shows that most American adults have been depriving themselves of the amounts of sleep they need.

Dr. William Dement, the director of Stanford University's Sleep Center, says, "Most Americans no longer know what it feels like to be fully alert." In his landmark book *The Promise of Sleep*, Dr. Dement unequivocally states that, "like bricks in a back pack, accumulated sleep drive is a burden that weighs you down. Every hour that you are awake adds another brick to the pack."

The Brain Keeps Track

"The brain keeps an exact accounting of how much sleep it is owed," Dr. Dement says. "Each successive night of partial loss is carried over, and the end effect appears to accumulate in a precisely additive fashion …. The size of the sleep debt and its dangerous effect are directly related to the amount of lost sleep. Until proven otherwise, it is reasonable and safe to assume that accumulated sleep loss must be paid back hour for hour."

He goes on to say, "In just a few decades of technological innovation we have managed to totally overthrow our magnificently evolved biological clocks and the complex biorhythms they regulate."

How important is sleep to you in your quest to win back your time? Vitally important. How important is it to your overall health and effectiveness? (Hint: See above.)

CAUTION

Pause!

A *Prevention* magazine survey showed that 40 percent of U.S. adults—tens of millions of individuals—"suffer from stress every day of their lives and find that they can sleep no more than six hours a night."

Short-changing your sleep on any given night (provided that it's only one) won't cause you much harm. You might feel crummy the next day, but you can compensate by taking a nap or going to bed early the next evening.

Sleep Deprivation: A Disaster in the Making

In *The 24-Hour Society*, sleep-researcher Dr. Martin Moore-Ede found that repeatedly getting less sleep than you need day after day can lead to disaster. He contends that a rash of transportation mishaps can all be traced back to insufficient sleep on the part of those in control of the vehicles.

How much do you need to sleep each day? It all depends—for some people, seven hours a night is great; for others, it's eight; for still others, nine. Most adults need about eight hours. College students may need an average of nine to nine and a half hours (whether or not they stayed up until 3:00 in the morning, they'd still need more sleep than a 35-year-old). As people age, some need more than eight hours a night; some need less.

CAUTION

Pause!

Don't use naps to catch up on sleep if you habitually short-change yourself each evening. It doesn't work.

Dr. Jack Edinger at Duke University's Sleep Center says, "The older one gets, the less smooth one's sleep pattern. It is normal for someone between 40 and 70 to be awake some part of the night." As you age, you may need more than eight hours of sleep nightly if it's punctuated by wakeful periods (not uncommon).

You've long known that you need to get enough sleep to function effectively. Who, or what, is the culprit? Here's a lineup of the usual suspects.

Habits Hang Heavy

If you've gone to bed at 11:00 or *midnight* for the past several months, chances are good that you'll go to bed around the same time this evening. If you feel compelled to turn in after Jay Leno does his monologue, you've developed a habit of retiring late.

Alternatively, if you have magazines, newspapers, CDs, and all manner of things to read and listen to, it's tempting to stay up yet another 20 or 30 minutes—which can balloon into 40 to 60 minutes.

If you're among the lucky ones who doze off as soon as you begin reading, be thankful. Many people remain awake longer when surrounded by information stimulants.

Coming to Terms

Midnight originally meant halfway through the night because people went to sleep when it got dark around 7:00 or 8:00 P.M. and got up when it became light around 5:00 A.M.

Eyes Wide Shut

If you use drugs (including alcohol), your sleep patterns will be disrupted and you're likely to get too little sleep. Alcohol might knock you out faster, but it can cause sleep difficulty and frequent wake-ups.

Coming to Terms

Your eyes actually make **rapid eye movements** while your eyelids are closed; these correspond to various levels of brain activity that are essential to sound sleep.

Getting Your REM Sleep

You've probably heard of REM—*rapid eye movements* that are a crucial part of your overall sleep cycle.

If you sleep too little or are awakened at inopportune moments, your REM pattern can be disrupted; hence, even eight hours in the sack may not yield the benefits of a solid eight hours of sleep. To win back your waking time, protect your sleep time:

♦ Don't sleep with your head by a telephone that can ring aloud. Remove the phone from your bedroom, or install an answering machine and switch off the ringer. Some people sleep with their heads by the phone because, for instance, they have aged loved ones far away; they worry about that one call in 15 years that might haul them out of bed at 3:00 A.M. Stop doing this; there's not much that anyone can do at that hour. You'd be far better off getting 15 years of sound sleep.

◆ Once a week, get to bed by 9:00 P.M. Your body will thank you. Let yourself go to dreamland for 9, 10, 11 hours—whatever it takes. Remember, you're probably going to live longer than you think you will; to get to old age with grace and ease, allow yourself at least one weeknight in which getting sleep is your only objective.

◆ One Friday night each month, crash right after work and don't get up until the next morning. Have dinner or skip it, as suits you. If you want to experience a fabulous weekend, this is the way to start.

◆ Avoid caffeine for the six hours before retiring. This means that if you're thinking about going to bed around 10:00, then 4:00 in the afternoon (or before) is the last time to imbibe any caffeine. But hey, why drink this drug-in-a-cup anyway?

◆ Avoid alcohol in the evening. Sure, it'll put you to sleep quickly, but it tends to dry you out and wake you up too early. Then you have trouble getting back to sleep, your overall sleep time is reduced, and the quality of your sleep is poor.

> **CAUTION**
>
> **Pause!**
>
> Dr. Martin Moore-Ede notes that if you stay up too late one evening, you are borrowing from the next day.

◆ If you fall asleep when you read in bed, then do so to induce drowsiness. Don't overdo it, though. Dr. Edinger says that it's important to make your bed and bedroom for sleeping (and, of course, sex) only. Don't set up your bed as a command station with your CD player, TV, or other appliances that reinforce alertness.

◆ Go to bed when you're tired. Let your body talk. It'll tell you when it's tired. Have you ignored the message?

◆ Don't fret if you don't fall asleep right away. You may need some time. After 30 consecutive minutes of restlessness, do something else until you're tired again.

◆ If you're kept awake by your spouse's snoring—or if you're the one snoring—you need help. I recommend a snore-control device. Whenever your snoring is above a certain decibel level, you receive a gentle vibration that breaks the pattern and helps you return to quiet sleep.

◆ Moderate exercise several hours before sleep aids in getting sound sleep.

◆ Moderate intake of proteins, such as a glass of milk, also aids in sound sleep.

Catching Up on Sleep: Myth or Reality?

If you've been depriving yourself of sleep for the last three years, you can't literally add back all the hours you missed. That kind of "catch-up" sleep won't support the continuing need that you face each day.

Nevertheless, your body is extremely forgiving. Many ex-cigarette smokers know this. Even lungs abused by years of smoking begin to cleanse themselves once the smoking stops for good. The effects of 10 years of abuse can greatly diminish in as little as 1 year. So it is with chronic undersleeping.

Getting enough sleep, as with engaging in other healthy practices, is a habit. Albert Gray, a successful businessman of yesteryear, said, "Every single qualification of success is acquired through habit. Men (and women) form habits, and habits form futures. If you do not deliberately form good habits, then unconsciously you will form bad ones."

> **The Time Master Says**
>
> Even if you've deprived yourself of sleep for a prolonged period, if you devote the next month to giving yourself all the sleep that you can get, you'll be in reasonably fine shape.

You can rationalize about it until doomsday, but depriving yourself of sleep is a bad habit. Of course, you have a lot to do. No one will debate that. You'll get it all done more effectively and more efficiently with sufficient sleep, not with less sleep.

Here are several suggestions to develop (or perhaps redevelop) the habit of getting sufficient sleep:

- ◆ Let others know about your newfound quest—this means family members who might otherwise impede your progress.
- ◆ One weekend day (or more) per month, linger longer in the morning before getting up—you know, sleep in!
- ◆ Any time that you're traveling for work, give the TV remote control to the front desk at the hotel. You can't afford to be clicking away at midnight. Get sleep when you're on the road (more on this shortly).
- ◆ Schedule extra sleep any time you're on vacation as well. An extra 30–45 minutes can make all the difference in the quality of your vacation.
- ◆ Recognize that, at first, you may have to force yourself to get into bed, even if it's 9:00 or 9:30 on a weekday evening and you'd rather be up and around.

You may have to break the flow of your normal evening activities to get that sleep.

Got Sleep?

Your sleep deficiency probably ranges between 45 and 90 minutes daily. If you're deficient by more than 10 hours a week, as a benchmark, it'll take you about a month to "recover." Again, this doesn't mean that you can replace all the hours that you've lost. It means that you can get to the point at which you're fully functional and can minimize (maybe eradicate) the effects of past deprivation. To get there, start at square one: Make a list of indicators that you're probably not getting enough sleep. Some of these may be familiar; some may be news to you:

◆ You bump into things more frequently than is normal for you.

◆ You slur your words.

◆ You have trouble digesting food.

◆ You're short with people when normally you wouldn't be.

◆ Your eyes are tired.

◆ Your *joie de vivre* is missing.

◆ You don't enjoy sex as much as you used to.

◆ You need to wake up by alarm clock (many people wake up when they want to, on their own).

◆ You don't want to face the day.

◆ Even small tasks seem to loom large.

◆ Your life has achieved a level of fine monotony.

◆ You find it easier to engage in tasks that don't involve talking to others.

◆ As much as you hate going to the dentist, you find leaning back in the dentist's chair rather relaxing.

◆ You find yourself nodding off in what are otherwise interesting or important meetings.

◆ You zone out for unknown periods of time while working.

◆ You engage in *microsleep* (the body's attempt to compensate for undersleeping) throughout the day. Drowsiness comes in waves. You can be alert one moment and drowsy the next, and not know the difference. Having too little sleep the night before (and certainly on an extended basis) increases the probability that you'll engage in microsleep.

Coming to Terms

Microsleep is a 5-to-10-second episode during which your brain is effectively asleep while you are otherwise up and about. Microsleep can occur while you are working at a PC or (omigosh) driving your car.

To Sleep Some More or Not?

Only you can determine how much sleep you need. I know I've had all the sleep I need when I bolt out of bed in the morning, ready to face the day. To determine your optimal sleep time, consider the following:

◆ Experiment with the number of hours that you sleep each night for a week. Start with eight hours, say, 10:30 P.M. to 6:30 A.M.

◆ If eight hours feels good, stay right there; no need to move on. If not, increase the amount by 15-minute increments.

◆ If you're waking up before you've slept eight hours (and you're not napping excessively during the day), perhaps you need less than eight hours. (More on naps in a moment.)

◆ To make your test valid, give up your alarm clock! Yes, give it up (any time you can afford to—not, of course, when you have a plane to catch). Any time it wakes you up, you don't truly know how long you would have slept.

Daytime Snooze Rules

If you have the opportunity, taking naps throughout the day (even on a weekday) can enhance your overall effectiveness and put you in the driver's seat of winning back your time.

Some people nap without problems; others can't nap at all. One study found that if you nap for 30 minutes each afternoon, you actually have a 30 percent lower incidence of heart disease than people who don't nap at all—such a deal. Napping increases your alertness for the rest of the day. Although many people feel a little groggy for a few minutes after a nap, it gradually subsides and they feel more alert (and in a better mood—try it).

Surprisingly, short naps are more productive than long naps. A short nap will leave you refreshed, whereas a long nap may interfere with your sleep that evening. The experts say that the best naptime is between 2:00 P.M. and 3:00 P.M. Any later, and your nap may be too deep, interfering with your nightly sleep. If you can, nap in a bed or a cot, but not a chair. Your quality of sleep will be much higher, and the immediate benefits will be more apparent. The only caveat: Naps are not a substitute for the proper amount of sleep.

The Time Master Says

The extra edge that napping provides can last for 8 to 10 hours. So, if you can steal one, you could be good for hours! However, naps are not designed to be substitutes for missed nocturnal sleep.

Coming to Terms

When you're **hydrated**, your body's tissues are sufficiently filled with water. To be **dehydrated** is to be parched.

Sleepy, Dehydrated, or What?

Hydration and *dehydration* play important roles in how much sleep you need.

About half the time I feel tired during the day, I haven't taken in enough water. Nutritionist David Meinz of Orlando, Florida, says that every chemical reaction that occurs in your body requires water. In fact, your brain is 75 percent water.

Meinz says that your thirst mechanisms lag behind your true need for water on a continual basis. Even a 2 percent reduction in your amount of body water will render you less productive than normal. A 5 percent reduction can seriously decrease mental functioning. Here are Meinz's suggestions for ensuring that you're sufficiently hydrated:

- Eight cups of water a day is the standard, but don't wait until your thirst reminds you that you need water. Drink before you're thirsty.

- If you work out a lot, your body requires a full 24 hours to regain the water supply that you need. Hence, you have to have much more water than you think when you work out.

- Drink eight ounces of water before starting your workout. During your workout, drink as often as you can.

- Sign on with the best water-delivery service in your area, or buy bottled water. The best choice for bottled water is spring water.

- If you use tap water, let it run about 30 seconds so that any sediments can clear out.

Meinz also says to take a multivitamin every day to reduce feelings of lethargy and ensure that you're getting most of the basic nutrients. Along with sufficient water intake, this will help you feel more vibrant more often during your day.

Get Rested

In addition to previous recommendations, here are other ways that you can get more rest throughout the day without putting a dent in your overall output:

1. Find a quiet place in your office, such as an empty conference room or a coworker's office, where you can simply sit in a chair for a few minutes and be still without fear of interruption. Even two or three minutes can help recharge your batteries.

2. Walk outside to a bench, your car, or some other safe haven where you can do the same.

3. Don't bolt right away from the table after eating your lunch. Linger for an extra minute or two; give your food a better chance to be properly digested.

4. Rest while you walk. This sounds like a contradiction, but you can walk hurriedly or restfully. On your way back from the restroom, a coworker's office, or lunch, stroll mindfully down the hall in a rhythmic fashion, fast enough that no one will accuse you of being a zombie, but sufficiently slow that you're hardly exerting yourself. This can work wonders.

5. Practice the same restful habits outlined here on Saturday and Sunday as well as during the week. Who says that you have to go all out during the weekend? Obviously, the opportunities for outright naps are much greater on Saturday and Sunday, so take them.

What about when you're feeling drowsy but you have to be awake and alert? In that case, think light and cool. With bright lights, your sense of alertness is enhanced and your brain is switched on. In essence, brightness equals wakefulness.

If your office or work space is somewhat on the chilly side (say, 68°F or less), you're also likely to stay more attentive and alert. As a rule of thumb for making presentations, it's better to have an audience cool and awake rather than warm and sleepy.

Road Rest

Although it may be harder to get a sufficient amount of sleep away from home, it's still just as important, if not more so. *On the Road with Hampton*, published by Hampton Inns, states that there were 43,900,000 individual business travelers in 1998 (one out of every five American adults). Suppose that you're one of them. You're bedding down for the night in a hotel and you need a good night's sleep so that you can summon enough energy to hold your own at the meeting the next day. Unluckily, the guest from hell is in the next room and apparently is trying to break the decibel barrier at 2:30 A.M. Normally, you're a sound sleeper, but this time you find yourself tossing and turning for four hours before you finally doze off. What can you do after checking into your hotel room to make sure that you get a good night's sleep every night, regardless of the quality of your sleeping accommodations?

Oh, Manager

Noise is invading the room that you've rented. If it's easy enough to determine the direction of the sound, and if the intrusion is from the room to the left or right, you could try tapping (gently but noticeably) on the wall. This alone sometimes works. In many hotels, the phone system allows you to readily dial adjacent rooms. If the noise is from across the hall or above or below you, you can call and ask the night manager to handle the situation.

Sleep Tools

To maintain greater control of potential sound disturbances, there are some essential items that you can use before checking into any hotel room: a *sound screen*, earplugs, and a timer.

Coming to Terms

A **sound screen** creates a sound "barrier" that breaks up, masks, or mutes the effects of louder sound from beyond the barrier by using white noise (a sound much like that of rushing water).

1. The Sound Screen is a portable white-noise device developed by the Marpac Corporation. It emits different frequencies and amplitudes of a droning, nondisruptive blanket of sound. You can use this device to minimize the effects of startling or disruptive sounds outside your room. By placing the screen about 10 feet from your head in the direction of any disruptive noise, you are able to minimize the intrusive effects immediately. If you're interested in this product, contact the Marpac Corporation at P.O. Box 3098, Wilmington, NC, 28406-0098. You can call them at 1-800-999-6962, or fax your order to 910-763-4219.

2. Create your own white noise. If you're awakened and the offending noise isn't too outrageous, use an empty channel on your TV set or radio as a white-noise machine. If you're using a TV this way, turn down the brightness to nothing, or cover the screen with a blanket or towel to minimize its light. If the TV isn't bolted down, put it between you and the noise. Experiment with your room's thermostat. Perhaps you can turn on the fan.

3. Space-age earplugs called Noise Filters are available from the Cabot Safety Corporation. They cost little and weigh even less. Airline gate and runway crews (employees who guide planes to and from their gates) use these industrial-strength plugs to shut out heavy-duty noise; they can provide you with a near-silent world. The plugs expand in your outer ear canal, blocking out sound in ways that traditional earplugs cannot. You can get these godsends in Walgreens and CVS pharmacies.

4. The fourth essential device is your own alarm clock or timer, instead of requesting wake-up calls. You can wake up on cue and be free from having to keep your room phone plugged in. This way, you won't receive other calls during the night. When you remove the plug from the phone, be sure to position the cord so that the end is exposed to you; it will remind you to plug it back in when you get up.

Well-Rested and Ready

If you're committed to getting back to the level of sleep and rest that you need—and if you're looking forward to being more awake, alert, and refreshed during the workday— you're already well on the way to making this happen. You'll feel the difference. Nevertheless, here's a checklist of indicators that let you know you're getting the amount of sleep that you need:

- You look forward to facing the day.
- You no longer need an alarm clock to get up.
- You awaken with energy, feeling great.
- Your eyes look clear, not red and bloodshot.
- You put in a full workday and have a deep-down satisfaction about what you accomplish.
- You have sufficient energy for activities after work as well.
- You look forward to sex.
- Your *joie de vivre* is back.

CAUTION

Pause!

Although sleep needs to vary, people who sleep about eight hours, on average, tend to live longer. "There will always be people who think that they can handle the effects of fatigue or believe that they can train themselves to get by with less sleep to get more work done," says William Dement, Ph.D. "All scientific evidence available says that this isn't so."

The Least You Need to Know

- Within a month, you can recover from a prolonged pattern of insufficient sleep. Start tonight.
- Insufficient sleep has a heavy impact on your effectiveness. Don't pretend otherwise.
- Safeguard your sleeping area by removing the phone and converting your bedroom back to a bedroom (not a den or a living room).
- You may need to take a nap during the workday. Get some type of brief rest. You definitely need to drink more water.
- You know that you're getting enough sleep when you bolt out of bed in the morning without having to use an alarm clock.

Part 3

Taking Back Your Turf

Does it feel sometimes as if you're being boxed in on all sides at work? One day you're working in an office, then it's a cubicle, then a smaller cubicle, and finally you find yourself working from benches.

Okay, so maybe that's not your situation. Nevertheless, you've likely incurred some encroachment of your time, space, and figurative as well as literal room to maneuver.

If you can reduce requests for your time, you'll finally be able to tackle your office and desk. (A desk, you may recall, is not a filing cabinet; window sills and the corners of your room are not permanent storage locations.) Then you can learn to manage piles and trials with smiles, and investigate some low-cost technology that won't drain your brain to use. When you make it to that point, we can move on to clever ways to handle all the messages that have been hounding you.

11

Loaning Yourself Out Less and Being Happier Because of It

In This Chapter

- ◆ What to do when your boss wants you to be a workaholic
- ◆ Defend your calendar because it's your life
- ◆ Learning to say "no" with grace and ease
- ◆ How to get off—and stay off—mailing lists

Actor Robert Redford once said, "Washington is a receptacle for workaholics." Of course, he could have said that about New York, Chicago, or any other major metro area! The ever-growing array of widely available office technology provides you the opportunity to do far more in a day than your predecessors of yesteryear. Concurrently, it also gives your boss and your organization the opportunity to get and expect more from you.

You used to be able to generate a handful of letters each day, if you were lucky. Now, with a few keystrokes, you can crank out 1,000 letters and still have time to work yourself to exhaustion before the end of the day.

Finished? Here's More!

CAUTION

Pause!

You know that you're a good worker. You're only too happy to help your organization in meaningful ways. Unfortunately, not all organizations make meaningful or reasonable demands, especially if their businesses have been slow lately.

The great paradox of today's work environment is that the more you can do, the more is expected of you. Unfortunately, expectations about what you can accomplish rise immediately with the introduction of tools that facilitate greater accomplishment. This explains why you frequently feel squashed in the gears of your work life like a present-day version of Charlie Chaplin in *Modern Times*. Instead of working on a real assembly line with which you can't keep pace, your "assembly line" is digital, byte-size, and cyber-driven at nearly the speed of light.

Survivors of Downsizing

The Families and Work Institute conducted a survey of workers who remained after downsizing efforts by their respective organizations and found some interesting statistics:

- ◆ 54% feel overworked.
- ◆ 55% feel overwhelmed by the workload.
- ◆ 59% lack time for reflection.
- ◆ 56% can't complete their assigned tasks.
- ◆ 45% must multitask too often.

With these findings, no doubt, those who remain after a downsizing face a tough road fraught with time pressures and anxieties. Yet, even in organizations in which downsizing has not occurred, or at least has not recently occurred, many of the same feelings among staff predominate!

The Time Master Says

When Colin Powell became the head of the State Department, he gave a closed-door, stirring speech wherein he talked about the mission of the agency and his own personal vision. He also discussed the importance of going home at a reasonable hour, not working on weekends, and maintaining a sense of balance. It would be interesting to know if he, along with his top staff members, actually followed suit, especially months into the job. Unfortunately, since September 11, 2001, we can assume all bets are off.

If a department or division is caught shorthanded, or if someone retires, makes a career change, or simply departs for some reason, the workload is often assumed by those who remain. In companies, or within tightly run departments, the absence of employees temporarily results in an uneven, unfair workload for those present.

Whether your organization has experienced a downturn or you simply are asked to do too much too often, let's explore how to further take charge of your turf and win back your time. We'll start with the vital challenge of managing your boss.

Teach Your Boss

Whole books have been written on this subject! Fortunately for you, I'm going to encapsulate them into the following single sentence: Ultimately, you'll be treated by your boss in the way that you teach your boss to treat you.

There, I've said it. A gross oversimplification? Look around your organization. Who gets stepped on the most? Who is handled with kid gloves?

Generally, the office wimps get used as doormats, and those who are a bit more particular as to how their workday unfolds are treated with a tad more respect. The key to not having your boss consume the time in your life beyond the normal workday involves re-examining the issues discussed in Chapter 1, "The Overtime Epidemic: How to Nip It in the Bud," and learning some specific phrases that you can offer as needed. Read on.

 Pause!

You don't want to be an office wimp, a routinely unsung hero who's asked (or is that commanded?) to perform great feats of productivity simply because you can, with no regard to your personal well-being and balance.

Workaholics Wanted

You've got this great position in this great organization. There's only one itty-bitty little problem: Your boss is a workaholic and expects you to be the same. This situation requires great tact and professionalism because you're not likely to change your boss's nature. You are likely to be confronted with his workaholism and its effects.

Here are key phrases that might help unstick you. (They work even better if your boss is not a workaholic!) Commit these to memory; in many cases it's essential that your retort be automatic:

◆ "I'm overcommitted right now, and if I take that on, I can't do it justice."

◆ "I appreciate your confidence in me. I wouldn't want to take this on knowing that my other tasks and responsibilities right now would prohibit me from doing an excellent job."

- "I'd be happy to handle this assignment for you, but realistically I can't do it without foregoing some other things I'm working on. Of tasks A and B, which would you like me to do? Which can I put aside?"

- "I can do that for you. Will it be okay if I get back to you in the middle of next week? I currently have A, B, and C in the queue."

- "The number of tasks and complexity of assignments that I'm handling is mounting. Perhaps we could look at a two- or four-week scenario of what's most important to you, such as when the assignments need to be completed and what I can realistically handle over that time period."

Even workaholic bosses are appreciative of your efforts on occasion. When the boss knows that you naturally work hard, he is not as likely to impose on you so often.

Shine When Others Will Slack

A great time to make a sterling effort is when the boss is away. Most people follow the old adage, "When the cat's away, the mice will play."

Be the one who's able to go into the boss's office after he returns and say, "Here's that big report you wanted. It's finished."

Reflect and Win

If you're the one who works hard when the boss is away, you help to convey a message that he doesn't need to constantly heap on assignments.

When the boss is outside the office, perhaps on travel or simply downtown fulfilling appointments, that's when he is most likely to monitor who's doing what back at the office. That's when the boss calls in more frequently, inspects things a little more closely upon returning, and is more on edge, knowing that most employees tend to slack off. Hence, this is your chance to shine, to teach this workaholic that you don't need to be overmonitored—and to make great strides toward controlling your time.

Calendar, Calendar on the Wall, Who's Overcommitted Most of All?

When you review your calendar months in advance and there's nothing scheduled, that's when you fall into time traps. Suppose that Jim comes in and asks you to volunteer with him three months hence for a charitable cause he supports. You open your appointment book or look on your scheduling software and see that there's nothing going on that day. So you say, "Sure, why not?" You mark it on your calendar. You even intend to honor your commitment.

Two months pass. As you approach the date on which you promised Jim you'd volunteer, you notice that you have responsibilities in and around it. A day or two before the time that you're supposed to help Jim, your schedule is jam-packed. Suddenly, Jim's long-standing request looks like an intrusion. Yet, when he asked and you agreed, it all seemed so harmless. All of which leads to Jeff's Law of Defending Your Calendar, which states (among other things):

> An empty calendar is not such a bad thing.

Defend Your Calendar

Why are you inclined to schedule tasks, responsibilities, and events for which you volunteer, but you aren't inclined to schedule leisure-time activities, particularly those on a weekday after work? Hopefully, you have no trouble scheduling a vacation. What about scheduling calendar pockets of fun, leisure, and relaxation throughout your week? You need to defend your calendar on a continual basis.

Your life (as discussed in Chapter 1)—as well as your career, year, month, workweek, and workday—are finite. If you are similar to other professionals, your calendar essentially is your life—therefore, you need to defend it.

As an exercise, review old calendars and examine the appointments, activities, and tasks that you scheduled. You'll gain perspective on how many things you scheduled that you could've done without.

In reviewing my own prior calendars (before I got all this wisdom), I observed that 40–50 percent of my activities were nonessential. Some could've been cut given my knowledge of their results. Most could've been cut simply because they weren't in accordance with my priorities and goals. I either yielded to the whim of the moment or I hadn't developed the ability to say "no."

Reflect and Win

For sure, volunteering to help someone is a good thing. Services and contributions by volunteers propel society and institutions. On the heels of 5,000 other things that you have to do, however, it may not be appropriate or even feasible for you to take on another task at this time.

Future Commitment Checklist

Here's a quick list of techniques to help you determine whether you can safely avoid adding some future commitment to your calendar:

- ◆ Is it in alignment with your priorities and goals?
- ◆ Are you likely to be as prone to say "yes" to such a request tomorrow or next week?
- ◆ What else could you do at that time that would be more rewarding?

Pause! _____

CAUTION

If you don't defend your calendar, it will surely be filled in with all manner of *worthwhile* activities that you don't have time for.

♦ What other pressing tasks and responsibilities are you likely to face around that time?

♦ Does the other party have options besides you? Will he be crushed?

♦ Do you like the person asking?

♦ If none of the above works, make your decision in three days hence, particularly when you can respond by phone, mail, or fax. It's much easier to decline when you don't have to do so in person.

A Graceful "No"

The bigger your organization, the more requests you receive to attend or support various functions. If you're an entrepreneur, a student, or a retiree, you still are likely to face a number of requests, most to be handled aptly with a polite "no." With Edgar's retirement party, Megan's baby shower, Kevin's summer bash, Aunt Sarah's sixty-fourth birthday party, the Little League parade, and who knows what else, it would be easy for you to fill up your calendar and never get your job done—let alone do the things that you want to do in life.

You don't need to bone up on the teaching of Amy Vanderbilt, Letitia Baldrige, or Miss Manners to say "no" with grace and ease. If you simply employ any of the following responses as they apply, you'll be in great shape:

♦ The easiest technique that you can use to decline a request is to say that your child's birthday/recital/graduation will be occurring at that time, and you couldn't miss it. Undoubtedly, your child will be doing something that merits your presence!

♦ Closely related is anything that your family has planned. For example, "Oh, that's the day our family is taking our annual fall foliage trip. We planned it months ago, and the hotel reservations have already been made. I do appreciate your asking."

♦ You may be able to work up enough guts to say, "You know, I'd like to, but I'm so overcommitted right now that I couldn't work it in and do it justice, or be fully attentive, or offer the level of support that I know you'd appreciate."

♦ "I wish you had asked me a couple of days ago. I already committed that time to helping XYZ accomplish ABC."

♦ "Could I take a rain check on that one? I've been working myself dizzy lately, and I've scheduled that time to be with my sex therapist/masseuse/bookie."

If you have no legitimate prevailing circumstances, here are other possible responses:

- ◆ "Let me get back to you by tomorrow on that." Tomorrow, use the aforementioned phone, mail, or fax to politely decline.
- ◆ Offer a gently worded "Thanks, but I'll have to pass."

Simplification = Freedom

You face so much that competes for your time and attention—perhaps a workaholic boss, an overfilled calendar, or scads of future commitments. Don't volunteer to have others hit you with even more tasks that will compete for your attention. Do you open your intellectual kimono willy-nilly and permit newspaper, magazine, and newsletter publishers to sign you up?

The effect of all this is feeling overwhelmed and having no sense of control over your time. The next time somebody calls with a highly worthwhile publication to which you can subscribe, use what you've learned in this chapter to politely decline. In addition, the following techniques for handling magazine subscriptions may be of use to you:

- ◆ As each of your magazines subscription expires, don't immediately renew. Wait three months to see if you miss having the magazine. If you don't, then you've saved some money and lots of time. You can always view several issues at a local library. In a society where information flows abundantly, no particular magazine (unless it's highly specialized) is that crucial anymore.

- ◆ If you do miss it, then resubscribe. The publication will take you back, I promise— in many cases, you'll even get a better rate.

- ◆ For the magazines that you currently receive, immediately strip them down; tear out or photocopy only those articles or passages that appear to be of interest to you. Then recycle the rest of the publication. (More on this in the chapters that follow.)

Reflect and Win

Without thinking, do you add your name to mailing lists, openly surrendering yourself to more data and more offers? If you make yourself aware of which organizations or businesses sell their client or membership lists, you can avoid the mailing-list blues.

- ◆ For existing subscriptions, experiment with giving away every second or third issue. Even chemists, engineers, and highly technical types agree that they could skip every third issue of their technical publications and not be less informed; most periodicals have an inherent redundancy.

◆ Each year, many magazines publish a roster of all the articles that they featured in their final issue of the year. Such indexes can be invaluable; you can highlight exactly which articles you would like to see.

◆ Some publications maintain a readers' service or an online version whereby you can acquire the specific articles you desire.

Eliminating Unwanted Mail

By extending the principles of reducing your magazine glut, you ultimately can save even more time. To get off—and stay off—mailing lists, write to the addresses listed here and ask to be removed from the list. Those organizations represent some of the most formidable mailing lists in the United States.

Advo Inc.
Director of Lists
239 West Service Road
Hartford, CT 06120-1280

National Demographics & Lifestyle
List Order Services
1621 18th St. #300
Denver, CO 80202-1294

Donnelley Marketing
1235 North Ave.
Nevada, IA 50201-1419

Mail Preference Service
Direct Marketing Association
P.O. Box 9008
Farmingdale, NY 11735-9008

Metro Mail Corporation
901 West Bond St.
Lincoln, NE 68521-3694

R.L. Polk and Company
List Services Division
6400 Monroe Blvd.
Taylor, MI 48180-1884

A Little Effort Goes a Long Way

Some strategies follow; you can use them to ensure that your name is removed from the mailing list(s). Some of them may seem involved, but once you get rolling, the peace of mind and time savings that you reap from having less junk mail cross your path will be well worth the effort!

- When you write to these organizations, include all variations of your name, such as Jeff Davidson, Jeffrey P. Davidson, Jeffrey Davidson, J. Davidson, J. P. Davidson, and so on; do this for all others in your household, for maximum effectiveness.

- Thereafter, write to the organizations every four months with a follow-up reminder; any purchase that you make by credit card or check is likely to get your name back on the direct-mail rolls.

- Create a printed label that says:

  "I don't want my name placed on any mailing lists whatsoever, and I forbid the use, sale, rental, or transfer of my name."

- The Direct Marketing Association in Washington, D.C., has published a pamphlet titled *Direct Marketing Association Guidelines for Ethical Business Practice*. It offers a comprehensive review of your rights regarding unsolicited third-class mail. For example, consider Article 32 on "List Rental Practices."

  Under the heading "Use of Mailing Lists," the DMA states, "Consumers that provide data that may be rented, sold, or exchanged for direct marketing purposes periodically should be informed of the potential for the rental, sale, or exchange of such data." It further states, "List compilers should suppress names from lists when requested from the individual." To reach the ethics department of the Direct Marketing Association, write to this address:

  Ethics Department
  Direct Marketing Association, Inc.
  1126 6th Avenue
  New York, NY 10036
  Phone: 212-768-7277
  Fax: 212-768-4546

- When you are besieged by third-class mail from repeat or gross offenders, and when such offenders have included a self-addressed bulk-mail reply envelope, feel free to use the envelope to request that your name be removed from their lists. Also, review their literature to see if there is an 1-800-, 1-888-, 1-877, or 1-866-number (toll-free) by which you can make such a request, at no cost to you.

- For those who do not heed your request, lodge a complaint with the Direct Marketing Association or the U.S. Postal Service.

- Sometimes the fastest way to deal with repeat offenders is to simply write the words "Speed Reply" right on the communication from them that you've received, and underneath those two words write this message: "Please remove me from your mailing list now and forever." Sign your name, date it, and send back the items or communication that you received. Be sure to address it to the mailing list manager of the offending organization.

- Inform the parties with whom you do business that you do not appreciate having your name added to a mailing list and being inundated by catalogs, announcements, brochures, and fliers. This is essential if you place an order by fax, purchase by credit card, complete a magazine subscription form, or procure any other type of good or service other than by cash.

Going to Extremes

As an extreme measure, I once carefully wrapped up a brick, and on the outside of the wrapper included this note to a gross offender: "I respectfully request that you remove my name from your mailing list. This is my eighth [or whatever the number] request, and, if unheeded, I shall send 10 bricks next time." After wrapping up the wrapped-brick-and-message, I affixed the bulk-mail-postal-reply face of the envelope sent to me in the latest mailing. I taped it securely to the package and dropped it in a mailbox.

Technically, of course, the post office didn't have to deliver it (I had defaced the reply envelope), but the delivery went through. It seems that I made a dramatic, costly impact on the original mailer, who then chose to heed my request and eliminate my name from its rolls. (The mailer called me and surrendered.)

The less unwanted mail you receive, the more time you have in your life. Period.

The Least You Need to Know

- If you're overscheduled, remember who invited all that into your life: you.
- If you have a workaholic boss, memorize key statements to spring at appropriate moments.
- Defending your calendar is synonymous with controlling your time. Beware of future commitments: They get vexing as their time draws near.
- Practice saying "no" with grace and ease. Use legitimate reasons (such as your kids, family, or prior commitments) to respectfully decline requests from others.
- Manage your magazine subscriptions. Keep your name off mailing lists.

The Efficiently Organized Office

In This Chapter

- ◆ Managing your desk and guarding the flat surfaces of your life
- ◆ Handling paper more quickly and easily
- ◆ Self-stick labels and long-life stampers yield maximum advantage
- ◆ What to chuck and what to keep

On the road to taking charge of your turf, you've learned two major principles thus far. In Chapter 10, "Becoming a Snooze-Savvy Sleeper," you read about the dramatic impact that sleep can have on the quality of your life and your effectiveness, both on and off the job. In Chapter 11, "Loaning Yourself Out Less and Being Happier Because of It," you saw some ways that you volunteer (perhaps unwittingly) to have more assignments, commitments, and information thrown your way—and that it's possible to keep much of this at bay.

Crack That Whip

Now it's time to tackle the vital notion of whipping your office into shape. You can rule an empire (okay, a little empire) from a desk if you know how to do it correctly. Too many people neglect their offices and their desks.

Ten reasons to stay disorganized:

1. A busy desk signals a busy mind—doesn't it?

2. The more stuff you have on your desk, the more likely people will leave you alone.

3. All those files and documents—you must be important!

4. Didn't somebody say that getting organized takes work?

5. Besides, doesn't it stifle creativity?

6. You have a ready-made excuse for not being able to find anything.

7. Accumulating piles is an art form.

8. There are others with worse messes than yours.

9. Building up huge piles shields you from visitors.

10. Consider all the decisions that you get to delay because the data is buried some-where.

A study among American Women Business Association members revealed that 43 percent of members spend 75 minutes a week looking for misplaced information. That amounts to more than 55 hours a year—like spending eight days simply looking around your office to find a document. Clutter is rising at an alarming rate at home and in the office. Many people now have more than one inbox. Keep your desk clear!

Control Your Desk, or It Will Control You

Have you seen the mid-1980s movie *Top Gun?* In it, Tom Cruise plays a Navy fighter pilot. Among his many responsibilities in flying some of the nation's most expensive air-crafts is landing Navy jets safely on aircraft carrier decks.

The Time Master Says

Your desktop, exhausted reader, is like the deck of an aircraft carrier. If you take the next pile of stuff that you get and simply park it in the corner of your desk with some vague notion that an organizing fairy will come by and do something with it, good luck when the next thing lands!

A few months after seeing the movie, I read an article in *Smithsonian* magazine about how aircraft carrier decks have to be completely clean and clear before a plane can land. "All hands on deck" on an aircraft carrier deck tradi-tionally meant that everyone—even senior officers—picked up a push broom and swept the deck completely clear when a plane was due to land. Now they have giant blowers and vacuums to do the job.

The goal is the same: to leave nothing on the surface of the deck, not even a paper clip. This ensures the highest probability of a successful landing. What happens if there is debris on the deck as a plane approaches? Or—oh boy—if an earlier plane has not left the landing strip? The likelihood of a mishap increases.

Nobody is coming to help you manage your desk; each new item that you pile on will add to the glut, like adding more files to an already over-loaded computer. If you don't take care of the files and delete them when completed, the computer will not have enough memory to handle new info—it will be slower, and it may say "disk is full."

All other things being equal, if you have but one project, one piece of paper—whatever you're working on—in front of you and the rest of your desk is clear, you're bound to have more energy, focus, and direction. If all manner of distractions compete for your attention—piles of reports, memos, and faxes—how can you have the same focus, energy, and direction on the task at hand? I think you know the answer.

Your Desktop Is Not a Filing Cabinet

What to keep on top of your desk is uniquely individual. As a general rule, anything that you use on a daily basis (such as a stapler, a roll of tape, or a pen) gets to stay on top of your desk. Remove anything that you can safely eliminate from your desktop. Where does it go? You might have a credenza behind you. In case you're thinking, "You asked me merely to shift my stuff from one surface to another," you're right. And it works!

Inside your desk, retain items that you use at least weekly, if not daily—but don't start storing supplies there. Those belong farther away from you, in file cabinets or supply lockers. Your goal is to maintain the optimal number of items on and in your desk—enough so that you work efficiently every day, but not enough to clutter up the works.

After you've cleared your desk of what's unnecessary, apply the same principle to the top of your filing cabinet, closet shelves, and other areas. What about your dining room table, a work bench, or the trunk or glove compartment of your car?

Your goal is to have in front of you what you need and not much more. Oddly enough, once these flat surfaces are under control, you also gain a heightened sense of control over your time. Such a deal!

Reflect and Win

The fewer things you have in these vital places, the greater sense of control you have over your immediate environment. So clear out the unnecessary items and start enjoying a new, more efficient work life.

Items Worth Acquiring

The following items can help you keep your office in shape:

◆ Color-coded file folders, tabs, labels, and long-life stampers.

Long-life stampers that say "draft" or "for your information" or some other oft repeated message can cut down on the time that you spend handwriting or organizing material.

Long-life stampers can cut down on the time your spend handwriting or organizing material.

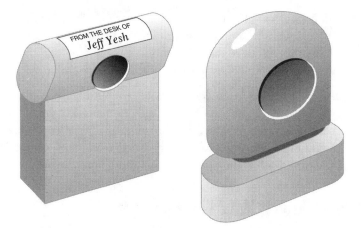

- ◆ A few three-ring notebooks for storing and maintaining similar items.
- ◆ A mechanical arm that hoists your monitor over your desk. You can use it to bring your monitor closer or move it aside, depending on how much room you need for your work. (If your computer's disk drives are in a tower case, you've just freed up another square foot or so of desk space.)
- ◆ A larger wastebasket.
- ◆ Magazine holders for your shelves.

Near your desk—but not on it—go the loving and familiar items, such as pictures, plants, and motivators. Also, if an item supports your productivity, efficiency, and creativity (from full-spectrum lights to ocean-wave music, or whatever) install it near—but not on—your desk.

Cardboard magazine holders help you stay in control of incoming items.

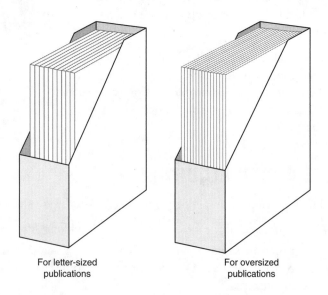

For letter-sized
publications

For oversized
publications

A Workout for the Cyber Set

Time out. As a quick aside to computer users, because you sit at your desk so often, for so much of your workday, in many instances facing the monolithic computer monitor, here are a few tips for overcoming the sedentary inclinations that facing a PC tends to support:

◆ Breathe in slowly through your nose, hold it for two seconds, and then exhale through your mouth. Repeat this several times, and you'll likely experience an energy boost.

◆ Roll your shoulders forward five or six times using a wide circular motion; do the same thing, this time rolling in the opposite direction.

◆ Turn your head slowly from side to side and look over each shoulder. Count to three. Repeat the exercise 5–10 times.

◆ While in your chair, slowly bend your upper body between your knees. Stay this way for a few seconds, and then sit up and relax. Repeat this once or twice to stretch your back.

◆ Hold your arms straight out in front of you. Raise and lower your hands, bending them at your wrists. Repeat this several times; it stretches the muscles in your fore-arms and gives your wrists relief.

◆ Fold your arms in front of you, raise your elbows to shoulder level, and then push them straight back. Hold this for a couple of seconds. This gives your upper back and shoulder blades some relief. Repeat 5–10 times.

Reflect and Win

Hereafter, manage your desktop as if it's one of the most important elements to winning back your time—because it is.

Take a break now and then. Ultimately, you'll get more done. And if you do even a few of these exercises, you'll feel better about your time during the workday and afterward.

Be the First on Your Block: Master Your Shelves

Shelves are one of humankind's greatest inventions, right up there with fire and the wheel. Do you ever consider what goes on a shelf versus what goes in a filing cabinet? Because filing is the subject of Chapter 14, "Becoming a Filing Wizard," let's focus on the first part of the question here: What goes on your shelves? In a nutshell, your shelves are the home of the following items:

◆ Items that you're bound to use within the next two weeks

◆ Items too large for a filing cabinet (or collections of such items)

◆ Projects in progress

◆ Supplies that can go in supply cabinets

Let's examine each of these individually.

For Use Within the Next Two Weeks

These include reference books, directories, phone books, manuals, instruction guides, books, and magazines (especially large ones, like annual directories and theme issues).

If It Doesn't Fit, Shelve It

Because it's difficult to file some thick items such as books (and some magazines) in a filing cabinet, any such item is better housed on a shelf. Any oversize item that simply won't fit in a file cabinet (and any item that is part of a continuing series) is probably best housed on your shelves.

If you receive a key industry publication and it makes sense for you to hang on to back issues, these also belong on your shelves. In this case, you could acquire magazine holders—essentially precut or preassembled boxes (corrugated cardboard or plastic) that hold about 24 issues of a monthly magazine. The box itself enables you to stay in control. It's visual; you can stick a face-up label on it. It's easy to grab one issue from among the many that you're retaining; it's easy to replace the issue.

Cardboard magazine holders help you stay in control of incoming items.

Projects in Progress

Similarly, if you're working on a project that requires a variety of items, the magazine boxes work well. If you keep your shelves behind your seat at your desk, keep one shelf compartment clear so that you can lay incoming file folders flat on it. You'll have a place for new stuff while keeping your desk relatively clear. It's better to have these materials behind you than right in your immediate work area. Undoubtedly, you face many demands during the day; you may have to draw upon several folders for different projects or tasks. It makes sense to have a single flat surface (even among your shelving units) readily available to accommodate active files.

Supplies in Supply Cabinets!

Most professionals today have little difficulty filling up their shelves. Supply catalogs, a Chamber of Commerce directory, guidebooks, or new software manuals all are capable of consuming a few inches of precious horizontal space.

Your inclination might be to get more shelves, but it's best to avoid that. Your goal is to keep your office in shape within reasonable parameters—using the desk, filing cabinet, shelves, and supply cabinet that you already have. If any of these is always overfilled, okay, I'll concede: Perhaps you need to go get another one. More often, lack of space is an excuse for not being able to manage an office.

Keep supplies in a supply cabinet (isn't logic beautiful?) because you can store them in bulk. Stack them horizontally, vertically, or with one type of item on top of another. Treat your shelves as somewhat sacred; align them so that you can pull out key items at will. If it takes you longer than 30 seconds to find something on your shelves, refine your system.

Filing Finesse

While "filing for fun and profit" will be covered in detail in Chapter 14, it's important to look at the relationship between your files and your office in general. Filing is a dynamic process. Items that you place in your file folder today may find their way onto your shelves, re-emerge in some other form, or be chucked.

What's on your shelves may (in some mutant form) find its way into your files. If you have a big reference book on a shelf, you may have to extract a few pages from it, discard or recycle the larger volume, and retain only a few essential pages in a folder in your filing cabinet. The relationship among all your storage areas is dynamic; your prevailing quest is to boil down what's crucial for you to retain—keep only the essence.

Are you fearful about tossing something because you just know that you're going to need it tomorrow? Chapter 23, "Treading Lightly— And Loving It," will help you here. Accept this: If there are no discernible negative consequences to tossing something, toss it. Most of what you're retaining is readily replaceable anyway. Office efficiency experts claim that 80 percent of what executives file, they never use again. Even if that's only partially true, it still means that a significant chunk of what you're retaining is deadwood.

Clearing this deadwood out of your desk, files, and office keeps your work space in shape. That enhances your capacity to properly handle new demands (and, as you read in Chapter 4, "Time-Binding Dilemmas That Can't Be Ignored," you know that more is coming). It also improves the

Reflect and Win _____

Information is power; if you can't find what you've retained, it's of no value to you. Worse, the time that you took to read and file the items is then wasted.

Pause! _____

You could employ stacking trays, but they tend to become semipermanent collections of paper rather than projects in progress.

The Time Master Says

The great paradox of keeping house is that getting things in shape takes time. Persevere. The small time investment that you make in developing your newfound efficiency will pay off repeatedly down the road.

odds that you'll be able to locate those items that you actually need.

Consider the cumulative time savings that you could potentially chalk up if you cut your search time in half—let's say that you'll save 12 minutes per day, at minimum. That adds up to an hour per week and 50 hours per year. That's like creating an extra week for yourself. As a kicker, others in your office get a clear message that you're someone who is able to remain in control, find things quickly, and stay on top of situations. So, you get a multiple payoff for keeping your files (and your office, in general) in shape.

The Least You Need to Know

- ◆ Your desk is among the most important areas of your life. Take charge of your desk, and you help take charge of your time.

- ◆ Refine your office set-up so that you can find whatever you're looking for easily. (That's right, easily.)

- ◆ Everyone faces a barrage of accumulated scraps and information tidbits. Corral these and copy them all onto a single page or into a file on your PC.

- ◆ Continually and ruthlessly discard what does not support you, and acquire what does.

- ◆ Getting things in shape takes time but pays off over and over again.

Surround Yourself to Win

In This Chapter

- Is your office equipment hurting you?
- Websites to set you straight
- Your office layout counts for much
- Establishing a secret workplace hideaway

The office equipment that you use, and how you use it, has an impact on your health, well-being, productivity, and, ultimately, your use of time. Healthy workers make more efficient workers. When the physical requirements of a job don't match the physical capacity of the workers, musculoskeletal disorders can result. *Ergonomics* is the science of fitting the job to the worker.

The Ergonomics of It All

An ergonomic office is essential to helping prevent injuries due to cumulative trauma from repetitive tasks, such as typing. If you work in a progressive organization that is interested in promoting wellness, see if you can have your

Coming to Terms

Ergonomics is the science that examines how devices should most smoothly blend to the human body and human activity.

seat, desk, and computer monitor aligned so that they are at the proper height and the correct settings for you.

If you're having back problems because of the chair that you are sitting in, because your wrists are hurting, or because something else is askew, you are certainly not going to be at your best. You won't be as productive as you could be. You may end up taking sick days that you otherwise could have avoided. Not getting a good night's sleep every night compounds the problem.

Pre-Empt the Pain

If you manage others, before your staff complains of sore forearms, aching wrists, or lower back pain, invest in making your office ergonomic. The fact that you are willing to invest in their well-being can also help build loyalty, boost morale, and improve retention. If that's not incentive enough, consider these statistics from the U.S. Occupational Safety and Health Administration:

Pause!

The costs of cumulative trauma injuries can be considerable. Avoidable afflictions such as carpal tunnel syndrome and back strain cut into workers' productivity, sometimes forcing employees to miss work or even change careers altogether. Experts estimate that the hidden costs (lost productivity, absenteeism, turnover) of cumulative trauma injuries are *two to seven times* greater than the visible costs!

- ◆ Work-related musculoskeletal disorders account for 34 percent of all workday illnesses and injuries.
- ◆ 1,800,000 workers experience repetitive stress injuries each year.
- ◆ Workman's compensation claims due to physical stress have tripled since 1980. Sixty percent are estimated to relate to poor ergonomic conditions.
- ◆ About half of every dollar spent on medical costs will be for treating cumulative trauma disorders.
- ◆ Indirect costs (overtime, replacement, attorney fees) from work-related musculoskeletal disorders to U.S. businesses may run as high as $45 billion per year.

Prevention Pays

A study sponsored by State Farm Insurance indicated that clerical workers' performance improved as much as 15 percent with ergonomically acceptable workstations and seating. The Occupational Safety and Health Administration proposed standards to force employers to make their offices ergonomic, but it was tabled in early 2001.

Buying ergonomic furniture or other equipment and hiring consultants to teach your workers how to protect themselves against injuries can be expensive. However, the costs incurred by not making those investments are much higher.

Becoming "EC"

Fortunately, there are a wide variety of resources to which you can turn to ensure that where you work and the way you work are "EC"—ergonomically correct. Listed here are a variety of websites that offer useful information.

Health and wellness-related websites:

www.virtualpsych.com	Advice for emotional coping and wellness
www.asda.org	American Academy of Sleep Medicine
www.americanheart.org	American Heart Association
www.amtamassage.org	American Massage Therapy Association
www.apa.org	American Psychological Association
www.awhp.org	Association for Worksite Health Promotion
www.ayurveda.com	Aurvedic Institute
www.jazzercise.com	Dance exercise
www.cdc.gov	Center for Disease Control
www.tifaq.org/ergonomics/office.html	CTD Resource Network
www.ergonomicresources.com	Ergonomic Resources, Inc.
www.ergo-2000.com	Ergonomic Resources
www.ergoweb.com	ErgoWeb, Inc.
www.office-ergo.com	F-One Ergonomics
www.mayohealth.org	Mayo Clinic
www.ncbtmb.com	National Certification Board for Therapeutic Massage
www.cdc.gov/niosh/ergopage.html	NIOSH
www.officeworld.com	Office World
www.sleepnet.com/depriv.htm	Sleep deprivation links
www.sourceequipment.com	Source Equipment
www.mmm.com/cws/newsletr.html	*3M Ergonomics Newsletter*
www.workspaces.com	Work spaces

Massage and bodywork sites:

> www.mediconsult.com
> www.naturopathic.org
> www.polaritytherapy.org
> www.yogaclass.com

If you suspect that your office ergonomics are lacking, here are five steps to improve them:

1. **Set up computer stations properly.** Desks are made for writing, not for computing. The standard desk height is 30 inches; consultants recommend 27- or 28-inch work stations for people who spend at least half their work time at a computer. The wrong keyboard height can lead to wrist, back, neck, and shoulder strain. Monitors should be set up so that the top line of type is between eye level and 15° below eye level. Proper positioning can prevent neck and back problems.

2. **Buy adjustable chairs.** Make sure that your chairs have adjustable heights, rotating five-wheel bases, tilting seats, and adjustable back rests. Staff should familiarize themselves with their chairs' features so that they can position them for maximum comfort. Knees, hips, and elbows should be kept at right angles when sitting. If staff members share workstations or are frequently moving to different desks, encourage them to always adjust the height and backrest of whatever chair they are using that day.

3. **Keep muscles loose by providing support and adjusting position.** Proper support for sensitive body parts encourages blood flow, which carries oxygen to muscles and carts away waste. Consider buying forearm rests and wrist cushions to use while typing or footrests for employees whose feet don't rest squarely on the floor. Tell all staff members to adjust their positions repeatedly throughout the day so that they don't continually fight gravity with the same muscles.

4. **Set up desks so that workers can avoid repeating difficult tasks.** For example, a worker shouldn't have to make an awkward reach for a frequently used folder.

5. **If someone experiences physical discomfort at work, act at once.** Even a small delay can turn a small problem into a major one. Don't hesitate to call a consultant, if one is needed. A single appointment could prevent a serious injury.

Setting Up Your Home Office

Just as ergonomic alignment of your office furniture and equipment can keep you healthy and more efficient, the layout of your office (and, if you're working from home, location within your home) can make a significant difference in your effectiveness, your marketing, and how others perceive you.

As you undoubtedly know, affordable PC-related technology enables more people to flourish in a home-based office environment. If you're already operating a home-based office or business, you've probably discovered many benefits of working from home. These benefits include the following:

- No additional rent or lease expense
- Reduced wardrobe expense
- No warming up the car
- No time lost commuting, and no commuting stress
- No auto mishaps, fewer car repairs, lower fuel expense, and longer car life
- No need for extra keys, security cards, parking passes, or lock combinations
- Moderate expenses for extra phone lines; moderate increases in utility costs
- Enhanced ability to make and receive after-hours work calls
- Use of other equipment at will; more flexible hours in general
- Enhanced ability to relax, rest, or nap at will
- Enhanced potential to eat more nutritious, well-balanced meals

Working from your home office, particularly if you hold another job outside the home, helps define and separate your two jobs. Lengthened workdays with less fatigue become possible because you control many of the environmental factors.

Ahem ... Is There a Downside?

The disadvantages of working at home, in many cases, stem from not having the discipline to capitalize on the advantages. For example:

- Making and answering phone calls at odd hours may become the norm rather than the exception. Many of these calls may prove to be disruptive.
- Napping, snacking, and home distractions may cut into vital working time. The capability to snack whenever you choose often leads to an increased belt size.
- The stress and tension of working in a traditional office may be supplanted by a different kind of stress—that is, attempting to do too much, being unfocused, or, ironically, becoming too successful as a home-based marketer.

Working from a home office can disrupt home life, and small children can distract a parent from business activities. What's more, the typical home office is often crammed into less space than it would be in a commercial building or elsewhere outside the home.

Making It Work

If there's a pattern to successful time management in a home-based office, achieving it likely entails much of the following. The entrepreneurs …

◆ Are persistent.

◆ Base their decisions on factual information as often as possible.

◆ Make continual, total commitments to the needs of the business.

◆ Quickly identify their immediate supporting environment—suppliers, customers, employers, friends, and relatives.

Despite everything that's going on around you, when you're working, your home-based office should become the center of your universe. How you feel about working in your home office actually is more important than where it is located within your home.

Your office needs to be comfortable and accessible for you. It has to be designed to support you, and if you choose to greet coworkers, clients, or customers at home, it needs to favorably influence them.

Variety Rules

Regardless of whether you live in a detached single-family home, a high-rise condominium, a garden apartment, or any other structure, the office layouts that you can devise to support your efforts vary widely.

> **Reflect and Win**
>
> You need quiet on the business front. Even in a custom-designed, home-based office, you need to control communications with the outside world. Between the telephone, fax, and email, the potential exists for an environment with as many interruptions as you would experience in a commercial office.

The Den Office

The den office (or an office set up in a spare bedroom) is the most popular among home-based workers and provides the greatest number of advantages. If you have a den or spare-bedroom office or a detached office, you are apt to enjoy more benefits than with an office in another part of your home, such as the attic, basement, or dining room. Heating, cooling, and ventilation are likely more easily controlled from the den-type office.

Proximity to the front door is useful when greeting visitors and making your own quick exits. Proximity to the bathroom cuts down on time away from your desk and opportunities to be distracted as you walk through the house.

If you live alone, any portion of your home that you carve out for home-office purposes can ably serve to support your efforts.

A den or spare-bedroom office in a home with a spouse or children (or roommates) may not give you the privacy and silence that you need to do your best work. If this is the case, many options exist to soundproof and cordon off your office space. Room dividers and sound barriers are available in a variety of shapes and sizes. Placed in front of your desk or outside the door to your office, they can improve any existing sound barriers.

Various white-noise and sound-dampening gadgets are available today through direct mail catalogs and at popular electronics stores. They mask the sounds behind them (such as noisy kids) and quickly pay for themselves.

The Detached or Semidetached Office

The detached or semidetached office is often mandatory, particularly if you are a lawyer, a doctor, or a dentist. A semidetached office is a completely finished room, or set of rooms, adjacent to or part of your home's overall structure that is otherwise not a part of your home. Ideally, you have both an entrance for clients and a passageway to the rest of your home.

The detached office offers privacy, can be decorated and furnished in complete contrast to your home, and provides most of the advantages of a commercial office.

The Attic Office

Depending on the specifics of your location, there are some distinct advantages to maintaining an attic office.

Advantages:

◆ If space is sufficient, you will be able to lay out several projects at once.

◆ You can set up substations for specific tasks (helpful when using part-time staff).

◆ It may offer excellent privacy and desirable isolation.

◆ Your view from on high may foster creative thinking.

Disadvantages:

◆ You tend to hear and be aware of all changes that take place under you (such as someone coming in the front door).

◆ Lack of proximity to the entrance can be annoying.

◆ The office may not be suitable for meeting clients.

◆ Rain, branches striking your roof, and a whole new cast of disturbances may arise.

◆ Heating and air conditioning may pose special problems.

The Basement Office

The advantages of maintaining a basement office in terms of supporting your efforts include these:

◆ If space is sufficient, you will have the ability to lay out several projects at once.

◆ You can create substations for specific tasks, which is helpful if using part-time staff.

◆ It can offer the right amount of privacy and isolation.

The disadvantages include these:

◆ Basements tend to be cold. (Cold air falls.)

◆ You tend to hear and be aware of all changes that take place above you (such as someone coming in the front door).

◆ Lack of proximity to the entrance way, bathroom, and other areas can be an irritant.

◆ The office may not be suitable for meeting clients.

The Dining-Room Table Office

The dining-room table, another table, or a corner of your home can effectively support you in your home-office efforts under the following conditions:

◆ You're a sales representative for a company with headquarters elsewhere.

◆ You're a part-time entrepreneur or the revenue that you derive from your home-office venture is not crucial to your income.

◆ Your venture doesn't require a lot of paperwork, notes, files, materials, and so on.

◆ You have a few key accounts, and the work that you do for them can be performed in a small area.

◆ You derive most or all of your income via online connections.

◆ You are an extremely organized person and have supporting resources.

◆ You live alone or have a very understanding spouse.

Here is a quick summary of the advantages of the dining-room table home office:

◆ It's a reasonable option if no other space is available.

◆ Work materials can quickly be assembled and disassembled.

- It usually provides sufficient table space to spread out work-related materials.

- Lighting is usually excellent.

- It provides a chance to be near other members of the family, if that is an objective.

- Assembling and disassembling work materials, if handled correctly, can actually promote orderliness and efficiency.

- It's close to all household amenities.

The disadvantages are these:

- It quickly and frequently leads to clutter.

- Generally, it is not conducive to sustained growth or expansion.

- It can be disruptive to home life.

- You become subject to distractions and lack of privacy.

- Files and paperwork can be lost or stained.

Home Offices Require Quiet

Many first-time home-based workers are in for a huge surprise—disturbances in and around the home can be as disconcerting as in a traditional office! Michael Korda, the famed publisher at Simon and Schuster and successful author, set up an office in his country home in an attempt to get more work done, avoid the commute, and have a life. In his book *Country Matters*, he discusses how invariably someone would drop by in the morning, there would be an unexpected phone call, an important fax would come through, and then some other matter in the household would need tending. Before he knew it, half the morning was consumed.

Essential Boundaries

Korda learned, as do all successful home-based workers, that you need to establish physical, psychological, and auditory boundaries. For example, what are the hours in which you don't wish to be disturbed? Perhaps you need to post them. Establish your routine so that you work the same hours every day and so that everyone in your household knows it. Noise is a whole 'nother matter. (See Chapter 10, "Becoming a Snooze-Savvy Sleeper," for information on noise reduction.)

Reflect and Win

Many home-based workers find that their highest productivity comes early in the day, perhaps before everyone else wakes and often after everyone else departs.

In my own home-based office, I maintained a policy for many years of "Nobody enter; I will be coming out on occasion, and at that time you may hit me with whatever matters I need to know."

Your Secret Hideaway

If you have enough space, set up two work centers. (I know, this could lead to more expense and shuffling items back and forth, but read on!) Alternatively, find a park bench or far library table where you can work undisturbed. I find it highly advantageous to have an administrative office where I answer the phone, read email, check the fax machine, work with part-time staff, receive mail, and so on.

When I need to have utter quiet for writing, composing an outline for a new speech, or simply engaging in creative thought, I have a different setting where I go. In my quiet domain, there are no phones, fax machines, or emails to disturb me. Talk about managing your time to the max and achieving your greatest productivity!

I greatly look forward to retreating to my sanctuary (in my case, a rented space) and feel that I can't spend enough time there in the course of a week. Fortunately, I do manage to get in several hours every couple of days. Often, those hours tend to be the most rewarding from time and productivity standpoints, and they also offer a deep sense of satisfaction.

The Least You Need to Know

- When the physical requirements of a job don't match the physical capacity of the workers, musculoskeletal disorders—pain—can result.
- Workman's compensation claims due to physical stress have tripled since 1980, the year PCs started becoming popular. Most of the claims were related to poor ergonomic conditions. Ensure that your desk, furniture, and equipment are properly aligned.
- Adjust your working positions repeatedly throughout the day so that you don't continually fight gravity with the same muscles.
- Home-based workers need a comfortable and accessible work space designed to support them and, if applicable, to favorably influence any coworkers, clients, or customers at home.
- Disturbances in and around the home can be as disconcerting as a traditional office! Establish barriers and boundaries so that you can remain productive.

Chapter 14

Becoming a Filing Wizard

In This Chapter

- ◆ As the world grows more complex, filing becomes more important
- ◆ The essential tools for mastering the high art of filing
- ◆ It's both what you file and how you file it
- ◆ Design your filing system to uniquely serve the way you work

Do you look upon filing as drudgery? If so, you're not alone! You don't see people shooting movies, writing Broadway plays, or producing hard rock albums on the topic. It's rather mundane, even pedestrian. Yet it's an unheralded key to winning back your time.

As discussed in Chapter 12, "The Efficiently Organized Office," when you're in control of your desk, your office, your files, and the resources you've assembled, you are a more focused, efficient, effective professional. In this chapter, I focus exclusively on filing. Don't give me that look; it's going to be engrossing, and it'll give you a career edge. Moreover, in the long run, it will help you manage your time better.

To File or Not To File

It's important to ask the question: Why file?

1. Files have future value. You file items because you believe that they will come in handy. (You seek to avoid filing items that don't have a future.)

2. There are consequences for not filing. You save receipts from business expenses so that you can be reimbursed by your organization and, heh, heh, comply with IRS regulations.

If you're in sales, you file information that will enable you to make greater sales in the future. This includes notes on customers and perhaps their catalogs, brochures, and reports.

Pause! _____

Most of what confronts you will have exceedingly little impact on your career or your life. Most of what crosses your desk is a clog that dares not find its way into your files.

Everything that you've ever filed presumably had (or has) future value, if only enabling you to cover your derriere. People often avoid filing because they don't see the connection between filing and its future impact on their careers and lives.

Starting the filing process is time-consuming—I won't kid you. It is one of those necessary tasks, however, that saves time later. Rather than spend hours searching for an item, you'll be able to find it—pronto. So, it's well worth a day or two during downtime to create a system that supports you.

Tools to Help Simplify

Filing requires only a few simple tools and the proper mind-set. The tools include:

◆ **A chair**—You can file while standing if you have a four-drawer filing cabinet and you're dealing with the top drawer. Usually, your filing activity is easier if you're in a chair—particularly a swivel chair. If you're way behind in your filing, you won't want to be on your feet.

◆ **A desk or flat surface**—This comes in handy when you staple or unstaple, paper-clip or un–paper-clip. Often you'll have to mark the folders that you insert into your file cabinet, making notes on what you're filing, folding, ripping, or taping together. A flat surface means never having to work in midair.

◆ **File folders**—These are essential. Rather than the manila folders that have been around since God enabled Moses to part the Red Sea, you can get folders in blue, green, brown, red, pink, or black—any color you want.

- **File folder labels**—These can be color-coded as well. You don't have to order the same old white labels. You can easily have subsections within your green file folders by using labels of different colors.

- **Filing cabinets with ample space**—The next time you visit your doctor or dentist, ask to see how the patient files are stored. Healthcare providers often use a modular stacking shelf system that gives them immediate access to the record needed.

- **Color-coded dots**—These help you find files quickly, even if you're already using color-coded files and labels. You could put a small red dot on files that you anticipate using in the next week or two. The real value of the dots, however, is that you can leave these current files in the file drawer instead of on your shelf or desk.

- **Staplers, paper clips, and other fasteners**—Keep these on hand; you never know when you'll need to fasten or unfasten items before you file them.

> **The Time Master Says**
>
> Unlike the Ten Commandments, what you file is not etched in stone. You can move things around, chuck them, add or delete files ... go wild. Your goal for now is to get things into their best apparent home.

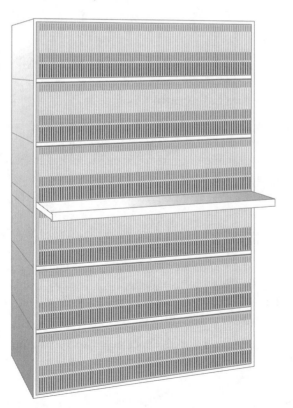

A shelf system like this one provides the room you need to set up any kind of filing system.

Paper Abounds

Even with PCs, fax/modems, email, and the Internet, paper will continue to be the dominant means of communication and the scourge of your career. Daily, the most repetitious task that you face could be handling paper. (See Chapter 4, "Time-Binding Dilemmas That Can't Be Ignored.") In many respects, to win back your time is to win the battle with paper.

The Facts of Faxing

Despite the awesome use of email, depending on the nature of your job, faxes may come in intermittently or all day. They may each require urgent and diligent efforts, or they may be more random in nature. In all cases, you want to be in an ever-ready state of preparedness. If faxes represent an intrusion, as opposed to the bailiwick of your daily tasks, notice at what times during the day you're most amenable to responding to them.

Perhaps it makes sense to let several accumulate before dealing with them all. The common denominator to addressing paper intrusions is to handle them in accordance with the energy that you can muster for their swift resolution.

Stripping to Success

When you receive a catalog, magazine, or other thick publication, strip it down to its essence. What few articles, pages, or items of interest do you want to retain? Once you identify them, recycle the rest and reduce the potential for office glut.

Immediately reduce books, manuals, and long reports to their essence; manually scan the entire document (using your eyes, not a hand-held scanner). Copy the few pages that you wish to retain, along with the title page, table of contents, and any critical addresses and phone or fax information. Your goal: Retain the few pages that seem important and recycle the larger document.

Your Copier Can Help

When new items arrive in your office, consider the creative ways that you can strip them down, particularly using the copier. Can you create a single sheet, perhaps front and back, that captures the essence of the larger document? Can you create a single sheet that captures the essence of several small scraps or tidbits that you want to retain?

When I speak at conventions, sometimes I ask the audience members to hold up their wallets. This gets a chuckle, but everyone plays along and the exercise is well worth undertaking; if their wallets are thicker than half an inch, they're carrying too much in them. My guess is if their wallets are thick, their files are overflowing.

Mr. Lakein's Junk Drawer

Alan Lakein, a management specialist of yesteryear (see Chapter 28, "Keeping It All in Perspective"), had a nifty idea about what to do with the mounting piles of stuff that you can't deal with now but want to review when you have a chance. He suggested putting everything in what he calls a C drawer, meaning that it's not an A or B item. You can't chuck it, but you certainly can't deal with it at the moment, either.

In this drawer, you temporarily house what you want out of sight and out of mind. Go back to your C drawer when you have the time (and mental and emotional strength!). Take out the items and see what needs to go into your file system (probably not much), what you can immediately chuck or recycle, and what goes back into the C drawer. I maintain a C drawer and find it helpful, particularly when I'm working toward a deadline and I encounter something that I don't have time to review immediately. I pop it into the C drawer and get back to what I was doing.

 Pause!

When confronted with too many scraps and information tidbits, it's easy to fall into the habit of parking them in your wallet, on your desk, or in your drawers.

Questions About Paper

When you're confronted by yet another report, document, or who knows what, ask yourself these questions:

◆ **What is the issue behind this document?** What does the paper represent? Is it an information crutch (data that you already know)? If so, chuck it. Does it represent something that you think might be important in the future? If so, put it in the C drawer.

Often the issue behind the paper flood is, in retrospect, too minor to merit your attention. Sure, it looms large at times, but what doesn't seem important when it arrives in screaming headlines? For years, newspapers have been able to sell their wares simply with clever use of language and font size. The issues addressed often have precious little to do with the typical reader.

◆ **Did I need to receive this at all?** This can be an insightful question to ask yourself. In many cases, the answer is "no;" that means that you don't have to spend another second on the item. Now and then, something that you didn't need to receive comes your way and is of interest. (Rare, but possible.) You can chuck most of these items immediately.

◆ **How else can this be handled?** Can you delegate what needs to be done regarding this new piece of paper? Referring back to Chapter 9, "Buying Yourself Some Time," is there someone else in your cosmos who can handle this for you and free up your time for more important things?

If no one else but you will do, how else can you handle it so as to have (in good old computer biz-speak) "quick and easy throughput"? Can you fax instead of mail? Can you email instead of fax? Can you pay by check instead of in person? Can you pay by faxing your credit card number instead of by check? Can you highlight the five items in the important company memo that merit discussion at the next meeting instead of trying to get a handle on all 22 pages?

◆ **Will it matter if I don't handle it at all?** This is a critical question. Much of what confronts you requires no action on your part. For example: announcements regarding upcoming publications, ads that tout prices or services, and anything addressed to "current resident." If you don't pay your rent or your mortgage, you'll be contacted by someone interested in collecting the money. If, however, you don't participate in the office pool, don't attend the local charity ball, don't make an extra copy of that recipe, or don't learn about that software game, your life will not change.

Discarding the Discardable

Without equivocation, march through your office on a search-and-destroy mission. Round up any suspects that fit these categories, and trash or recycle them:

◆ Outdated manuals.

◆ Back issues of publications that you haven't touched in more than two years.

◆ Drafts, earlier versions, and outdated versions of letters, correspondence, memos, reports, and documents that have already been produced as final (unless you're in the legal department of your organization—then it's your job to hang on to such—ahem—material).

◆ Carcasses of once-useful stuff: dead bottles of white-out, dry pens, pencil nubs, or business cards whose vital information is already logged in your database.

◆ All scraps and tidbits of information, used post-on notes, and the like that have accumulated around your desk, in your wallet, and elsewhere. Put them on a single sheet or log them in to a file on your computer.

◆ Excess vendor supply catalogs.

- Manuals that you will absolutely never open again.

- Outdated catalogs, flyers, annual reports, brochures, and promotional materials.

- The hoard of thumbtacks, pushpins, pennies, and paper clips that gathers in the corners of your desk drawers.

- Take-out/delivery menus from restaurants that you never visit (or visit so frequently that you've memorized the bill of fare).

- Lingering stacks of irrelevant documents and extra copies of relevant documents. Retain what you need. Toss the rest.

Filing to Preserve Your Sanity

Suppose you face a mass of items (probably more like a mess of items) on your desk. How would you tackle it? How would you whip that stuff into shape?

Toss It and Forget It

Wade through everything rapidly, and determine what can be tossed, as well as any duplicate or outdated items you don't need. Some items won't fit in your file folders anyway; it's best to copy the handful of pages that you need from them, file those pages, and recycle the rest.

"When in doubt, throw it out." These immortal words, uttered two decades ago by efficiency expert Edwin Bliss, are still true. If you're not sure whether you need to keep something, in most cases you've already answered the question: no. If you're like most professionals, you have a tendency to overfile, which gluts your system and contributes to obscuring anything that you need to find. If you ever file too much stuff, use the C drawer discussed previously as a pit stop for potential file items.

If you question whether to file an item, put it aside for a day or two and look at it again. Often the answer will present itself. Ask yourself, "What will happen if I pitch this?" If there's no significant downside, gleefully chuck it.

Sort for Similarity

In that great mass of stuff before you, if eight items refer to delegation, that's a clue to start a file folder labeled Delegation. Do the same with other groups of like items.

Reflect and Win

If you haven't ordered file folders before, you're in for a revelation. They come in colors. You can use green file folders for anything that relates to money, red for government, blue for (true blue) customers, and so on to stay organized more easily.

Plow through the entire pile; toss what you can, and group like items until everything is tossed or grouped. Yes, some items will stand alone. Not to worry.

When approaching each of your minipiles, ask yourself these questions:

- ◆ Can I consolidate each pile by using the backsides of documents, single-page copies, and shorter notes?

- ◆ Can I consolidate scraps and tidbits by using the copier to create a dossier page or stapling them into a packet?

- ◆ For piles that have only one or two items each, is there a way to group them? (An article on office chairs might join your notes on using room dividers in a pile called Office Furniture.)

Few Large Files Versus Many Small Ones

Go through the materials that you've put in minipiles; see if any of them should go into all-encompassing files, such as Copiers or Insurance. Always, always seek to have a few large files of like items, not a gaggle of small files. It'll be easier to find what you want in the course of your day, week, year, or career.

Use date stamping, if it suits you. Some efficiency experts suggest putting a date stamp on every item that you file. If you've been holding on to an item for months on end and haven't used it, maybe it's time to chuck it.

It's not mandatory to use date stamping; an item's future relevance isn't always linked to how long you've had it. Generally, the longer you've held on to an item without using it, the smaller the chance that it will be of future importance.

File Headings That Convey Meaning

This is the part where filing gets to be fun. (You're laughing. See? I told you.) By using customized file headings, you can devise compartments that enable you to give the materials that cross your desk a good home, while you remain anxiety-free, guilt-free, and fat-free. If you often don't know where to file items, you can create a file called Where to File This? (I use one called Check in One Month).

Other handy file names that you could use include these:

- ◆ Read or Chuck
- ◆ Read When I Can
- ◆ Review for Possible Linkage with ABC Project

Saving Time with Tickler Files

You can benefit greatly by creating file folders for each month. Then, when something crosses your desk in December but you don't have to act on it until February, into the February file it goes.

You can have a 31-day tickler file as well. If you receive something on the second day of the month but you don't have to deal with it until the 14th, put it in the file marked the 14th—or give yourself some extra time and put it in the file marked the 13th. (Think about it.)

You can use this system to pay bills on time. Write the checks in advance, sign them, seal them, stamp them, and put the envelope in the appropriate folder of your 31-day rotating tickler file. Review that file at the start of each week and perhaps once or twice during the week; you'll know automatically when it's time to pay a bill or address a date-filed item.

The monthly files and 31-day tickler files will help you reduce clutter while offering you peace of mind. Simple? Yes. It's also remarkably efficient.

When you view something several days, weeks, or months after first filing it, you often have greater objectivity and a new chance to act on it, delegate it, or toss it. If a lot of stuff gets tossed, fine; at least you had those things out of your way.

> **Coming to Terms**
>
> **Tickler files** automatically remind you of when you need to deal with a particular task. When the request for the task hits your desk, you can place it in the tickler file for the appropriate future date. Every day of the month, check your tickler file for that day to identify tasks to take on.

Creating Files in Advance

Suppose you're planning to go to graduate school for a Master's degree. One way to accommodate the growing body of literature that you'll be assembling is to create a file folder in advance of having anything to file. When stuff comes in that appears worth saving, it'll have a home.

You might think that this is merely a way to collect more stuff. It's not! Creating folders in advance of the need can be a potent reminder and affirmation of your future goals.

Suppose you come across a brilliant article on how to finance your degree in a way that considerably reduces your burden. Where are you

> **Reflect and Win**
>
> You can start a new file folder, label it, and park it in your file drawer without anything in it! Are you insane to do so? Nope.

going to put that article? Park it on top of something else, where it will sit for weeks or months? You still won't know what to do with it, but you'll want to hang on to it—right?

What are some files that you can create in advance of having anything to put in them—merely because it makes sense, based on where you're heading in life? Here are some suggestions:

◆ Your child's higher education fund

◆ Your retirement home

◆ Your vacation next year to New Zealand

◆ Assistance for your aging parents

◆ Evolving technology that interests you

◆ A new medical operation that might affect you

If a new project is about to start, create a directory for it on your hard disk. Suppose that Bart, a new employee, is going to start in a few days. The first thing I do is create a directory named Bart. As the days pass, I move files into Bart's directory so that I already have assignments for him. As he takes them on, others develop; I move them to his directory.

> **The Time Master Says**
>
> At least 50 percent of dealing with all the piles of paper that you confront is simply making room for them!

I have a directory called "Inprog" that I go to at the start of each day; from there I might move an item to "Bart" or (once it's finished) elsewhere on my hard disk. See?

Sheltering Homeless Files

In housing your files, your goal is to keep closest to you the items that you use frequently; keep rarely used items farthest from you. Much of what you file won't be used often.

Of course, certain factors—the nature of your work, tax laws, or other regulations—may require you to hang on to more than you'd like. Whatever you have to hang on to—plus what you want to hang on to—can be stored away from your immediate workspace. I'm going to take the leap and assume that your organization already has systems and procedures for storing files.

What about you? Are you hanging on to all kinds of stuff that you cannot bear to pitch? Here's a plan of attack:

1. Group like items, put them in a box or storage container, and mark the box with something descriptive, such as "Check again next April" or "Review after the merger."

2. Before storing a container, quickly plow through it once more to see what can be removed. This will simplify your task, and you'll thank yourself later.

3. Once the box is out of sight, build a safeguard into your system. Put a note in your "April" file that says to review the contents of the box located at XYZ.

Sometimes, instead of storing vast volumes of material, you can simply scan it and keep it on disk.

Can anyone else in your organization or family harbor such items so that you don't have to? If the box holds reminders of some dear, departed one, perhaps the best solution is to rotate it among the siblings—four months a year at your sister Samantha's, four months at your brother Todd's, and four months with you.

Money for Storage

If the stuff you've boxed is valuable and compact, maybe it makes sense to put it in a safety-deposit box in a bank. If it's voluminous, maybe consider putting it in a commercial *self-storage unit* (available in most metro areas).

Paying to store materials brings up the issue of what you're retaining. Is it worth it to pay a bank or a company to retain the stuff? If it is, then you'll feel all right about forking over the dough. If it doesn't seem worth the cash, you have a viable indicator that you can chuck it.

Coming to Terms

When you rent a **self-storage unit,** you get a garage-like space that you can cram full of any items that you don't need on a daily basis. For example, you may want to store old files in a small self-storage unit. See "Storage" in the Yellow Pages to learn what storage options are available in your area.

Winning Through Recycling

Watch constantly for what can be recycled. Can you give a report, memo, or article to a key associate or junior staff person who it will benefit? If so, it's far easier to let go of what you're retaining.

Can you use the clean back sides of sheets for rough drafts, scratch paper, internal memos, notepads, and hard-copy fax responses? If so, it will be easier for you to recycle materials that come across your desk. In this case, you're supporting the environment by getting double use out of your materials. All the folders that you use are potentially reusable. Label them over again and give them new life. Recycling also gives you a quick and socially acceptable means of dealing with much of the paper and clutter that arrives during the day.

If you don't take control, you're setting yourself up for glutted files, glutted systems, and glutted thinking. Rather than winning back your time, you'll be giving it away. You're at your best when you're a lean, mean, working machine.

The Least You Need to Know

- Filing is a necessary response to working in an environment of continual overload. Effective filing is an opportunity for you to devise a personal information-retrieval system that supports the way you work and live.

- When you're in control of your desk, your office, your files, and the resources that you've assembled, you're a more focused, efficient, and effective professional—and you're certainly more in charge of your time.

- The tools for effective filing are simple. Colored file folders, labels, and dots help you organize what you're retaining. Purchase them with reckless abandon.

- Remove anything from your immediate environment that you don't need to encounter for weeks or months.

- Recycle whatever you can of the stuff that comes across your desk. This will automatically help you win back your time, keeping your files lean and mean.

Top Time-Management Tools Revealed

In This Chapter

◆ No need for guilt and anxiety

◆ Technology time traps

◆ Speakerphones, headsets, and two-way recording

◆ Simple technologies, affordable prices

The only time you have to adopt a new tool or technological device is when: your organization or boss requires it, your clients already use the technology, or you'll gain a strategic competitive advantage.

Getting Ahead of Yourself?

While there's no denying the awesome power of online information, it's important to keep things in perspective. "Driven by our obsession to compete, we've embraced the electronic god with a frenzy," says Bill Henderson, leader of the Lead Pencil Club. "Soon, blessed with the fax, voice, and email computer hook-ups and TVs with hundreds of channels, we won't have to leave our lonely rooms—not to write a check, work, visit, shop, exercise, or make love. We will have raced at incredible speeds to reach our final destination—nothing."

Have you been caught in the trap of gathering information or acquiring an item far in advance of your ability to use it? I'm talking about hardware and software, instruction manuals, scanners, additional printers, adapters, cassettes, videos, CD-ROMs, phone systems, fax machines, and who knows what else.

Ten Times the Advantage

Peter Drucker, Ph.D., the noted sage of management, once made the observation that for new technology to replace old, it had to have at least 10 times the benefits of its predecessor. Neil Postman, Ph.D., in his book *Technopoly,* says that the introduction of any new technology into your life brings both benefits and detriments. The manufacturers, advertisers, and dealers are adept at helping you focus on the benefits—especially in the rare case that you happen to become one of the world's expert users of the system that they're offering. How often, however, do you read about the downside of acquiring new tools and technology in your life?

Some Good, Some Not So Good

Consider the cell phone: If you're the parent of three children, it can give you great comfort to call them after school from the car. There's a downside, too. By having a phone in your car, what else have you added to your life that perhaps you didn't want? (Note that more than half of these developments have an impact on your time.)

- The ability of anybody to reach you at any time
- Disturbance of one of the last sanctuaries you have
- The need to change your brochures and business cards to reflect your cell phone number
- The now documented, tremendous potential for driving less safely
- Added expense as you engage in unnecessary conversations
- The annoying habit of making one extra call before reaching destinations—to make sure that plans haven't changed …
- … thereby leading to heightened insecurity and anxiety
- Another expense to pay at the end of the month
- Involuntarily opening up your receptors to notice other ads about other cell phone systems
- The annoying feeling that your system is insufficient and that you need more range, more power, and less cost per call

It seems paradoxical that a device created to make you more efficient or to save you time holds nearly equal potential for doing just the opposite.

The Revenge Effect

"The Revenge Effect is the curious way the world has of getting even, defeating our best efforts to speed it up and otherwise improve it," says Professor Edward Tenner of Princeton University. The failure of technology to solve problems, Tenner says, can often be traced to the interaction between machine and man. Freeways, intended to speed travel, lead to suburbs—urban sprawls out instead of up, and so commuting times climb. Computers make it easy to copy and print files, so you end up copying and printing many more files, and your paperless office fills up with paper.

I, Rulemaker

With a cell phone, you could make the purchase with predetermined rules of use, such as making calls only to loved ones and for crucial appointments, limiting calls to under three minutes, or not listing your cell phone number on business cards or brochures.

The crucial element is that you define your personal set of rules for using the tool.

Many types of "neat tools" follow. Some represent sophisticated technology, and some are rather simple. Each represents great potential for you to win back your time. With your own rules of use, you'll feel better about how and when you use the tool, and you'll avoid potential time traps.

Reflect and Win

When you view each new technological tool as both beneficial and detrimental, you're in a far better position to stay in control of your time.

Speaking of High Productivity

To be more productive in your office and make maximum use of your travel time, use a pocket dictator or, as the capabilities broaden, speech-recognition technology. I've used dictators to capture notes, offer immediate thanks to people I meet, and produce whole books—yes, even this one.

If you are already proficient in using your own personal computer, laptop, or notebook computer for word processing, there still are many advantages to becoming skilled in using portable dictation equipment—particularly if you have other staff members who can transcribe your golden words. By using portable dictation equipment or speech-recognition technology, you can approach your productivity potential. Few things in life will have this type of dramatic impact on your ability to manage your time.

Benevolent Dictators

Portable dictation equipment allows for mobility. You can dictate almost anywhere. Microcassette recorders accommodate up to an hour of taping on each side. If you compose directly on a word processor, you may be able to type between 40 and 80 words a minute. With a little practice, you can dictate at 100–140 words a minute. When you type while you are thinking, your mind races ahead of your fingers. Many of the ideas and phrases that you compose in your mind are lost.

Once you become familiar with the ease of operation and the pure joy of finishing written items in one-third of the previous time, there is no returning to old ways. With dictating, you can handle whatever you wanted to write but never found the time to actually do.

In Your Own Words

Speech-recognition technology enables you to speak into the system's headset and dictate at a slightly slower speed than you're used to talking. In 20–40 minutes—depending on the system and how adept you are at it—the software "learns" your voice pattern and from that discerns what words to throw on the screen as you speak.

With practice, you'll soon be able to speak at a normal speed and spend little time "training" the system—perhaps five minutes or less. Systems will be available soon enough on which no training is necessary and anyone's voice can be interpreted.

The Time Master Says

In a few years, you won't have to talk. You can simply don a headband, issue thought commands, and have the computer diligently obey!

Pause!

Speech-recognition software is not ready for prime time. The software needs to be fine-tuned to eliminate the frequency of errors and the bugs in the system.

A Better Deal

Currently, speech-recognition software is convenient when it comes to dictating brief letters and email responses, creating lists, and developing other documents that are not voluminous. As the mighty microchip continues to decrease in size and become more powerful, the software will be ready right out of the box and will have awesome capabilities, such as discerning 300,000 or 400,000 words instead of 20,000 or 30,000, have automatic syntax and idiom checkers, and, in general, take the pain out of composing new text, much like word processors took the pain out of making corrections to text. The instruction booklet—if there's one at all—could be four pages or less. Perhaps you'll need just a single card.

The landscape is changing so quickly that it will pay to monitor developments and perhaps begin to get your feet wet in the technology. Here are two websites that offer resources and support:

www.synapseadaptive.com

www.voicerecognition.com

No Peeking

Much as with dictating equipment, you're better off not looking at the screen while using speech-recognition software. Continual monitoring is going to only hamper your progress. If the wrong word was inserted here or there, or you want to make a correction, do it afterward.

Reflect and Win _____

Soon, my words here will all become moot, and speech-recognition systems will be developed to the point at which you may regard them as a godsend. Freed from keyboards, your productivity and creativity may rise in ways that you have rarely experienced in your career. There will be tremendous time savings for those who master this process.

Reflect and Win _____

If you avoid dictation because you can't write without being able to visually review what you've written, consider this: A good outline is a prerequisite to any effective writing. When dictating with a good outline, key words can readily be expanded to sentences and paragraphs. And the pause feature allows you to easily start and stop, to gather thoughts, and to articulate complete sentences and paragraphs.

Perpetually Pausing

Dictating in 20- or 30-second blocks what may have previously required 2 to 5 minutes to write negates the need for visual review. If you are able to file and extract materials readily—and if your desk is well organized and your shelves are neat (you followed all my advice!), chances are good that you'll be good at dictating with portable equipment.

Useless Options

When you call another party these days, you're subject to a nearly endless round of voice-mail options. When it's *finally* time to leave a message, make sure that it's detailed so that the other person knows specifically why he should call you back.

The Time Master Says

To save your time, and the time of the people you are calling, write down a few key words in advance of making a call, perhaps using contact-management software with the questions typed into the party's record. By succinctly conveying your message in a minute or two and slowly and clearly stating how you can be reached, you've done yourself and the other party a big favor—and saved both of you a lot of time.

With contact-management software, you can log in when you made a call and what the recipient's response was. There is also software available that can log in phone calls and faxes sent and received.

Use of the telephone is an area ripe with potential time savings, and you don't need any modern technology to be effective. Without being short with callers, convey an urgency in your voice that lets them know that you're not going to prolong the conversation:

- "I hear you. Let me get back to you later in the day when I ...."
- "Gotta run, thanks for keeping me posted."
- "I'll ponder that one; I'll get back to you via email."
- "That sounds intriguing, but I'm not the right person. Take care."

On personal calls, you have more leeway for deflecting the discussion until later:

- "You've caught me at a bad time. Can we ...."
- "Let's talk this evening, when I have more time."
- "I'll catch up with you on the weekend."
- "I'm knee-deep in paperwork right now, but let's ...."

Look Mom—No Hands!

Whether you use the telephone five times a day or all day long, simple, inexpensive technology is available to immediately double your phoning efficiency. If you need both hands free to take notes or maintain better organization during a phone call, the typical phone receiver is not practical. Speaker phones aren't much better, and the sound quality is still less than desirable even on higher-end models.

Cell phones free your feet, not your hands. A far better solution? The telephone headset.

Headsets include a set of lightweight earphones with a long prong bending toward the mouth. This ear-and-mouthpiece set is attached by a cord to a desktop dialer.

Headsets for the Downtrodden

When you wear a headset, your hands are free to take notes, shuffle papers, or open file drawers. Yet, the sound quality of your voice equals or exceeds that of a traditional hand-set phone.

Less Fatigue, More Vim

An advantage often cited by headset users is less fatigue. If you make and receive many phone calls, a most efficient way to handle them is to reserve a specific block of time—say, two hours in the afternoon—to return and generate calls. Repetitive phone use, however, is tiring. A telephone headset alleviates this strain. Ten to fifteen calls need not be drudgery.

All Headsets Are Not Equal

The simplest models sell for as little as $49.95, while the most elaborate can climb to $300 or more.

Here are some suppliers. I suggest getting their catalogs first.

- ◆ GN Netcom Incorporated, 10 Victor Square, Scotts Valley, CA 95066; phone 1-800-995-5500 (a full-line supplier)
- ◆ Plantronics, P.O. Box 635, Santa Cruz, CA 95061-0635; phone 1-800-544-4660 (a full-line supplier)
- ◆ Ziehl Associates Inc., 115 Meacham Avenue, Elmont, NY 11003-2631; phone 1-800-654-1066

Reflect and Win

You can respond to questions much faster when your hands are free to look through the files for answers. And when the task of making phone calls is more comfortable, you don't give in to the temptation to waste time between calls.

Pause!

Headsets with cordless capabilities are not a match for the best corded products. Nevertheless, with noise-canceling microphones and higher-frequency communication, the cordless headset is clearly a time-saving device whose time has come.

Flying the Quiet Skies

Along the same lines of donning a headset, if you fly frequently, you might want to consider a new generation of active noise-cancellation headphones. The Sharper Image version is designed to generate "antinoise" waves that neutralize the irritating drone of an airplane engine and surrounding cabin sounds. With fewer distractions, you can get more work done and be more in control of your time.

If you fly from New York to Los Angeles nonstop, at the end of your flight, you'll actually feel rested and relaxed. Noise does a number on each of us, often in ways that we can't discern. Some models of noise-cancellation headphones allow you to use a two-prong adapter so that you can listen to the in-flight music or programs offered while receiving the benefits of hearing less engine and cabin noise. In fact, you can hear every word of the programs being offered.

Many systems simply run on AAA alkaline batteries. The systems are lightweight and pack easily. They're also affordable, at less than $100. If you fly at least 20–30 times a year, noise-cancellation headphones could be a godsend for you.

> **CAUTION**
> **Pause!** _____
>
> Noise-cancellation headphones do not diminish all noises around you, such as other people talking to you, an announcement over the plane's public address system, or at other times when you're near a radio or ringing telephone.

> **Reflect and Win** _____
>
> A common misconception about two-way recording is that it's illegal. Not so. You may tape-record any conversation at any time in all 50 states. What's illegal is when neither party knows that the tape recording is being made. That's called wiretapping or eavesdropping, and even law-enforcement officials who engage in it first need to secure permission for doing so.

Conversation Worth Saving

Some people have used two-way phone conversation recording for years as a means of keeping a log of conversations to help document highly complex transactions.

I'm all for reversing any perception that using two-way recording is anything other than a marvelous timesaver. As a speaker and author, I find it convenient to be able to record conversations, both ways, with the touch of a button. When a meeting planner is giving me essential information over the phone, my ability to capture those words on tape can mean all the difference when it comes to delivering a dynamic program. There's no way that I can take notes as fast as I way can capture the meeting planner's words via taping.

When the Sparks Fly

When I'm interviewing someone way for a book, letting other people simply talk—at whatever speed they wish—facilitates effective conversation. The sparks fly. I ask a question, and the other person answers. Later, when I review the tape at my own speed, I am able to glean the essence of what the person said—not what my half-baked notes reveal or my even less effective memory recalls. Often when reporters call me and they're not armed with two-way recording equipment, I volunteer to tape the conversation for them and mail them the tape.

With two-way recording, I can offer a lot more information in a lot shorter time. It'll be higher quality information, and it flows in the manner in which I intend.

There are countless instances in which you could tape-record a conversation, play it back, and be more effective at what you do. This could include conversations with coworkers, clients, suppliers, and so on.

> **CAUTION**
>
> **Pause!**
>
> Detectives, snoops, and spies have long recorded conversations for purposes of collecting evidence or for entrapment. Clearly, there's a negative connotation to the notion of two-way telephone conversation recording among the underinformed.

The Ethical Question

While legally you don't have to tell the other party that you're recording the conversation, you may feel that ethically it's best to do so. I eliminate this potential dilemma by simply saying to the other party at the outset, "Let me capture this on tape," or "Do you mind if I capture this on tape?" Only a handful of times in hundreds of recordings has anyone said, "I'd prefer not," and I've respected that.

Otherwise, I've been able to capture conversations from mentors giving me advice, peers brainstorming with me on a problem, and the aforementioned meeting planners and journalists.

Any consumer electronics store carries a vast array of phone systems with two-way conversational recording capability from which to choose. Most models sell for less than $100, so there's really nothing to stop you.

Mobile Data Phones

The first generation of mobile data phones represented a product whose time hadn't come. They were overpromised and they underdelivered. This situation was short-lived, however, as new phones started offering faster connections, better browsers, and crisper interfaces. You can't expect the experience of surfing the Internet or a desktop or note-book-size computer to be matched in any way by a mobile data phone whose screen size isn't much larger than two thumbprints. Nevertheless, the quicker, louder, increasingly clear connections make for a far more enjoyable experience and will attract more users.

Email can be retrieved as little time as 10 seconds. Stock quotes can come in under 60 seconds. Because the graphics are better, more words and more lines of text can appear on the screen. And color screens make all the difference.

Options Galore

While cell phone email is still in the early stages, faster wireless networks and higher-capability handsets will all but guarantee that you will be sending and receiving email at your discretion, all day long, where ever you go.

Most mobile phone service companies presently offer either free or for-fee email services over your cell phone. With some, it is part of their overall wireless Internet packages. Usually, you can't use such a service until you activate the carrier's wireless Web service, which is for a fee. Users have discovered that, in many cases, their phones already have email addresses assigned to them, usually on the order of yournumber@yourcarrier.com.

Increasingly, you have the option of creating a customized email address that enables you to forward your emails to other accounts.

Pause! _____

Email over a cell phone can be cumbersome. You end up typing with your thumbs. You can view only six lines of text at once. On some systems, you can't open attachments; you are limited to text messages. You want to keep your messages short, since wireless transmits between 14k and 56k.

To compose messages, some phones use a touch screen; others have a virtual keyboard, and still others allow for handwriting recognition. Nevertheless, composing and sending messages can be real work.

Soon enough, most systems will have "predictive text input," which essentially enables you to type in the first few letters of a word and the system will spell out the rest. Some carriers are also developing stock answers, such as "I'll get back to you in a little while." Eventually all carriers will offer some kind of voice reply options. What a world!

The Least You Need to Know

- ◆ Adopt new technology when your organization requires it, your clients use it, or you see strategic, competitive advantages.
- ◆ Buy portable, expandable, flexible technology.

◆ Each tool designed to increase your efficiency carries the seeds of both great benefit and significant drawback.

◆ Learn most technologies when you need to—no need to feel anxious from advertising designed to make you feel inadequate.

◆ Simple technologies such as dictation equipment, headphones, and two-way telephone recorders can also benefit you greatly.

Part 4

Connecting to Others

Once you're in charge of your turf—or a least know what it takes to get there—it's time to get into a higher and more efficient gear when it comes to staying in touch with others. The chapters in this part examine the ridiculous to the sublime in terms of options available for staying in touch.

The key to making the most of these options is to recognize that, while technology marches forward, each new development isn't always to your benefit. In other words, you can both save and waste oodles of time using office gadgets, beepers, email, the Internet, and snail mail. Since you'd rather save oodles of time, we'll focus on that.

Your quest is to appropriately use or apply the tools and methods of communication discussed here. Otherwise, you may quickly find yourself behind the no-time 8-ball faster than you can say, "The dog ate my homework."

Let's begin with an eye-opening, but entirely thoughtful look at a small gadget that can dominate your life (but only if you let it) and turn those people all around you into techno-dweebs.

WHY SUPERHEROES COULDN'T EXIST TODAY.

Chapter 16

Staying in Touch Too Much

In This Chapter

- ◆ Voluntary versus involuntary beeper enslavement
- ◆ The Faustian bargain
- ◆ Keeping in touch, or fanning anxieties?
- ◆ Beeper use is a negotiable issue

It's safe to say that information overload is a much greater problem today for most professionals than information scarcity. Information overload also introduces new mental, emotional, social, and interpersonal issues. For example, while many researchers believe that attention deficit disorder (ADD) is a purely biochemical phenomenon, a growing number believe that ADD can also be influenced by environmental factors, such as the onslaught of too much information. I agree with the second camp.

Interruptions Abound

The typical worker is confronted by 6 interruptions every hour, averaging 1 every 10 minutes. The average number of messages received in a day by the typical U.S. office worker breaks down as follows:

Phone calls	52
Email	36

Voice mail	23
Postal mail	18
Interoffice mail	18
Faxes	14
Post-it messages	13
Pager messages	8
Cell phone messages	4
Express mail	3

Source: Intertec Publishing, Stamford Connecticut © 9/99

The same study showed that 68 percent of email and instant-messaging services users cite that their long-distance bills have decreased. The study also showed that an exceptionally high segment of women 55 and older benefited the most from these email and instant-message savings.

Messages received via pager and cell phone are on the rise. Chances are, the typical office worker will experience a decrease in actual phone calls, postal mail, faxes, and interoffice memos, while receiving more email, pager messages, and cell phone calls.

Disturbances We All Could Do Without

In the last five years, every time I give a speech to an audience, whether there are 50 or 500 people in attendance, about 30 minutes into it, somebody's pager sounds. It happens so frequently that I'm used to it, and it neither upsets me nor throws off my timing. I find it curious, however, that someone could sit down to a scheduled presentation of 45 minutes to several hours seemingly oblivious to the fact that his pager may sound.

When a pager sounds, wouldn't you expect the offender to stand up and go dashing out of the room? After all, if someone has paged him, he took the time to set the darned thing, or he merely allowed it to beep at the same time every day, you'd think that the alert signals something important.

In all the times, no such offenders in my audiences have gotten up. I guess that most people invest in technology that they never fully understand, let alone master. If you can't control when one of the devices you're wearing beeps, I wonder, what chance do you have of controlling your time?

Voluntary and Involuntary Servitude

In this world are two types of pager (or, as I like to call it, beeper) enslavement: voluntary and involuntary. It's voluntary when you buy a beeper of your own accord and no one made you do it—this is the most *insidious* kind of enslavement.

When the World Was Young

Once the world was not populated by people with beepers—and, for that matter, cell phones. You could attend a movie or a play and not have a beeper-clad patron in the row behind you demonstrate the essence of crassness by allowing his pager to sound during the performance.

Coming to Terms

Something that is **insidi-ous** is downright treacherous.

In the late 1970s, wearing a beeper was a mark of distinction. It meant that you were a top executive who made major decisions that impacted thousands of people or millions of dollars. Or, perchance, you were in the healthcare field and every day made crucial decisions, some of which meant the difference between life and death for your patients. Or, it signified that you were in the military, perhaps in command of strategic operations.

Today, some people wear beepers in the name of being in touch with others at any given moment. Any darned fool can wear a beeper—and practically every one of them does. Being "locatable" by beeper, however, is not much different in concept than a pet who's kept within the bounds of a back yard via an invisible electrical fence.

The "In" Thing

In 1995, 1 in 14 teenagers carried a beeper. By 1997, it had climbed to one in seven, and, by 2002, one in five.

One high school on Long Island, which had allowed students to wear beepers in class as long as they were on "vibrate" instead of "beep," reported that about three-quarters of the students started wearing them! Does anyone in civilized society believe that students need beepers in class? Does anyone believe that beepers don't interfere with education?

Beeper Message Codes

Code	Message
423	"Call me now."
00100	"I feel very alone."
121	"I need to talk to you alone."

continues

Beeper Message Codes (continued)

Code	Message
50-50	"It's all the same to me."
007	"I have a secret." (as in Agent 007)
1040	"You owe me big time."
0001000	"I'm feeling mighty alone right now."
099	"I've got something to tell you."
05-05	"Margaritas, dude!" (Cinco de Mayo)
020202	"Just thinking of you."
04-04-04	"Happy holidays." (Read upside-down)
080808	"Kisses and hugs."
1	"You're the one" or "You da' man."
10	"You're perfect."
11	"You're perfecter."
1-1	"Thank you."
13	"I'm having a bad day."
1-8	"I ate."
101	"I've got an easy question."
10-4	"Is everything okay?"
141	"I'm with you."
180	"I love you."
10-20	"Where are you?"
10-2-1	"It's possible" or "There's a chance."
13-30	"I'm having a bad day and it's getting old."
1492	"Let's go sailing."
1701	"Live long and prosper."
1776	"You're revolting."
100-2-1	"The odds are against you."
13579	"This is odd."
121212	"Happy birthday!"
10000001	"Miss you."
11111111	"Congratulations!"
–2	Used as a suffix to convey "I'll second that" or "Me, too."
21	"Let's have a drink."
2-2	"Now we dance, shall we?"

Code	Message
222	"Pick me up after school."
2001	"You're way out there."
2468	"You're terrific."
30	"This is getting old."
360	"I love you back."
4	"Let's play golf."
411	"Need some information."
5	"Hi."
5-0	"Are you booked?" (Or, "Let's go to Hawaii.")
55	"Let's cruise."
54321	"I'm ready to explode."
66	"Let's hit the road."
710	"I'm out of gas." (Read upside down)
747	"Let's fly."
86	"You're finished."
87	"You're late" or "I'm late." (Read upside down)
8642	"I'm gonna get even with you."
9-5	"It's quitting time."
99	"Good morning."
911	"This is big; this is an emergency; call me now."
98-6	"Hope you're feeling better."
90210	"I'm feeling kind of witchy."
99-44-100	"I'm almost totally completely bored."

Is Constantly Keeping in Touch Too Much?

The prevailing argument is: "If I'm electronically connected to the great mass of humanity at all times, then I can be available when people need me, respond to emergencies, and, in turn, be in touch with others when the need arises." It's a *Faustian bargain*, however, because the price for this sense of security is the elimination of the following luxuries:

Coming to Terms

Shady deals have been called **Faustian bargains** because the lead character in *Dr. Faustus*, by Christopher Marlowe—named Faustus, of course—sold his eternal soul to the devil for a better time on Earth. Generations later, the German philosopher Goethe expounded on this theme.

◆ Being alone

◆ Dwelling on your own thoughts without fear of interruption

◆ Working in harmony with your own internal rhythms, with no break in the action

◆ Becoming comfortable, happy, and even content with the entity known as yourself

Connected in Spirit?

The typical yet odd reasoning behind wearing a beeper all day long is to stay connected to others. Is this being connected to others in a meaningful way? Or is it a disguise for individual and mass anxiety?

The need, however, to constantly keep in touch about everything ranging from the magnificent to the utterly mundane, from that of utmost importance to that which is absurdly trivial, spells a much deeper and insidious problem. *Overcommunication* is not necessarily *effective* communication.

Pause!

Is it any wonder that attention spans have dropped to all-time lows? Is an entire generation doomed to believing that being chained to a beeper is normal? Will anybody be left who can go for hours—let alone days—without getting all bent out of shape because they're not "in touch"?

"Let me put it this way," said a 17-year-old whose day was apparently shattered when in 1998 the communications satellite Galaxy 4 beeped out, "every other minute you're getting beeped, and then all of a sudden, you not getting beeps at all; it's like silence."

A generation of people is experiencing little sense of being spiritually in touch with one another because they are electronically in touch around the clock. Consider that the people whom you love and like and are most in touch with in this world. Sure, an occasional message via a beeper—similar to an occasional email or an occasional phone call to someone who wasn't expecting it—can help brighten their day.

Beep Together, Keep Together?

Some people profess that families who beep together keep together. Some families maintain codes that indicate everything from "Come home in time for dinner" to "Pick up a loaf of bread." This is a seemingly positive development. After all, bread is a staple of the American diet.

Still, you can't help wondering if the beeper isn't overused by a factor of, say, 15. Some people talk all day long because they have some things to say, and some people talk all day long because they're anxious. Is this the case with beeping, too?

I'll Concede, a Few Valid Uses Exist

To be sure, there are valid uses of beepers by people who need to have information on demand. Volunteer firefighters use beepers for a quick response to a fire—and, if your house is burning, you're darn glad of it.

> **Pause!**
>
> Dr. Peter Crabb, a professor of physiology at Pennsylvania State University, has been studying technology's impact on behavior. He says that the instant gratification brought on by beepers can end up enslaving the user. Those who voluntarily—or, for that matter, involuntarily—wear a beeper essentially are giving the message to all others that it's okay to interrupt whatever is going on with them.

A Cell Phone Fetish?

Alas, now nearly everywhere you turn, you see someone talking on a cell phone, fiddling with a beeper, or deploying an electronic scheduler—and the phenomenon isn't limited to the business world. Consider the true story of Elizabeth, a full-time college freshman. Her mother, Teresa, was extremely concerned about staying in touch with her daughter. Because of this concern, Teresa armed Elizabeth with a cell phone with capabilities galore, as well as a laptop computer.

As a result, Elizabeth spends most of her time in lectures playing games, buying movie tickets, or reading the latest e-news on her cell phone. When in her room, Elizabeth is a true child of the twenty-first century, downloading movies and videos from MTV onto her computer. The technology that her mother wanted to keep her child safe and informed has isolated Elizabeth from the surrounding college world and distracts her from her studies.

What about Teresa? As a corporate executive, she preaches the importance of "staying connected." Maybe you've seen her, speeding down the highway, haphazardly weaving in and out of traffic; all the while, a cell phone headset rests atop her head.

Beach Leash

Do you know someone like David, the manager of a sales team for a small food manufacturer? David's company supplied him with a cell phone and a laptop to keep in touch with him on his trips out of town. As a result, even when on vacation, David finds himself connecting with his boss "just to remain in sync." On a romantic getaway with his wife to St.

Thomas, David spent oodles of time in his hotel room instant messaging his boss about an upcoming deal, instead of parasailing or cliff gliding with his wife.

Bit by Bit to Death

When the big book of human civilization is written, someone will look back and say that the beeper was among the most dubious developments in the course of humanity. We don't need drips and drops, tiny bits of information coming to us all day long. It's not the best way to function—and, indeed, it may be harmful to effective functioning.

Reflect and Win

In *The Artist's Way*, Julia Cameron recommends that when someone who is trying to be creative feels blocked, there is a simple cure. Rather than being bombarded by the thoughts and words of others, for one week give up reading (except, of course, this book), watching television, and listening to the radio. This exercise encourages the person's own ideas and creativity to emerge.

The Time Master Says

Some theaters in London request that attendees turn off beepers and cell phones before the performance begins. In the United States, many business establishments, such as restaurants, are adopting strict policies regarding the use of beepers and cell phones, with some places regarding them with the same disdain as smoking.

Beeper Intrusions

As you've learned throughout this book, the most effective way to manage your time is to stay in control of it, to protect yourself from unwanted intrusions. Receiving mail, email, phone messages, or beeps around the clock all disrupt your potential for highly productive, clear, cool thinking. You need peace and quiet when you're pondering how to best make a new product or service offering, reflecting on what you've accomplished, or fathoming where you or your organization is heading.

The following letter, which I received from a man after a speech that I gave, is one of the saddest commentaries on working in contemporary society that I've ever encountered:

> While you were lecturing, my cell phone, pager, and voice mail (mental and physical torture device) vibrated no less than three times. Usually I leave the room to listen to the voice mail and return the calls. During your presentation, I just let it vibrate. However, I can't turn it off. I carry the phone as a requirement of my job. I must carry it whenever I am officially on the job. Yet, I know peers who are on call 24 hours to their organizations. They are interrupted by pages and cell phone calls at dinners, church, the theater, everywhere.

If this scenario even mildly describes your situation, it's time to take control in major ways. And if you don't take control, who else on the planet will do it for you?

Use and Not Abuse

Okay, so let's actually talk about ways to decrease the use of these devices while still having them available for use when the situation merits.

E-Etiquette

Dr. Jaclyn Kostner, author of *Virtual Leadership*, advises displaying proper etiquette when you wear a beeper or take a cell phone with you:

◆ Turn off your device when attending face-to-face meetings.

◆ Turn off your device during lunch, dinner, or other professional occasions.

◆ Turn off your gadget in nonbusiness public places, such as restaurants, movies, and performances.

◆ Turn off your beeper or cell phone to be with your family and friends.

Put It in Writing

If your employment is based on a contract—and, increasingly, this is true of top managers and executives—then you have options for not being enslaved to your beeper. When renegotiating your contract, insert a clause allowing for specific times throughout the day or week when you expressly are not responsible for being on call.

If performance reviews or appraisals don't occur frequently enough for you where you work, or if one is not slated until the distant future, arrange a meeting specifically to address this issue. Depending on how long you've been wearing the beeper, how many beeps you receive per day, the nature of your work, and how disruptive the overall effects have been, you don't want to let too many more days or weeks pass before elucidating your views to those who would otherwise have you wear a beeper around the clock and never have another word on the topic.

> **Reflect and Win**
>
> Whether or not your employment is based on a contract, negotiate to achieve the same results. Whenever it's time for a performance review and appraisal—be it yearly, semi-annually, quarterly, or monthly—take the opportunity to discuss with your immediate supervisor the potential disruption to your psyche and physiology of being constantly on call.

Pause!

Knowing that any non-work activity can be disrupted is harmful to your breathing space. When you can't eat, sleep, make love, or go to the bathroom free of beeper- or cell phone–related anxiety, you're not free to live.

Energizer Bunny No More!

As tactfully and professionally as possible, inform the powers that be that maintaining ever-ready responsiveness with a beeper diminishes your capacity for creativity in those tasks and responsibilities where it's needed.

A Message Hierarchy

If most of your beeper messages originate from a central source, such as an executive assistant, instruct that person on when it's okay for you to be contacted and when it's not okay. For example, you could use a system such as the one laid out in this table.

Redirecting Beeper Messages

Level 1	"Contact me now."
Level 2	"Contact me within X hours."
Level 3	"Contact me sometime today."
Level 4	"No need to contact me at all."

To make this system work, you decide in advance precisely what represents Level 1, so that Level 1 summoning of you is indeed rare. These would be absolute and dire emergencies where your input is absolutely essential. Everything else does not require beeping you every bleeping minute!

Lower-Level Stuff

Level 2–4 issues can wait. Level 2 represents important bits of information but those that are not necessarily urgent. Level 3 represents messages that you could receive at any time during the day because they're not time-related in any way. Most of the messages that you receive in a day undoubtedly will fall in this category. Once your assistant becomes adept at recognizing that most messages are Level 3, you'll find that you have more stretches of uninterrupted time during the day.

Level 4 represents those messages that your executive assistant might have sent previously but now, based on a clearer understanding of what needs to be transmitted and what doesn't, fall into the "no need to contact me at all" category. These represent questions that are already addressed by existing printed materials, such as these:

- Policies and procedures manuals
- Memos
- Faxes
- Other items that the assistant can retrieve on his own

With Crystal Clarity

You want to admonish the assistant anytime he sends a Level 4 message because, indeed, you didn't need to be contacted. You can curtail your assistant's behavior in this category by pointing out, "That was a Level 4 message," whenever you receive one.

Using this system, you'll find that in a matter of weeks—and, more often, in a matter of only days—your assistant will understand with relative accuracy what level to assign to information that potentially could be beeped your way.

Relay and Forwarding Options

Another measure on the road to managing your time and staying as beep-free as possible is to use all relay and forwarding options available. Leave instructive messages on your voice mail or telephone-answering devices that let callers know when and where you can best be reached.

Also leave instructive messages that enable callers to have a higher probability of being served by you without necessarily having to contact you immediately. This can be done by employing the various voice-mail boxes available on many systems: "Press 1 if you have a question about XYZ," "Press 2 if you have a question about ABC," and so on.

Deflect for Defense

Get in the habit of specifically announcing that such-and-such person can take care of ABC, that you'll be reachable Tuesday from 2:00 P.M. until 4:00 P.M., or that the best way to handle XYZ problems is to send an email to accounting. In this manner, you may be able to deflect half or more of the messages that would otherwise disturb you.

Beyond Beeper Range

At certain times on some days, don't wear your beeper or carry a cell phone at all, and inform others that you will not be so equipped. Once the umbilical cord is disconnected, certainly your staff, and many others, learns new ways to proceed on matters without instinctively and incessantly beeping you.

Are You Sending Messages?

How about the situation where you're supervising others, and you're the one continually sending messages to them so that they're beeped all day long? You've gotten through this chapter thus far, so perhaps you have a newfound appreciation for what you're putting your staff through.

Can you find it in your heart, and does your newfound awareness lead you to the conclusion that you could be sending fewer messages per day? Chances are highly likely that you could. In most professions, effective managing does not encompass micromanaging around the clock.

If you've selected the right people, have trained them accordingly, have given them the opportunity to develop on-the-job skills, have given them appropriate feedback, are available for coaching, and give them adequate tools with which to perform their assigned tasks, why the heck do you need to be beeping them all day long?

The Least You Need to Know

- The need to constantly make contact with others is not necessarily effective communication; it is anxiety.
- If you lack a spiritual connection with someone, beeping and other e-communication is unlikely to create one.
- Tell your immediate supervisor about the disruption to your psyche and physiology. Bargain for time off the beeper.
- If primarily one person beeps you, indicate when it's okay for you to be contacted and when it's not.
- Sometimes don't take your beeper with you, and inform others that you will not be so equipped.

Chapter 17

Email: No Worse a Curse (Than Beepers)

In This Chapter

- ◆ Coming at you at high speed
- ◆ Not making email the most urgent thing in the morning
- ◆ Put spam in its place
- ◆ To send or to call—that is the question

Perhaps you're not among those who are chained to a beeper or obsessed with a cell phone. The odds are much better, however, that you do send and receive emails every workday—and sometimes in between. The advantages of email are abundantly clear. Email is fast; it's transmitted nearly instantaneously after you click on the Send button. Only the Internet service providers (ISPs) on your end and on the recipient's end have any real say as to when the email actually shows up in the other person's mailbox, but, in most cases, it's under a couple minutes.

One of the many dangers of email, which is now being documented, is that it has become an obsession for many people. Some people check their email 200 or 300 times a day—no kidding! Some incessantly send mail merely to receive mail. Some, God forbid, spend oodles of time actually pondering the legions of spam that they receive.

Email seems to lend itself particularly well to various forms of addiction. Still, if you are using it appropriately, it can be useful. Where else on this Earth can you get a message from somebody or to somebody so easily and so quickly nearly anywhere on the globe? No paper, no toner cartridge, no stamps, no envelopes. No trip to the mailbox, no second guessing as to whether you had the right postage, no nothing. It just goes—which is why, as you've already undoubtedly concluded, you receive so many of the darned things every day. It's too easy to send!

> **CAUTION**
>
> **Pause!** _____
>
> Theoretically, you can become addicted to or obsessed with almost anything.

> **CAUTION**
>
> **Pause!** _____
>
> It's no trick to receive many more emails than you can possibly respond to. It's also easy for you to send emails to others when no message is needed or wanted. Are you unknowingly glutting the mail inboxes of others? The more you send, the more you get in return. As a guiding principle, send as few as possible to do the job and still have a life.

The Email Avalanche

The number of emails that you receive is probably growing at a frightening pace. Actually, among those with email accounts, the number of emails that everyone is receiving daily is escalating.

Since the start of the century, the annual number of emails to members of the U.S. Congress now exceeds 80 million. This excess results in members routinely ignoring most of them. The Associated Press reported that some senators receive up to 55,000 emails a month, whereas House members only get about 8,000.

While millions of emails come from their constituents, most of the emails that members of Congress receive come from advocacy groups and corporate lobbyists—generally people from outside their state or congressional districts. That's what happens when anybody can send to anybody with the click of a mouse! Simply because you can send to anyone doesn't mean that you should.

Spamination (Spam-a-Nation)

Okay, so you're not in Congress. Nevertheless, depending on which study you encounter, the typical executive today receives 150–190 emails a day, much of it spam! More than 35 percent of the 400 managers polled by the American Management Association and Ernst & Young say that they use email the most of any communication tool.

Despite software filters and ISP crackdowns on offenders, mass delivery from spammers has risen dramatically. And why not? Using unsecured, third-party servers, a spammer can target nearly every email address found on the Internet at practically no cost, since the ISP pays for the transmission.

According to Jupiter Communications, there are far more email accounts on record in the United States than the size of the U.S. population. The spammers know this and do their best to try to get their junk into everyone's inbox.

Email *spam* has become such a problem that the U.S. House of Representatives has introduced four bills to stop spammers in their tracks. In the works: a "Can Spam" bill, which would require spammers to offer legitimate reply addresses and easy *opt-out* instructions. Several bills also allow ISPs to refuse unsolicited commercial email, penalize spammers for ISP policy violations, and forbid transmission of unsolicited advertisements to mobile phones and other wireless devices.

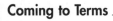

Coming to Terms

Spam is unsolicited email messages sent out in bulk to thousands of recipients in the quest to sell something.

Coming to Terms

Opt-out capability means that someone hit by spam could easily select to be removed from the spammer's list.

Nearly all of the four bills introduced require spammers to provide inclusion of easy opt-out instructions and forbid them to employ false or misleading headers or subject lines. Violators could incur civil—and potentially criminal—penalties, be barred from using ISP lists, and be subject to individual suits for damages. Sounds good to me.

Bamming Spam

Independent of which bills become law and what effect they may have on your inbox, undoubtedly you need time-saving strategies for dealing with spam right now.

Here are some tips about spam that may help:

- If you respond to a spam message by choosing "opt out," you only confirm that there is an actual person behind your email address, which *increases* the amount of spam that you receive. Maddening, isn't it? Do not respond to the spammer in any way.

- By posting your email address on the Internet through chat rooms, message boards, directories, and web pages, you're making it available to spammers. Do so sparingly. It may also be useful to have a second, more private email account.

Pause!

It's vital to understand that responding to spam increases the volume of spam that you receive. Although it may seem like a good offer, resist the temptation to respond to any spam.

- Spammers' lists run alphabetically. Because they're often cut off when an ISP notices an attack, addresses at the end of the list often get less spam than those at the beginning. Therefore, Zach@xdomain.com gets fewer spam messages than Allyson@zdomain.net.

- The more complex the email address is, the less spam it receives. BillJ@yahoo.com or Quatrina67@Hotmail.com, for instance, will get more spam than 23rxt98@ yahoo. com or dfW32ly668@hotmail.com.

- If you send any spam messages that you receive to your ISP's abuse email address, along with the source code from the original spam message, your ISP may be able to take action.

- Different websites have different policies about the privacy of your email address, so be selective when registering online. When in doubt, don't.

Beyond these tips, any time that you receive mail that has lots of X's or all capitals (which is regarded as shouting), or that otherwise makes excessive claims, don't waste a nanosecond on it. One writer commented, "You can safely bleep anything that has lots of exclamation marks, assorted promises, and come-ons, or if it looks like it was written by someone who pants for a living."

After accounting for spam, you're still looking at 80 to 120 emails per executive each day. That's an awful lot of communication coming at you at high speed.

In the context of managing your time, keeping your job, and having a life, how do you handle email? Let us count the ways ....

> **Reflect and Win**
>
> A Gartner Group study reveals that "employees are emailing their coworkers so much, including so many people on their 'cc' list, that the result is productivity-sapping 'occupational spam.'" Do you need to cc so many others? Probably not. Likewise, you don't need to be on a lot of cc lists.

Our First Subject: The Subject Line

Don't get caught up about the subject line. For reasons that I'll probably never fathom, some people go bonkers when it comes to composing the subject line for their email. They stare and they stare, and they still don't know what to type in. Why bother? Your email will go through whether you include a subject or not.

If you can't live without listing a subject, wait until you have first composed your message. Then look at what you've said, and extract two or three words (usually together), making a phrase that you can throw into the subject line. Voilà! You've got it. That's one small step for you, one microscopic step for humankind.

Friendly Subjects

If your email is nonwork-related, then you've got it made in the shade. All you have to do in the subject line is put something like "Hi," "Greetings," "It's me again," "Hey," "Good day," "Long time," or something equally harmless. A friend is a friend and is probably glad to hear from you. What does he care if you say "hi" in your subject line? It probably suits your message well, anyway.

Censor Yourself

When you employ the same type of words in your subject heading that spammers use, you run the risk of having your email message getting discarded before it's even read. Hence, you've lost the time that you spent composing the email—and you'll waste yet more time trying to get a reply from a party who never read your message to begin with. What are the banished words? You already know most of these:

The Time Master Says

The most efficient use of your time, when compiling email messages that you intend to be read, is to offer a vibrant subject line or at least a passable one so that the other party will open and read your mail.

- Sex
- Money
- First time
- A one-time offer

- Free
- Exclusive
- Adults only
- Limited time only

- Naked
- Incredible
- Make money now
- Don't miss out!

Dead giveaways include anything with stars, plus signs, equals signs, or typographical "artwork."

Banished Words and Phrases

Don't use any of these words or phrases in the subject line of your email if you intend for any non-*Enquirer* subscribers to read your email:

Free Guide	Cyber Sex
You Were Carefully Chosen	Hot Nymphs
Consolidate Your Loans Now	Make $50,000 in Just Three Days
How to Stop Belching	More Web Hits Instantly
You Can't Ignore This	Pay Zero Taxes … Legally
A Friend Gave Us Your Name	Make More Money Than You Ever Dreamed Of
Limited Edition	You Can't Ignore This Offer

Amazing Pet Training System

Fly for Free

Stop Psoriasis Now

Make Money at Home

Your Dream Vacation Is Waiting

Don't Ignore This

Secrets Now Revealed

Lowest Air Fares Ever

Grand Cayman Tax Shelters

With Over Ten Million Email Addresses

An Urgent Message

ANNOUNCING …

Get into the College of Your Choice

Retire Now

Instant Web Site

We Believe You Would Be Interested …

CAUTION

Pause!

Treat any email that you ever send at work or at home as having the potential to revisit you. Even if you delete it from your system, it still may reside on your Internet service provider's system. If you write in disparaging terms about someone else and send it to a third party, expect it to come back to haunt you.

CAUTION

Pause!

The people who get obsessed with checking their email at every spare moment are often the ones not doing a great job anyway, sending off epistles to loved ones, seeking to pick up new acquaintances in chat rooms, and sending and receiving the latest jokes to and from the usual gang.

As *The Financial Times* reports, few email users recognize that "deleting a controversial email message from a desktop PC does not always get rid of it. In most cases, the message is also stored more permanently on an Internet server or network server computer. If the lawyers come knocking on the door with subpoena, this is the first place they will look."

Checking Twice or Thrice

Unless your job specifically calls for continual email monitoring or you're waiting for a critical response, it's best to check your mail about twice a day, and perhaps a third time, if you're feeling particularly ahead of the game.

Online Efficiency Through Offline Preparation

The "administrivia" that you tend to first thing in the morning, often before downloading new messages, enhances your productivity in both sending and receiving email.

- Perhaps you need to prepare files on your hard drive.
- Perhaps you have addresses to correct.
- Perhaps you've received phone and fax messages that will fuel your email responses.

I normally start my day at 7:30 A.M. Egad—I know it sounds like slave hours, but you have to consider that my boss is a pretty driven guy (I work alone!). Kidding aside, I start the day early, and I end earlier than most.

After clocking in, I usually work for 60 to 90 minutes before checking for new email. Once I do this, I allow anywhere from 30 to 45 minutes to handle the 15–25 messages that I'll have waiting for me.

Overall, if I'm free and clear of the morning administrivia and emailing before, say, 9:00 or 9:30, I consider that to be a great start.

Lunch Break

I confess to checking after lunch to see if anybody sent me anything, but then I log off rather quickly. I certainly check in at around 4:30 each day, to catch the closing emails that might be arriving from East Coast correspondence and from those on the West Coast who know to send their messages in before 2:45 Pacific Standard Time.

Follow the Instructions

As have other technologies, email usage has spread so fast that it has exceeded our ability to successfully adapt to this form of communication. Most people dash off emails at high speed. I'm not knocking the high rate of typos and grammatical errors—I make them, too, and that is not a huge issue regarding email use. However, have you ever teed off anyone because of an email? Your stark letters on the screen of your recipient can easily be misinterpreted, and, unfortunately, this happens all the time. Did you ever receive a disappointing or questionable email from someone you like?

Sometimes an email message can make you seem as if you're curt or abrasive. It's not that you intended to ruffle any feathers; it's just that email, unless worded carefully, can sometimes come off as impersonal, cold, and uncaring.

> **⚠ CAUTION**
>
> **Pause!**
>
> Michael Eisner says, "Email isn't just about speed, efficiency, and information. It is also about unscreened emotions, about options untempered by body language, about thoughts unrefined by reflection, about hostility, and provocation. At its worst, it is like talking in the shower with someone listening through the wall."

Pause Before Sending

"The Send button can prove an irresistible temptation to propel thoughts on their way to impress or titillate or even inflict pain," says Michael Eisner, CEO of the Walt Disney

Company. Too few people apparently are using the draft box and clicking the Send button nanoseconds after typing the last letter in their message. As with traditional writing, when possible, perhaps it's best to park emails for a day and revisit them before sending. With some email service providers, you have the option to delay sending until a prearranged time. With most providers, you have the option either to park an email message in the Draft Message box or to send it.

"The slowness of communication technology used to help protect us from ourselves. This is no longer the case," observes Eisner, who points out that, for enhanced communication and better relationships, you can always pick up the phone, get in a car, or board a plane. By using a variety of communications, he observes, we can "master email and not be mastered by it."

Make That Call

> **Pause!**
>
> Don't use email as a substitute for conversation because you will tie up endless amounts of time. It could easily take a dozen rounds of email for two people to achieve the same level of communication and understanding that's possible with two minutes of conversation.

If you rely on email too much—such as sending email when a face-to-face conversation was more appropriate—you may be seen as somewhat aloof. Managers looking for a way to avoid face-to-face conflict will often use email, says Linda Talley, author of *Business Finesse: Dealing with Sticky Situations in the Work Place for Managers*. "It's an easy way out," she says.

If you feel that a conversation is warranted, you're probably right. Make that visit or that phone call. If you need a yes or no answer, or to easily transmit the data that someone has requested or is waiting for, then proceed with email.

One-Way Messaging

Everything discussed to this point leads to the inevitable issue—is the message that you wish to convey appropriate via email? The answer is not always so clear cut. Email, like leaving a voice-mail message for someone, is a one-way medium. When you leave your message, communication is flowing in only one direction. Jaclyn Kostner, Ph.D., based in Denver, Colorado, offers the following list of *inappropriate* messages for one-way media, such as email and voice mail:

- The complex
- New ideas
- Issues requiring clarification

- ◆ Solicitation for agreement
- ◆ The emotionally charged
- ◆ Material that has a strong personal impact on the recipient

Other than these topics, it's probably okay to engage in one-way messaging.

Once you've determined that your message is suitable for one-way media, Kostner observes you have one more choice: Should you relay your message by email, or is voice mail preferable? Let's review her guidelines.

When Email Is Preferred

Kostner advocates choosing email (not voice mail) in situations when …

- ◆ A written record is needed.
- ◆ Language is a barrier. In multilanguage teams, written words are frequently easier to understand than spoken ones, especially when accents are heavy or language skills are less than fluent.
- ◆ The team's normal business day hours in each location do not match.
- ◆ You've been unable to reach the person interactively, but you know that the person needs the details right away.

The following also can represent appropriate use of email:

- ◆ One-word or short answers
- ◆ Approval or disapproval
- ◆ Forwarding of vital information to appropriate parties
- ◆ Articles, reports, outlines, and guidelines that have been specifically requested by the recipient
- ◆ Updated information such as price quotes, progress reports, and summaries of activities, again when the other party is expecting or requesting such

Pick Up the Phone

On the other hand (as the economists say), Kostner advises leaving a voice mail or answering machine message when your message is urgent or when the recipient is mobile. Voice mail is easier to access than email, in most cases. Also leave a voice message any time that the sound of your voice is key to understanding your message.

The Least You Need to Know

- Constantly checking for email or sending it has become an obsession for many people and a serious time drain. Actively seek to limit your email use.

- Avoid using the same type of words that spammers use; chances are, your email might get discarded.

- Posting your email address anywhere on the Internet makes it available to spammers. Be cautious and consider using a second, more private email account.

- Managers looking for a way to avoid face-to-face conflict often use email. If you rely on email too much, such as sending email when a face-to-face conversation was more appropriate, you may be seen as aloof.

- Skip email whenever the sound of your voice is crucial to understanding your message.

Mastering Email So That It Doesn't Master You

In This Chapter

- ◆ Skip the preamble and don't ramble
- ◆ The wisdom of pruning but not overpruning your messages
- ◆ Preparing stock messages to help convey your sense of responsiveness
- ◆ You're in charge of your email basket; it is not in charge of you

A good email message often requires only a few choice paragraphs. Because you're a fast typist doesn't mean that you need to ramble on forever and ever. Guy Kawasaki, author of *How to Drive the Competition Crazy*, says that most people send email messages that are too long. Most of the action is in the first and last paragraphs. If it's longer than four paragraphs, watch out—you're not using the medium for which it was intended, and you're tying up your time.

Brevity Is the Soul of Email Wit

Think about the email messages that you receive that go on and on for far longer than the first screenful. Particularly among those that are unsolicited, do you read them all? If you do, how many of them do you actually save? Chances are, the longer ones tend to get discarded more quickly.

Reflect and Win

When composing an email message to someone who's not expecting it but whom, nevertheless, you wish to influence, aim for one screenful or less. Pretend that the other person has a 14-inch monitor and that the area in which he receives emails represents roughly one-quarter of the screen. Given this narrow parameter, craft your message to fit neatly into the allotted space.

Pause!

If Internet abbreviations were universally known, used, and understood, they'd represent tremendous savings in terms of composing and reading email messages. The problem is that they are not universally known, used, or understood. When you use such abbreviations, you'll likely confuse the other party—and that's not a time-saver for anyone.

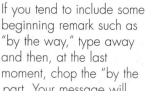

Reflect and Win

If you tend to include some beginning remark such as "by the way," type away and then, at the last moment, chop the "by the way" part. Your message will read cleaner and neater.

Undoubtedly, you can shorten many of your messages—and maybe you already do. If you don't, it's time to start practicing. Prune your prose. Say it once, and be done.

Prune, but Don't Overprune

Occasionally you'll get an email from someone who uses such cryptic language, chops key words from sentences, and uses so many abbreviations that the meaning of the message is all but lost. For example:

> looking fw'rd 2 c'ing u this eve. is 7 gd, or do u thk earlier is btr? Also, R U getting tix or me? I'll B in to 5. later, TGB

Don't be among those who prune beyond reason—and beyond the recipient's ability to extract your meaning. And forget all those semineat net abbreviations that you see in other books, such as BTW, which means "by the way." You're more likely to confuse the other party than communicate effectively.

People actually email back and forth regarding what the abbreviations meant! Now that's a waste of time.

Needless Drivel

If you want to get ruthless about the splendid use of your native tongue, why would you want to include something that began with "by the way," anyway? It tells the other party that what you're about to announce either is not important or that you didn't know how to effectively juxtapose the item with what you've already written.

"Net" Savings

Once you begin pruning your prose effectively, you'll find that email can be a valuable tool. After all, even if you're inundated with the number of messages that you receive daily, there is a net savings in the form of less mail, fewer faxes, and fewer telephone calls (hopefully) from these same parties.

If you're able to productively handle your email, you effectively reduce the time and tasks associated with other forms of correspondence.

Keep Your "CC's" to a Minimum

Some *netiquette* experts suggest that no more than three parties should receive any message that you're sending. So, you'd send to one principal recipient, with circulated copies to two others. If you're the manager of a small group of, say, 6, 8, or 10 people, perhaps it's necessary for you to send to all 6, 8, or 10. If you're the president of an organization of thousands and you want to send out an all-purpose email to all of them, let 'em rip.

In general, when you CC more than three or four parties in your email for a rather pointed message, you're signaling to most recipients that they can safely *ignore* your message. As with failure to prune your prose, you're doing more work than is necessary, such as rounding up more addresses in the CC line and potentially glutting other peoples' email inboxes. You don't really want to do that, do you?

Reflect and Win

Companies that implement Internet-based email services will be able to slash telephone call–related labor costs by 43 percent, according to Forrester Research, based in Canada.

Showing Your Responsiveness

With a multitude of email messages piling up in your inbox, even a brief time away from your PC means that you'll have scads of emails to respond to upon returning. A mere two days out of the office will result in your coming back to at least two to three times the normal number of email messages that you encounter, and much of it is spam—junk email. Barring the passage of broad-sweeping legislation (see Chapter 17, "Email: No Worse a Curse [Than Beepers]"), you have two basic strategies when it comes to dealing with your overstuffed email inbox. You can let it make you crazy, or you can practice *triage*.

Coming to Terms

Netiquette is the combination of *net* and *etiquette*, which means etiquette for those online.

Coming to Terms

Triage is the practice of quickly poring over a variety of items and allocating them based on what needs to be handled immediately, what can be handled later, and what can be ignored altogether.

Triage or Die

I advocate practicing triage for all email messages all the time. First, you want to quickly eliminate the inane. These include all forms of spam.

After eliminating the obvious, the next question is which emails you can park—that is, place in a holding folder, bin, file, or whatever your system calls them. Some are entirely worth saving but simply are not urgent. Some are from friends and loved ones, and you want to pore over what they've written. Some have told you in the letter that the reply time need not be immediate.

> **Reflect and Win**
>
> Even if a message isn't urgent, if you're able to respond to it quickly and effortlessly, why waste time parking it? If the message is staring you in the face, all you have to do is type a few words and hit the Reply button, then send it off and get on to the next email!

The last category is those email messages that you receive that require quick to immediate action. Quick means sometime during the day. Immediate, as I use it here, means that you should reply right now, while you're online. Hopefully the number of messages that you get that fall into the quick or immediate categories is small.

For those emails that mandate your present, earnest, and rather speedy attention, do your gut-level best to handle them so that they're out of the way and you're mentally—as well as physically—clear of them.

Stock Your Messages

If you've returned from several days away from your PC, or if the number of email messages in your inbox is ganging up on you, here's a viable temporary solution to this dilemma: Have stock messages ready—such as that you have recently returned from traveling and will respond by midweek, or anything else that conveys your sense of responsiveness.

When I receive an acknowledgment message from someone (even an automated acknowledgment), I regard that person highly. At least he took the time, or set up his system as such, to let me know that he received my message and intends to do something about it. That's a far cry from those you don't hear from for days, much of the time suspecting that you'll never hear from them.

Any of the customized email programs on the market enable you to save stock messages and easily retrieve them as needed. Also, many feature filters, which enable you to sort email as it arrives. The filters find and delete email that contains specific key words or that were sent from specific addresses.

Pssst ... Don't Pass It On

Are you one of the many people who participate in the constant forwarding of semiamusing jokes or the distribution of email chain letters? Occasionally, you receive a joke that is so funny that you want to pass it along to someone else. Okay, that's human nature. Still, passing chain letters is an utter and complete waste of time. The stories that you hear about people winning riches are baloney. Now, you'd never engage in passing on chain letter emails—would you?

Any type of dawdling when it comes to email is a potentially large time waster. When you dawdle in the office, there are greater repercussions. You may not have considered it, but extensive use of the phone, email, or any other gadget for personal reasons actually steals time from your employer.

If you're on commission, you may have a stronger argument that it's your time and that how you use it is up to you. The larger question is, what else could you be doing with this precious time? At day's end, what gets shortchanged that didn't need to be?

> **CAUTION**
>
> **Pause!**
> You can rationalize all you want about how much you get done in a day, how hiring you was a bargain, and all the other wonderful things that you do that don't get counted. When push comes to shove, reading, composing, sending, and filing email that is not work-related means that you are being paid for dawdling.

The Best Managers Still Delegate

Productivity consultant Laura Stack observes that email adds a second "pile" to your desk. You have to deal with not only the physical paper piles on your desk, but also the piles of files in your email inbox. "Your indecision about what to do with each email received compounds the problem," she says. Hence, she advocates the 6-D system to handle email. In a nutshell:

1. Discard it. Delete the email as soon as you receive it.
2. Delegate it. Forward it on to someone else who can take care of it.
3. Do it. Respond to the email and then delete it.
4. Dungeon it. File it someplace where you can retrieve it if you need to.
5. Don't see it again. Call the sender and get off the routing list.
6. Decide. When are you going to deal with it?

Among the important emails you receive, if you're a manager and have any type of administrative or supportive staff to manage well, you need to delegate and forward many of your email messages each day to your staff. If you're not delegating email, just as before the advent of email, you're not managing well. You're holding on to too much!

Not delegating has cost many an executive a vital promotion—and, worse, has led some to the unemployment line.

If you want to be efficient when forwarding email, use aliases. This essentially means that you make some modifications to your email address book; thereafter, all you have to do is type another person's initials, and his email address appears. Keep a copy of what you send in the online "file folder" that you maintain for messages related to that person. Thus, you're instantaneously able to forward tasks and catalog them. If you need to write anything in the body of the message at all, it could be as simple as, "Please handle this." Hey, what could be simpler?

Working Offline to Increase Your Productivity Online

When you arrive at the office each morning, do you check your email right away? If so, you may not be as productive as you could be. While in some professions checking email first is mandatory, many professionals have the option of checking email when they choose. Here's the case for *not* emailing until later in the day.

When you log on first thing in the morning, you're automatically compelled to pay attention to what's new, current, or tugging at your time and attention. Whatever you had planned for the day ends up taking second place to tasks that you feel obligated to perform as a result of the emails that you received. This is not to say that you are not receiving important emails that represent important tasks and require timely turnaround. The question becomes which is more important: to proceed based upon your personally crafted agenda or the one that transpires as a result of being hit by many, many emails?

An Offline Look

When I come into my office in the morning, I take a look offline at the emails from previous days that I have saved and arranged in various files and folders. Quietly and *unhurriedly*, I compose letters offline and put them into the Drafts folder. For those emails that I have received that merit a reply, I carefully cut and paste the elements of the message that I want to include in my reply and prepare my response underneath. I send it when I'm ready, not in a rush.

Much of what I receive consists of items that I want to copy and move into my word processing software because they are worth retaining on my hard drive. I also do this offline and at my own pace.

While remaining offline, I examine emails that I didn't know what to do with the first time around. Sometimes I delete them. Some I file for future examination. Most I deal with then and there, *formulating replies* and saving them in the drafts pile.

Ready to Go Online

When I'm ready to go online, I feel comfortable and secure. I have mastered my entire email file up to that point. I am in control. Granted, when I go online I'll be hit with a barrage of new messages that represent everything from urgent and important tasks to less important items and spam.

Coming to Terms

Formulating an email reply is different than simply responding to one. It entails ensuring to the best of one's ability that the message is clear and accurate, and that it conveys precisely what the sender wishes to communicate.

Because I have not logged on as the first activity in the morning and have not allowed myself to be besieged by all types of new messages, I'm in a more commanding position to take action as I see fit and stay in control of my time and my day.

Receiving Before Sending

When I first log on, before sending my drafted letters to their intended recipients, I press Get Messages. Why? Sometimes the messages received supersede the messages that I was ready to send to someone. A new message might resolve the issue altogether. As the new emails appear on my screen, I take a few minutes to review them, scanning the essence of what's involved and then moving on to the next. I eliminate spam immediately. Once I've reviewed the array of new messages, I turn to my draft files and launch all of the email in waiting. In most cases, this includes all the drafts, but occasionally I delay or eliminate one because of the new email messages that I've received checking new messages.

Always Triage

I then return to the messages that I just received and handle them individually. I quickly reply to messages when not much effort is needed. Those that can be answered with a short message and sent by simply hitting the Reply button are best handled in that fashion.

Some emails contain information that I want to save to my hard drive. Often, these contain attachments. In this case, I open the attachment, save the item in the appropriate folder on my hard drive, and return to my email screen. Now I'm left with the handful of emails that are urgent and that perhaps require significant attention. To handle the issue, I may have to round up information, cut and paste files from my hard drive, make a telephone call, or create a new directory.

Because I logged on later in the morning, after I had mastered all of my existing email files, purged the spam, taken care of the quick reply messages, and filed the information that I wanted to retain on my hard drive, I am generally left with only a handful of pressing tasks. This alone helps me stay in balance, feel in control, and give a higher level of attention to the remaining emails that merit an extended effort.

Coming to Terms

A **stock message** is one that you park in your templates, draft, or signature folder to reuse as the situation applies.

I'm Working on It

In situations when it may take me a while to resolve the issue, I sometimes send a *stock message* or short note back to the sender saying, "I'm working on it and will be back in touch on such and such day." This lets the sender know that I received the message, that I regard it as important, and, while I can't resolve the issue or meet the request at this moment, that I certainly am working on it.

The Elements of Effective Online Management

Making this system work requires discipline *not* to log on early in the morning or throughout the morning. It also requires an understanding of how you work best, what will help you to maintain control, and what yields the greatest productivity: to stay offline until you're ready to go online.

You may find my approach to be interesting and even stimulating, but you may still fall back into the habit of jumping online too soon—too soon to stay in control and too soon to be at your best.

If you're among the miniscule percentage of readers who understand the benefits of proceeding in the manner described, here are some additional components to make the system work effectively:

◆ Have plenty of online file folders available. Communication software packages enable you to create as many file folders and subfiles as you choose. Assign a file folder for each of your major projects and for each broad topic important in your work and your life, such as work, family, school, and so on.

◆ Create a variety of folders on a temporary basis, when an issue or project is at hand, and eliminate the folder when the significance of the issue recedes.

- Use all manner of filters to immediately eliminate spam and other types of messages that you don't want to receive, as well as messages from certain senders. The fewer unwanted email messages you see, the more effective you'll be in responding to those that merit a response.

- Whenever you have to give an answer more than a few times or disseminate a message to several recipients, use a template, a prewritten response. You can always eliminate templates that are no longer useful to you. It's far better to create a template and not use it than not to create one and find yourself having to repeat the same type of message over and over again.

- Whenever you encounter an interesting website address but you find you don't have time to visit it right then, send yourself an email containing the address. Better yet, create a draft email with the subject line "Interesting website addresses." As you gain each new address, go back to the draft and add it, resave the draft letter, and carry on. Later, when you feel more inclined, go to the draft and visit the websites that you deemed interesting.

> **Reflect and Win**
>
> Because you can rename, combine, or submerge folders with the click of a mouse, and because the nature of your work is probably dynamic, it makes sense to move folders in some way at least once a week. If you are not doing so, chances are, you're not using email as effectively as you could.

- Much like letting magazines and hard-copy information stack up when you don't have time to review them, when you return to the pile or draft, you find that some of what looked so interesting at the time has lost its appeal. Thus, you've saved time and are probably no worse off in your overall career progression and quality of life.

By using the techniques outlined, it need not be the burden that so many career professionals perceive it to be. At all times, the fundamental principle is that you're in charge of your email basket; it is not in charge of you.

Coordinating Your Software

For those who are overwhelmed by email, one writer, who shall remain nameless, suggested throwing away your whole inbox of messages every other week or even right now, claiming that "nobody will notice." While I can appreciate the idea of not letting email inboxes build up, there's a more efficient way to manage the information that comes into your life via the Internet.

Here's what I do: When I turn on my PC in the morning, I start up in my word-processing software. Then I click on my contact-management software. Third, I click on my email software without actually going online, as described earlier.

If there are email messages (previously downloaded) that need to be returned, I compose the message offline and transfer it to an email outbox, which will hold all the emails that I want to send until I get online and choose to send them.

Ready for Action

Once online, if any of the incoming emails that I receive contain vital information in the message section or attachment, I copy the information, then wheel over to my contact management software, and place it in the record of the person who sent me the information.

For example, if Ryan sends me an important list via email, I copy that list and then put it in my database file under Ryan. If I need to insert the list into a report, I copy and paste it into my word-processing software. Hence, I'm able to address the important emails that I need to, save key information from them, and keep my inbox relatively clear.

Sometimes I visit my contact-management software and, using the calendar or alarm, see who needs to be contacted on a given morning. Then I turn to my word-processing program, compose a message, copy the message into the Insert Notes section of the contact-management software, and then wheel around and send the message as an email to that person.

By opening these three software programs concurrently and cutting and pasting from one window to the next as necessary, I'm able to …

- Stay in touch with parties in an efficient manner.
- Keep my email inbox relatively clear.
- Maintain an easy way to find information sent to or from specific parties.
- Have less notes and clutter on my hard drive and surrounding desk area.
- Maintain peace of mind.

The Least You Need to Know

- When composing an email message to someone who's not expecting it, aim for one screenful or less.
- Delegate email as often as you possibly can.
- When practical, park emails for a while and revisit them before sending.
- Whenever you have to give an answer more than a few times or disseminate a message to several recipients, use a template, or a prewritten response.
- Create your own system for smoothly shifting from word processing to your contact-management software to your email, and you'll be supremely efficient.

An Internet You Can Live With

In This Chapter

- ◆ Getting onto the web: who uses it—and why?
- ◆ The rise of misinformation
- ◆ Search engines worth your while
- ◆ Living with the Internet

You're giving up pieces of your day when you surf the Internet for hours. Is what you do worth the time you spend? If you're finding key information quickly, then yes. Anything else, and the answer is suspect. The Internet—and, more specifically, the World Wide Web—puts more information at your fingertips than you can effectively handle. The key to maintaining control when you're on the Internet is to realize two things:

1. The sooner you quit trying to keep up, the better you'll feel.
2. You need to continually and carefully choose where to give your time and attention.

This chapter will help you achieve both those goals.

Who's on First

Nielsen-NetRating reports that, in mid-2001, there were 102 million active web users, compared with 62.8 million in mid-1999. This is an explosive increase and underscores the gargantuan affect the web has had on society.

Other findings also reveal sensational growth in web use: 58 percent of the United States, representing 165 million people, had home Internet access, up from 39 percent two years earlier. Those who go online are doing it more frequently and are spending more time staying online. The average Internet user spent 10 hours and 19 minutes online as of mid-2001, up from 7 hours and 39 minutes two years before.

Based on research conducted by Google.com, an astounding 70-plus percent of web pages are less than one year old, as of 2001, and more than 89 percent are less than one to two years old, as reported by the web servers. (The actual age can be greater.) For the far-reaching future, the rate of new data posted each day will continue to explode.

Your ability to keep pace with it all becomes increasingly difficult. You simply have too many alternatives, regardless of what you're seeking. Hence, you need to clearly establish your searching/browsing objectives by posing the following questions:

- Who are you trying to reach?
- What are you seeking to learn or gain?
- To what effect?

Anything less than careful consideration of these issues is likely to result in spending more and more time online.

The Web Is Different

For all the news and information that it provides, it's important to remember that the web is primarily a marketing vehicle for those who host websites.

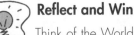

Reflect and Win

Think of the World Wide Web as an information guidebook and advertising directory with more than 100 million entries that is updated or changed every picosecond.

"Every other kind of marketing prior to the web has been 'push,'" says web guru David Arnold, Ph.D. "Direct mail, print and broadcast media advertising, telemarketing, billboards—they all involve pushing information at people. The message reaches an intended market and has an impact whether the communication is welcome or not." Websites, however, must draw visitors to them. Even the world's best site will have no visitors unless people are drawn to the site.

Don't Use Up Your Life

In the days of horse-and-buggy travel, drivers placed blinders on their horses to block their peripheral vision, thus keeping them from being startled by things that they didn't need to see. Similarly, you can choose to travel the information superhighway wearing electronic blinders that enable you to view only the information that affects your microniche.

Information Overload Exacerbated

Your house and garden plants need to be regularly shorn of dead leaves and stems to promote healthy growth. Likewise, you need to trim yourself of deadweight thinking: believing that you need to endlessly strive to keep informed and up to date. The web beckons at all hours. You know it's there, like television—an information drug available in unlimited quantities and ready to rob you of your time at any moment.

Before you log on, eliminate what is not useful to you. Here's how: Create a default Download directory on your hard drive, and specify this directory in the Preferences sections of your Internet software. This way, you will always know where to find freshly downloaded files instead of having to search your computer system. Then create permanent directories into which you'll transfer important files from your default Download directory—after you've confirmed their long-term usefulness.

Pause!

Much of the web is self-serving hype about the web itself. Many people are trying to show off the "cool" graphics that they can make, offering little else. That won't improve your life or end your workday any quicker. Don't waste your time on such sites.

Pause!

Before you face the mounds of new information, delete outdated documents and unnecessary downloaded files from your computer. Download from the Internet only the information that will truly support you in your work. Instead of downloading files that you'll use just occasionally, record their addresses and leave the information on the Internet.

Pay the Piper

The nature of many websites has changed; what was once free often costs money today. The "experimental" stage of the web is over, and companies are deciding that their efforts in building and maintaining websites need to turn profits. Understood, and expected. In a way, this change is good because it forces each one of us to decide which sites and fees are worth our time and money.

When you have to pay for something, you're more discerning. You are also more judicial in the use of your time. If every site cost money, multimillions of users would approach the web differently, potentially a positive development. Maybe the time spent online would diminish. (Of course, the great danger might be that people would return to television or some other sit-on-your-rear-end pastime.)

Customize the News and Information You Receive

Increasingly, websites and information services are available that enable you to cut down on bulky newspaper and magazine subscriptions by receiving your news and information in customized, byte-size portions. Some sites, such as *The New York Times*, at www.nyt. com, ask you to disclose personal information in exchange for free daily news and updates.

Somewhat similar to *The New York Times*, CNN, at www.cnn.com, requests information about you, your business, and your interests in exchange for allowing you to custom-design how your news is delivered.

Other sites, such as *The Wall Street Journal*, at www.wsj.com, enable newspaper subscribers to add an online component for a modest fee, while nonsubscribers must pay roughly double the cost.

Is Privacy Still Possible?

One of the more annoying developments on the web is the invasion of privacy. Websites plant *cookies* on your hard drive so that when you visit them more than once, your interests—as determined by what you visited previously—can quickly be catalogued by the site owner. However, chances are good that it is simply a mechanized catalog and that there may not be someone in particular who knows exactly what you look at once you stray into his website's territory.

Coming to Terms

A **cookie** is an electronic marker that a website places on your hard drive so that if and when you revisit the website, your PC is electronically recognized and you may be directed toward website features that presumably lie within your area of interest.

Cookies Crumble

On a positive note, Harris Interactive Surveys conducted a study in June 2000 that revealed that 39 percent of respondents knew what a cookie was and how to disable it. Men were twice as likely as women to know this information.

The banner advertising that you see, and even some of the features on the site itself, can literally change in nanoseconds based on what cookies have been stored on your hard drive. To me, this is a gross form of manipulation.

Fortunately, browser software comes with the capability to screen for cookies or eliminate them at the end of each visit or each day. The instructions are in the Help menu.

Unobtrusive and Secure

The larger, more troubling issue from a time standpoint is that you can hardly visit a site these days without some second or third screen popping up, banner ads waving messages, or unwanted sounds intruding your computer.

If you choose to do business at a particular website, such as order something, make sure that it is a secure site. That means that if you transmit any important information, like credit card data, third parties would have an exceedingly hard time trying to sift it. Most reputable sites have some type of privacy statement, although that is no guarantee that your information will remain private. Still, it is better to see a privacy statement posted than not.

> **CAUTION**
>
> **Pause!**
>
> If you are unsure as to how the information that you submit to a web vendor will be used, send that party an email first and ask. You want to protect your privacy, and you also don't want to waste your time dealing with annoying or exploitative vendors.

Ordering Online

Ordering online will only get easier. After 10 years of languishing, the idea of using electronic money has taken hold. Services such as CheckFree and PayPal have become standard payment options for many online shoppers. websites are lining up to secure shoppers' ability to pay over the Internet, slicing days off traditional bank transaction times.

Peter Thiel, founder and CEO of PayPal, says, "The ability to move money fluidly and the erosion of the nation-state are closely related." He believes that PayPal will be a vehicle of geopolitical liberation. Interviewed by *Wire* magazine, he explained that, with a PayPal account, any Internet user could transfer value with greater anonymity than he could by employing a Swiss bank account.

PayPal and similar e-cash transfer services act as seamless intermediaries in the exchange between merchant and buyer. To open a PayPal account, for example, you need to provide only your name, your email address, and a password. Once you register, you're issued a credit, debit, or checking account number, and then you're free to send and receive funds. Both parties to the transaction have to subscribe to the service.

Misinformation Is Not Pretty

Along with the products and services that you can order on the web and the wealth of useful information that you can tap into are volumes of misinformation. Vast stores of what passes for data are the opinions of those who post the web pages. Worse, too often the information is outright false—but it spreads at hyperspeed. The truth rarely has a chance to catch up.

In addition to false or misleading information, the web is rife with what is called "spoof data"—information spread as a joke but presented as true. Why does this abound on the net? Until the mid-1990s, the majority of web users were college students, predominantly male. A few of them with an immature sense of humor can create a huge swath of ruin. Spoof data, however, can come from anywhere.

A clever junior-high student can generate spoof data that appears to emanate from the White House. The good news is that the web—while massive and growing explosively— has the tools to help you become deft at securing the information that you need.

> **Reflect and Win**
>
> PC consultant and trainer Tricia Santos suggests visiting http://searchengine watch.internet.com to learn about mining for Internet informational gold. This site teaches you how to make the most of the search engines and how to get your own site listed. It also lists and evaluates all the major and specialty search engines out there.

The Search Is On

To find the information that you need, or to specifically learn more about a product or service, most people head for one or more of the online search engines and request a keyword search. "Some search engines scour the web, locating and indexing new sites as they appear," says David Arnold, Ph.D. "Others, like Yahoo! (www.yahoo.com), list only those sites that are submitted to them." Does this mean that you should use only those search engines like Yahoo! that are more selective? No.

Index-Savvy

Tricia Santos, president of IMP Training (www.triciasantos.com), explains that search engines are basically indexes. You type in words, and the search engine finds the web pages in its index with those words. To do this, they use what are called "robots" to index tens of millions of web pages.

Santos suggests several strategies to help you use search engines like a hard-core geek. One is to use a variety of engines with the same search criteria until you settle on the few that give you the best results consistently. A few of the more popular ones include these:

- ◆ www.google.com
- ◆ www.lycos.com
- ◆ www.infoseek.com
- ◆ www.nlsearch.com

nlsearch.com also includes the full-text articles from more than 5,000 journals and magazines (with more being added all the time). You can get the abstract for free and the full text for a reasonable charge. If you use this search engine more than a few times, you may want to pay the nominal monthly fee.

Metasearch engines submit your search criteria to a number of different search engines for you. One such metasearch engine is www.metacrawler.com.

With all these engines available, you want to find the most efficient way to use them. That's where word-searching comes in.

Check It Out: Multiple Word Searches

When conducting a search, the first principle to learn is this: The more words you use, the more accurate your results will be. Virtually all search engines use quotation marks to identify phrases. For many, you can put the plus sign before any word that you need to find included on the web page, and you can use the minus sign for those that should not be included.

When searching for entries on professional speakers, you might want to make sure to exclude the words *stereo* and *car*, or you'll get entries on sound systems. Each search engine is a bit different, however, so look for the buttons labeled Options, Help, Hints, Tips, or Advanced for online assistance on how to use the site.

Santos suggests that you turn to hotbot.com because that site uses drop-down lists and other simple tools to set up your multiple word searches. Look for other buttons that will expand your search for you as well. Usenet, for example, features thousands of newsgroups that you can tap into. (More on this later in the chapter.)

A Return Visit

When you find an information-rich site upon which you can rely, you're most likely to want to make a return visit. Everyone who's on the web regularly has their own favorites. Make sure to bookmark or add such sites to your favorites list. Here are a few ideas on what makes a site worth noting:

♦ **Periodic updates**—Something significant changes on the opening screen once a week, once a day, or more often.

♦ **Up-to-the-minute information**—Trends, breakthroughs, results, and so forth make it a place worth visiting daily for late-breaking news or public service messages.

♦ **Quickly engaging**—The site encourages immediate participation and gives visitors choices, such as the opportunity to vote for something or send an opinion.

♦ **Online tutorial**—The site teaches visitors something and offers short, to-the-point instructions or guidance on something of interest.

♦ **For members only**—The site offers exclusive features to its members. This is important if staying informed among such privileged users is important to you. You'll need a password to enter.

♦ **Article series**—The site gives readers continuing information.

♦ **Survey or polling results.**

♦ **Rating guide**—The site categorizes products or services that you might use.

♦ **Review service**—The site provides reviews of movies, books, software, programs, courses, or the web itself.

To learn about key sites, find others who are willing to trade site suggestions with you. Peers can help enormously, and clients or customers may be helpful. In addition, web specialists might know of sites that you wouldn't stumble upon.

The Best Leave Clues

Good websites have certain features in common. If you find a site that offers most of the features listed here, it will help to optimize your time online:

♦ **Keeps visitors from getting lost**—A good website includes multiple links that take you back to the home page, to the previous page, or to another value-packed page of your choice. It ensures that you can quickly return to something familiar or move forward to something new.

◆ **Goes easy on the graphics**—Many websites truly are works of art by master graphic artists. Smaller graphics and text-only hyperlinks, however, help you navigate much faster.

◆ **Includes multiple contact links**—Good sites contain clear links that point you to contact information such as email addresses, fax numbers, snail mail addresses, and phone numbers, if appropriate.

Much of what you find on websites is time-sensitive or is updated on a daily or weekly basis. Other sites post information for the long run. My site includes both dynamic and static information (see www.BreathingSpace.com). One feature called "Book Digest" summarizes nearly 100 books. Visitors may download book digest selections of their choice each month for free. I add to the digest periodically, but it is basically a static portion of the site.

The Time Master Says

A good website is visitor-focused. A good site focuses on your needs, ensuring the most direct access to information that is most valuable to you.

Hard-to-Find Information Though Newsgroups

What are newsgroups? How can they help you stay in control of your time? First, a little history. A network called Usenet started as an electronic bulletin board served by just two sites: the University of North Carolina and Duke University. Coincidentally, I live halfway between the universities.

Today, Usenet newsgroups have grown into a global collection of thousands of discussion groups where people post messages and replies on specific topics of interest.

Networking People

Usenet—short for "users' network"—is a connected network of people. Usenet newsgroups reside at specific, accessible computer sites and originally operated independently of the Internet. People stopped by, read comments, added their own, and checked replies much like a community bulletin board in a public hallway.

Reflect and Win

Server sites around the world use the Internet today to share newsgroups and pass the postings from server to server throughout the computer network. Tap into this rich informational resource.

Similar to the Internet, no particular person or group owns or runs Usenet. It operates according to certain conventions, using a system of universally recognized categories.

Newsgroups Newbies

If you're already browsing the World Wide Web, or if you intend to, you probably have what you need to access desired discussions. "The major web browsers come with built-in newsgroup readers that let you view, write, and reply to the postings of the groups you specify," says David Arnold. Software from online services usually includes a preconfigured reader.

Choose Your Weapon

Two basic categories comprise newsgroups, according to Arnold. The first, most highly controlled category contains the following headings:

- **comp**—Computers and related topics (hardware, software, technical discussions)
- **news**—Usenet itself (announcements, software, and other information)
- **rec**—Recreation and hobbies, entertainment, and the arts
- **sci**—Science (excluding computer science)
- **soc**—Social issues
- **talk**—Debates on controversial topics
- **misc**—Everything else, including "help wanted" postings

The second and less stringent set of categories includes these:

- **alt**—Alternative groups
- **bionet**—Biology
- **bit**—The most popular topics from Bitnet electronic mailing lists
- **biz**—Business, marketing, and advertisements

The major group headings under each category are further broken down into subtopics, each separated by a period in the address of the group. Arnold remarks that, as the separators grow, the topic area shrinks. For example, you may see a newsgroup identified as biz.books. Here you would expect to see information about all kinds of books on business. People participating in biz.books.technical, however, would be specifically interested in technical business books.

Making Newsgroups Work for You

Deja News, at www.dejanews.com, is a useful site for uncovering discussion groups. The Deja News search engine is devoted entirely to newsgroups, and the site contains information and tools to help you find and use the groups that interest you. After you've visited a few and gotten a feel for how they work, you may find the best to suit your needs.

- By following groups in a certain field, you can gauge trends regarding particular issues, products, or services.
- You can join a group and get to know it, and then let group participants know that you exist. Offer information that they'll value.
- When you become comfortable in the group, ask questions, solicit ideas, and request feedback.

The owner of an executive recruiting firm needed fresh ideas to increase business, so he posted a message with a discussion group for advice. From the numerous replies that he received, he found one that he put into practice. He figures that piece of advice brought in several thousand dollars of new business.

The Internet in Perspective

How many times before going online do you take a deep breath and get yourself focused? For the rest of your days, the volume of information available via the Internet and all other sources is going to accelerate. Allow yourself to acknowledge that it will always be that way, and give yourself the opportunity to pause for a moment and relax.

The Least You Need to Know

- Much of the web is self-serving hype about itself. Skip that part.
- Before you wade through scads of new information, delete old and unnecessary documents and files from your computer.
- Use top search engines (such as www.hotbot.com, www.lycos.com, www.infoseek.com, and www.nlsearch.com) to aid you in your searches.
- Usenet newsgroups have grown into a global collection of thousands of discussion groups where people post messages and replies on specific topics of interest.
- Far more information exists than you have time to keep pace with. Focus on what's vital, and let the rest go.

Part 5

Thinking Your Way Out of Time Traps

Consider what you've been up to in the first four parts of this book: leaving the office on time, understanding why time flies, and recognizing that we are all in the same boat. Then you decided to be in charge of your time and identified priorities, chose goals, sought help, and got more sleep.

Taking the bull by the horns (when the bull was sleeping), you volunteered a little less, whipped your office and files into shape, and used time-enhancing tools profitably.

Then, by golly, you re-examined how and when you communicated with others, gathered information, and stayed connected, with an eye on being far more efficient and effective.

Maybe none of the individual changes was too huge, but you've been busy. By contrast, you're going to like the next three chapters—these tips and recommendations require less work! You'll learn tips for uncomplicating your life. You can simply think your way through some situations, and they'll come out all right!

Okay, enough presection banter.

Chapter 20

Up Your Mail IQ

In This Chapter

- The old ways to transfer information and messages will linger on
- How to save two-thirds of your correspondence time
- The postal service is still worthwhile on some types of deliveries
- Employing a 31-day tickler file for timed responses

Most messages that you receive—whether in the form of email, faxes, or memos—will require your response. The faster and easier you're able to respond, the better your day, week, career, and life will be—and the greater control you'll have over your time.

Options abound for speedily handling message replies. Let's check 'em out.

The Cornerstones of Speedy Correspondence

I'll bet that, too often, correspondence that requires a prompt response falls by the wayside; you have to handle too many other things. Here's a secret to managing your time: When a response doesn't require formal business protocol (that is, when you know the other party well), or when the item merits only brief regard, remember that there are many ways to handle it quickly:

1. Some people use preprinted, plain-paper messages, such as, "Excuse the informality, but I feel that it's more important to respond promptly than to offer a more formal reply that would take much longer."

2. Retain the return address information on the envelopes from the mail that you've received. Thereafter, you can use this as your address label back to them and avoid having to engage your printer, copier, or label paper. Clip such addresses, or tear them out with the edge of a ruler.

   When I receive a package from someone, I clip the label from the package and attach it to the documents that came inside with a big paper clip or removable tape. When I'm ready to make a response, an address label to the other party is already available. (This will save you lots of time. When other people respond too slowly, often it's because they haven't devised a speedy reply system.)

The Time Master Says

It's a good idea to order office supplies by fax so that you won't have to stay on the phone and spell things out to somebody who writes at a blinding snail's pace. You won't have to worry that the other party will record the information incorrectly. A third- or half-page fax/modem transmission can present everything needed to convey in seconds.

Reflect and Win

Make a point of providing return address labels to your correspondents. Weeks later, you may begin to notice that you receive replies more promptly and that the other party is using the address labels that you provided. This tells you that they've bought into your system.

3. Order a rubber stamp from your office supply store that says "Speed Reply." I have one myself; it's oversize and prints in bright red. When you receive a letter that merits a quick reply, stamp it with "Speed Reply," and offer your reply on the space at the bottom of the letter. Alternatively, you could print labels that say "Speed Reply" and simply affix them to the page.

   You have the option of faxing the letter (the fax machine treats deep, bold, red ink as black), or you could copy and mail the letter. Techniques such as these enable you to get a reply to the other party quickly and give you a record of the correspondence. Such a response is helpful to recipients as well; it presents their message with your reply. Think of how many times you've written to someone, the person responded, and you couldn't remember why you wrote in the first place.

4. If you're mailing a response, insert one of your own address labels to help the other party keep in touch with you. I enclose my address label with nearly all correspondence I mail. If you surmise that you'll write the other party again, include extra address labels.

   When you've successfully trained your correspondents to communicate adeptly with you, you both benefit.

5. Order a rubber stamp, or create a label that facilitates your fax replies as well. At the least, include your name, phone number, and fax number—your essential contact information. You could use the stamp on any correspondence that you receive; it avoids using up the recipient's fax paper.

   Often, when you receive faxes from a free-standing fax machine, the other party uses a full page to announce that a fax is coming and then uses another page for a six- or eight-line message. The whole communication could have taken one-third of a page. When you initiate a labeling system, you let other parties know that you respect their time and resources—and you keep your costs down.

   And if you're using a fax/modem, the same principles apply. Keep your fax identification information concise and near the top of the first page. Keep your message brief; it makes a response more likely and keeps your transmission costs down.

6. For longer or more involved hard-copy correspondence, use the back side of the page that you receive. Make a copy of the front and back for your own hard-copy files. Sometimes you can consolidate the correspondence that you've received and do the same for what you send. For example, if someone sends you a two-page letter but you need to respond to only one key paragraph, simply clip that paragraph, include it at the top of your transmission, and reply below.

7. Feel free to number the points in the correspondence that you've received and address each point in your reply. This cuts down on the time and energy that it takes to reply. Otherwise, you have to quote chapter and verse in your reply.

   When you number the points in the correspondence that you receive, you can usually address everything in a one-page response. Formal responses that take two or more pages require copyediting and tedious tweaking. They suck time out of your day and life faster than a vampire at a slumber party.

8. Seek creative ways to use your fax machine, fax/modem, printer, and copier in combination to generate fast, appropriate responses to messages that you receive; don't let correspondence pile up.

> **Pause!**
>
> Most professionals today indicate that they need more time to get their jobs done, often because of the correspondence that they have to handle. That kind of thinking keeps you enslaved to the clock. More time is not on its way, and it's not the solution if you aren't operating efficiently.

> **The Time Master Says**
>
> While business and organizational protocol may often call for formal responses, your mission (should you decide to accept it) is to offer efficient, informal responses as often as appropriate.

9. Design forms to handle routine communication. Better yet, see if someone in your office has already created one, or assign that task to someone. Many office-supply stores carry books with predesigned correspondence forms. They're worth the $10–$15; you're likely to save enough valuable time to pay for them the first day that you use them.

The Time Master Says

Any time that you want to respond to someone's message but you don't want a lengthy conversation, you can time your transmission to arrive when the person isn't in. For example, if you're on the West Coast and it's 4:30 P.M., it's a safe bet that if you respond to someone on the East Coast by fax or voice mail, that person won't be in at 7:30 P.M. to receive it. Your party will receive the message the next day, which is fine with you because you didn't want to talk to anyone anyway.

Working with the Postal Service

You already know about the express-mail services because you probably use them often: FedEx, DHL, Purolator, Roadway, Airborne, UPS, and others. But it still makes sense to use the U.S. Postal Service, despite all its troubles, if you know how to use the system effectively. Here is a brief, alphabetical description from the public information at the postal service regarding standard services. The following is a description of services to safeguard, protect, and document your packages. Because the postal service is always changing its rates, I've left these out. You can call your local postal office and get somebody to give you the current rates.

Reflect and Win

The U.S. Postal Service has more than 26,000 stations and more than 10,000 special Express mail collection boxes in which you can deposit your parcels. Your letter carrier can accept prepaid Express mail shipments when he delivers your mail. The postal service can supply you with mailing containers (envelopes, boxes, and tubes) and the necessary mailing labels free of charge.

♦ **Certified mail**—This type provides you with a mailing receipt. A record of delivery is maintained at your receiver's post office. For valuables and irreplaceable items, the postal service recommends using insured or registered mail (they're coming up in this list).

♦ **Express mail next-day service**—This is the postal service's fastest service. To use it, take your shipment to any designated Express mail post office (generally by 5:00 P.M.), or deposit it in an Express mail collection box. Your package will be delivered to the addressee by 3:00 P.M. the next day (weekends and holidays included).

◆ **First-class mail**—This service is designed for letters, postal cards, greeting cards, and personal notes, and for sending checks and money orders. You cannot insure ordinary first-class mail. However, additional services such as certificate of mailing, certified, return receipt, and restricted delivery can be purchased. If your first-class mail is not letter-size, make sure that it is marked first class, or use a large green-bordered envelope.

The Time Master Says

Bar-coding makes first-class mail even faster: Chances are, your word-processing system already contains a simple bar-coding procedure.

◆ **Bulk business or advertising mail**—This may be sent by anyone but is used most often by large mailers. This class includes printed material and merchandise weighing less than 16 ounces. Two rate structures exist for this class: single piece and bulk rate. Individuals may use this class of mail for mailing lightweight parcels, and insurance can be purchased to cover loss or damage of articles.

◆ **Forwarding mail**—When you move, fill out a change of address card in advance at your local post office. When possible, notify your post office at least one month before your move. First-class mail is forwarded at no charge. Magazines, newspapers, and other second-class mail are forwarded at no charge for a limited time.

◆ **Priority mail**—This is first-class mail (more than 12 ounces and up to 70 pounds, with size limitations) to be delivered allegedly within two business days, although reports indicate that delivery times vary widely.

Reflect and Win

Insurance can be purchased up to a sizable sum (in the thousands) for standard mail, a certain maximum on registered mail, and a far less maximum for third- and fourth-class mail. Insurance can also be purchased for merchandise mailed at the Priority Mail or first-class mail rates. With articles insured for more than a threshold amount, a receipt of delivery is signed by the recipient and filed at the delivering postal service. The amount of insurance coverage for loss is the actual value, minus any depreciation.

Insurance, however, won't protect you from all losses. No payments are made for sentimental losses or for any expenses incurred as a result of the loss.

◆ **Registered mail**—The postal service regards this as its most secure mailing option. It is designed to provide added protection for valuable and important mail. Postal insurance may be purchased for articles valued at more than $100, up to a maximum of $25,000. Return-receipt and restricted-delivery services are available for an additional fee. Registered articles are controlled from the point of mailing to delivery. First-class postage is required on registered mail.

♦ **Restricted delivery**—Except for Express mail service, you can request restricted delivery when purchasing return-receipt service. Restricted delivery means that delivery is made only to the addressee or to someone who is authorized in writing to receive mail for the addressee. Such mail addressed to officials of government agencies, legislative and judicial branches of federal and state governments, members of the diplomatic corps, minors, and individuals under guardianship, however, can be delivered to an agent without written authorization from the addressee.

♦ **Return receipt**—This is your proof of delivery; it's available on mail that you send by C.O.D. or Express mail, mail insured for more than $25, or mail that you registered or certified. The return receipt shows who signed for the item and the date that it was delivered. For an additional fee, you can get an exact address of delivery or request restricted-delivery service.

♦ **Special delivery**—You can buy special-delivery service on all classes of mail except bulk third-class mail. Delivery happens even on Sundays and holidays, during hours that extend beyond the hours for the delivery of ordinary mail. This service is available to all customers served by city carriers and to other customers within a 1-mile radius of the delivery postal office. Note that special delivery may be handled by your regular carrier if it's available before the carrier departs for morning deliveries.

A System of Timely Responses

Chapter 14, "Becoming a Filing Wizard," discusses setting up a file for each month and also creating a 31-day rotating tickler file. These files offer a home for things that you don't need to deal with immediately or that are best dealt with at some future time (you know, like the turn of the twenty-second century!). To handle mail quickly, tickler files are just what the time-saving doctor ordered.

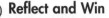

Reflect and Win

The tickler file is your answer anytime you have hard-copy correspondence that you need to address but that is best sent at another time.

Suppose that you receive correspondence that doesn't have to be answered now. What are you going to do? Let it sit in the black hole known as your inbox? Park it some place on your desk that is equally remote to a black hole? Create some new file for it that you never find again? All these temporary solutions are less than desirable.

While it may make sense to handle the correspondence now if it needn't be transmitted until later, do what you have to do with it and then park it in your tickler file.

For example, if you receive something on the 5th that need not be mailed until the 15th (to reach the other party by the 19th), take care of it today, while it's hot, fresh, and right in front of you. Seal it, stamp it, and put it in your tickler file for the 15th.

The electronic version of this technique is to type your email message and then enter the date and time that you want it submitted, or put it the Deferred mailbox for sending when you choose.

You may recall that a tickler file is an ideal way to organize bills without paying them too early (which can cost you if you have an interest-bearing checking account) and avoiding penalties for paying too late.

Here are some other ways to use your tickler file for timed responses that save you time and help put you on top of things:

- Stash tickets to forthcoming events in the appropriate tickler-file date.
- Store coupons, discounts, and promotional items until you're ready to use them.
- Park items that you want to read on your next plane trip in the tickler file for the day before your trip.
- Find temporary locations for notes, outlines, or other documents that you'll want to have on hand when someone visits your office.
- Do the same for forthcoming group, department, or company meetings.
- Place any mail that you receive but choose not to open now in your tickler file; choose a date that seems more appropriate for you.
- When you're waiting for someone's response, file a copy of your transmission in your tickler file or in a file labeled Awaiting Response.

The Least You Need to Know

- Temporarily put this book aside and order a long-life stamper that reads "Speed Reply" from an office supply store, or create labels using your PC and printer. Start using your speed-reply message on correspondence right away.
- Check out submitting legal contracts via fax. You can also become adept at negotiating via fax.
- Depending on what you want to send and to whom, the U.S. Postal System (for all its shortcomings) has a variety of services that may provide what you need.
- Set up a 31-day rotating tickler file system so that when you have correspondence to handle but prefer to send it later, you have a convenient place to park it.

21

Decide or Let It Ride

In This Chapter

- ◆ The growing number of choices and resulting decisions you'll face
- ◆ When it makes sense to refrain from making a decision
- ◆ More data can confound your ability to decide
- ◆ Using the power of your intuitive abilities

In a world of nearly seven billion people, volumes of information are being generated and sped your way by worldwide media and print coverage. The more information you're exposed to, the more choices you face and the greater the unrelenting pressure is on you to choose. Any way you cut it, you're confronted by too many decisions—at work, at home, on the weekend, while traveling, when you wake, when you retire at night, when you're on vacation, and when you're with either friends or enemies.

In this chapter we'll focus on how to make effective choices in a sea of too much information: welcome news on how to choose!

Choices (and Decisions) on the Rise

It's not hard to understand why you face too much information. Society spews it in abundance. When you go to the drug store to buy something as inconsequential as shampoo or skincare lotion, beware. More than 1,200 varieties of shampoo and more than 2,000 skincare products are on the market. Choices abound in other arenas as well. More than 11,000 popular videos are available for viewing (more than 78,000, if you include management training, aerobic fitness, and how-to's). Three thousand books are published in the United States each week—more than six hundred a day. Ten times as many radio stations exist today than when television was first introduced. If these examples don't indicate "choice overload," I don't know what does.

Americans were exposed to six times as many advertising messages in 1991 compared to 1971, and far more today than in 1991. The level of bombardment has passed the point at which anyone can absorb even a small fraction of what he is exposed to. In his 1969 book *Future Shock*, Alvin Toffler said that in the future, too many choices will compete for your time and attention. He was right. Manufacturers engage in mass-customization to offer you products with whatever bells and whistles you want (and ads that make you want them).

Theoretically, with the perfect information, after having whittled down your search to the essence of your needs, you could purchase any product you seek. There's only one problem: You hardly ever receive even semiperfect information (at least, in this life). So, you're forever besieged by too much information—much of it conflicting—and it impedes your ability to choose. To win back more of your time, identify the big decisions and make them quickly. Start by determining which decisions are worth making and which are worth forsaking.

Worth Making, Not Forsaking

Think back to Chapters 7, "What Matters Most to You?" and 8, "Sustaining Your Priorities for Fun and Profit"; review the discussion on establishing priorities and goals. What you establish as important in your life is immediately linked to decisions that are worth making.

When something will have a significant impact in the area of one of your life's priorities, that's a decision worth making. Many people mix decisions worth making with those worth forsaking, treat them almost equally, and wonder where the time went.

If your boss requests that you make a decision, the situation is clear-cut. Nevertheless, decisions worth making are often conditional. If you're single and trying to choose between two likely mates, your decision will affect the quality of your life in the foreseeable future—and perhaps the rest of your life. The following are examples of decisions worth making:

- The choice of a spouse
- The choice of a home
- Major work decisions that your organization requests of you

- Where you'll live
- With whom you'll associate
- What course of study you'll pursue
- Whether you wish to climb to the top of your organization or profession

Decisions worth making, while often conditional, are not always apparent. Consider the following five issues. Are they decisions worth spending any time on? It all depends. In the list that follows, mentally circle the decisions that you believe are worth making:

- The color of the next toothbrush you buy
- The next movie you see
- Whether to attend the next PTA meeting
- Whether to take your car in for a tune-up tomorrow
- What to eat for breakfast

Have you finished circling the items? Good. So what are the right answers? As you may have guessed, there are no right answers, per se.

Worth Forsaking, Not Worth Making

Decisions worth forsaking are plentiful. When you're faced with too many decisions anyway, your reflex action is likely to be an attempt to grapple with all decisions.

1. **The color of the next toothbrush**—For most people, this is a decision worth forsaking; it can't be that important. When might it be? If the decor of your home and bathroom is of utmost importance to you (don't laugh—it is for some people), then this becomes a decision worth making.

2. **The next movie you see**—It's likely that you go to only movies that you think you'll enjoy; when you see one that you don't like, it is a mistake, but the earth doesn't tremble. If you consider movies as just a way to pass the time, then which one you see is not of paramount importance.

   When would it be? If improving the cultural component of your life is among your priorities, and the movie is of the shoot-'em-up variety, your decision is clear: Don't go see it. Of the hundreds of movies that you've seen in your life, how many have truly had a significant impact on your behavior and activities? Few, if any. Seeing *Saving Private Ryan* may heighten your sensitivity to vital historical issues, but, more often than not, choosing a movie is no big deal.

3. **Going to the next PTA meeting**—Your child's education or the betterment of your community is likely a high priority, so you would attend. If your child is doing

extremely well in school, or if you're pleased about the school system in general, you could skip one meeting—or even a run of them.

4. **Putting your car in the shop tomorrow**—Has your car been running poorly lately? What is the cost of you being tied up on the highway and not getting into work on time, and causing 10,000 people to snarl at you? Can you bring work with you to the repair shop, or can the shop give you a ride back to work quickly after your arrival? Is preventive maintenance part of your overall plan to be ready and stay on top of things? The more people take care of their automobiles in advance of any failure of performance, the fewer breakdowns there are on the highway—which good is for everyone.

5. **What to eat for breakfast**—If you're already 32 pounds above your ideal weight and have no resolve of getting back into shape, what you eat for breakfast tomorrow morning matters less than the longer-term health concerns you're facing. Go ahead and have that (one) honey-glazed doughnut with your coffee. If becoming the first octogenarian to visit the moon is a priority for you, then, once again, the choice is clear: Go healthy instead.

What's a *low-level decision?* When a coworker asks you where you want to go to lunch today, your response will most appropriately be, "You decide." Of the couple thousand times you've been to lunch, can you recall any significant impact related to your decision on where you went? Okay, so one day you met somebody you started dating. Another time, you learned something new. In general, there hasn't been much impact. Other examples of decisions worth forsaking include these:

◆ The park where you'll take your children to play—let them decide

◆ Whether to catch the news at 10 P.M.

◆ Whether to get Del Monte or Bird's Eye frozen vegetables

◆ Whether to visit Colorado for five days or six

Coming to Terms

A **low-level decision** is one with few or no significant consequences, whatever decision you make. Don't waste time agonizing over low-level decisions—you have better things to do with your time.

You may be asking if there is any perceptible benefit to making fewer choices per day. Yes! When you go to a dinner party and the host has already assigned seating to the guests, it's an act of kindness. It reduces anxiety about who'll be in the chair beside you. This is a time-honored tradition from Walnut Creek, California, to the White House.

Action Is Invigorating

If you frequently find yourself overanalyzing situations , relent. You've been trained from birth to collect all the data, statistics, articles, reports, and information you could lay your hands on before making a decision that involves the outlay of any sizable sum.

When each individual in two groups of executives had to make a large purchase decision for their respective companies, the first group was armed with information—reports, data, statistics, and all that jazz. Understandably, each executive used all the information to make the purchase decision.

The second group consisted of individuals who had no such data or statistics. They used instinct, or intuition, or whatever you want to call it. Weeks after the purchases had been made and each executive got to see the results, which group do you expect was happier with its decision? (Well, okay, I did load the question a little to favor the second group.)

Honestly, you are more likely to have chosen the group that had the data and statistics. If given a chance to be in one group or the other, you would have chosen to be in that well-informed group, wouldn't you? How could the second group possibly be happier with its results? If you're 30 or 40 or 50 years old, everything that you've learned in your life up to now is summoned when you make a decision. There's far more to instinct or intuition than is generally acknowledged.

Reflect and Win

Much of the data that you collect may be redundant, reaffirming what you already know. Too often, you may unconsciously be collecting what you already know or believe, without seeing the data objectively.

Traps Lie in Waiting

There are also inherent traps in collecting more data on the path to making a decision. The more data you collect, the likelier it is that you'll get conflicting answers.

Sometimes the data that you collect is nothing more than a crutch. Or sometimes its only purpose is to cover your derriere (if the decision turns out unfavorably), by having an authority to cite: "It says right here blah, blah, blah."

Sometimes the data that you collect is a substitute for taking action. Studying a decision is a classic way to delay making it. (The government has done it for years.) In all cases, whatever data or information you collect has to be applied.

More data is not always the answer, but what's the alternative? I'll deal with intuition in a moment. For now, here are some techniques for making big decisions in record time—and getting the answers that you want with less effort:

1. **Three calls away from any expert**—If you can identify the single best person to call to start off your information search, you can get your answer within two more calls. Who's the first person to call? It could be your municipal or college library, an official of an industry or professional association, or an information service firm (such as market researchers). Perhaps you can find an expert within the government or an editor at *Consumer Reports.*

2. **Finding the trailblazer**—Have others already made a decision like this? If so, and if their circumstances are somewhat similar to yours, it would behoove you to learn what they have discovered. It pays to network with people in your field. Later you can tap them for their experiences.

3. **Consensus building**—Can you assemble a group, hash it out, and base your decision on the consensus reached? In many instances, this works fine. After all, you relied on the power of the group; if your decision crashes and burns, you can always point the finger at them (just kidding!).

4. **The answer will simply emerge**—This alleviates a lot of decisions. Often, as circumstances unfold, the decision that makes the most sense becomes apparent. If you suspect that this might be the case, sit back and let time take its course. The answer may become abundantly clear.

Listen to Your Inner Voice

Interested in the fastest way to make decisions? This involves using your instincts or intuition. You're already pretty good at this; you got this far in life and, hey, it ain't so bad. Write down your intuitive choice before making any final decision. Then, when enough time has passed to see the results of a more analytical decision, write them down and compare them to the results of your intuitive choice. As time passes, you'll begin to notice how frequently your intuitive choices were wise ones, and you'll find yourself trusting your hunches more easily and more often.

The Time Master Says

When you get adept at trusting your intuition, you can bypass many reams of data and information that previously impeded your ability to choose. You can call upon your still, quiet, and faithful internal guidance system.

How did you select your dentist? Did you open up the phone book and get the names of the 10–12 dentists nearest you, then call each of them, decide (based on the call) to visit 5 to 7, visit their offices, and grill each one on billing procedures, background, expertise, competency of their staff, office hours, prices, and overall philosophy? Then did you whittle down the list to maybe two or three, call them back or visit on another occasion, and do some background checking for reputation, longevity in the community, and professional standing? Then, and only then, did you decide on dentist A?

Or, did you choose dentist B on the basis of whom your parents or friends see, where some referral service sent you, or simply the clever ad that you saw in the phone book?

You probably used the latter method, picking a dentist by hook or by crook—and if that one didn't work out, you switched. In short, you used a combination of references and intuitive processes to come up with your dentist.

Why, then, do you overcomplicate so many decisions at work and in the rest of your life? When you base a choice on intuition, every cell in your body and every shred of intelligence that you've ever accumulated are brought to bear. There's a lot going on behind the solutions that you make.

New information is only going to hit you faster and faster as your life proceeds. You'll be able to absorb and use only a fraction of what you're exposed to. There's no time for exhaustive research on every consumer product that you buy (ever try counting how many different ones you use?). Trust your instincts.

> **Reflect and Win**
>
> Pay attention to your small voice, you know—the little munchkin behind the scenes of everything that goes on all day. That's your intuition talking, and it's there to support you if you listen to it.

Suppose, on the other hand, that you're considering whether to move to town A or town B. What factors would you logically consider? Try these out:

- Housing prices
- Taxes and demographics
- Schools
- Crime
- Community groups
- Family and friends
- Lakes, streams, and beaches
- Trails and mountains
- The business community
- Population density
- Education levels
- Nearby colleges
- Churches, synagogues, and mosques
- Road systems
- Major highway access
- Shopping
- Traffic patterns
- Deviant groups

You guessed it: There are dozens of factors that you could analyze and compare. In the end, your decision would probably be based on some combination of data (though not too much) and intuition (probably a lot).

Procrastination Is a Temptress

When faced with too many decisions, your natural inclination may be to procrastinate— or perhaps you fear making a mistake. Don't beat yourself up (that can be a way to delay action further); lots of people face this problem. Decisions that would normally roll off your back become more involved when there's too much on your plate—and chances are, there's too much on your plate. Here's a list of ways to break through the procrastination that stymies your decision-making process:

- **Face procrastination head-on.** What is blocking you? What is the real reason you don't want to choose? Write it down or record it on cassette. This exercise alone may dislodge something and help you decide.

- **Choose to easily begin.** Make a positive affirmation of yourself: "I can easily make this decision." This affirmation has power and is often enough.

- **Find the easy point.** Ask yourself, "What are three to five things I could do to progress toward the final decision without actually tackling it head-on?" Then initiate these "easy entry" activities. Often, they're enough to get you fully involved.

- **Set up your desk for a decision.** Set up your desk or office to enable you to focus on the decision at hand; ignore other (less important) matters. This might involve neatly arranging papers, file folders, reports, and other items. Working at a clear desk leaves only the issue at hand in front of you.

Most of your decisions will have only a minimal impact on your life; don't let the fear of being wrong shackle you unduly.

Decisions Disguised as Problems

Quite a few decisions that you have to make are based on problems. Modern management theory holds that problems can be approached productively when you see them as opportunities or challenges. In *The Path of Least Resistance*, Robert Fritz suggests that you view problems as your best friends. It often works!

How does facing a problem help you get to a higher ground? This view of problem solving works best when you're dealing with minor issues, not extremes—such as the death of a loved one. If the decision that you face is a disguised problem, pretend it's your best friend or a teacher with wisdom to impart. You may dislodge something in your decision-making process and proceed more easily.

Reflect and Win

If you come up with a decision that both addresses the immediate situation and provides long-term benefits, then you've got something.

Biographers have noted that Ben Franklin listed the pluses and minuses of one path versus another when faced with big decisions. Sometimes he gave weight to them; sometimes he didn't. While this is a basic approach to making decisions, listing your potential options on paper still beats merely weighing them in your mind; you can keep better track of them this way.

In *Feel the Fear and Do It Anyway*, Dr. Susan Jeffers suggests that when you encounter a decision that represents a hurdle or a roadblock, you need to let yourself feel all the emotions that arise. Are you uneasy? Quivering? Lightheaded? Is your stomach upset, are you trembling, or do you feel fearful? When you're honest with yourself about how you feel (namely, scared), initiate your decision anyway, Jeffers says. Often you're able to break through your fear and overcome the obstacle that loomed so large when you weren't being honest with yourself. (Hmm, sounds like it's worth a try.)

Shop and Compare

When you need to make a purchase decision, sometimes all you need is a good set of questions to ask. Without further ado, here's a checklist of questions for making sound purchase decisions more quickly:

- ◆ Are there quantity discounts or special terms?
- ◆ Are there corporate, government, association, or educators' discounts?
- ◆ Do they give weekly, monthly, quarterly, or seasonal discounts?
- ◆ Do they give off-peak discounts or odd-lot discounts?
- ◆ Do they offer a guaranteed lowest price?
- ◆ Do they accept major credit cards?
- ◆ Do they accept orders by fax? By email?
- ◆ Do they offer a money-back guarantee or some other guarantee?
- ◆ Do they have a toll-free ordering line and customer service line?
- ◆ Do they guarantee the shipping date? How do they ship?
- ◆ Do they offer free delivery? Free installation?
- ◆ Will they keep your name off their mailing list (unless you want to keep up with special sales)?
- ◆ Do they intend to sell, rent, or otherwise transfer your name and ordering information to others?
- ◆ Are their shipments insured?
- ◆ Are there shipping and handling charges? Are their prices guaranteed? Is there tax?
- ◆ Are there any other charges?
- ◆ Do they have free samples?
- ◆ Are authorized dealer/repair services in your area?

- Are references or referral letters available?
- Are there satisfied customers in your area?
- How long have they been in business?
- By whom are they owned?
- How long for delivery?
- Is gift-wrapping available?
- Does the product come with a warranty?

The Least You Need to Know

- As you age, you'll face more decisions—not fewer. Focus on decisions that advance your priorities and support your goals.
- Avoid making low-level decisions whenever possible.
- More data is not always the answer. Trust your instincts more often; they are there to serve you.
- If the decision represents a problem, see it as a friend and messenger. With that perspective, ask what the problem is helping you to do or overcome.
- Using a prepared checklist can enhance a purchasing decision. Feel free to copy the one given here.

22

Concentration: A Largely Lost Art

In This Chapter

- ◆ The fallacy of doing several things at once to "save" time
- ◆ The wisdom of doing one thing at a time and doing it well
- ◆ Your own interruption-management system

A study by Pitney Bowes reveals that 40 percent of workers are interrupted six or more times an hour by various messages, while another 37 percent are interrupted three to five times an hour. The study also observed that "the seemingly endless growth in communications is taking its toll."

In a society in which others seem hell-bent on providing an endless round of distractions, if you can continually hone and refine your powers of concentration, all other things being equal, you'll do a better job and have more time at the end of the day.

There is no greater efficiency than focusing on the task at hand, giving it your full concentration. As stated in Chapter 7, "What Matters Most to You?" the importance of concentration and focus cannot be understated. A friend of mine has a saying that is appropriate here: "Focus beats brilliance every time."

Multitasking Is Risky Business

People try to do too much at one time. Whether they're at home, at work, or even driving in their cars, too many people resort to multitasking too often.

Does multitasking enable people to accomplish more? Research shows that the opposite may be true! A study published by *American Psychological Association's Journal of Experimental Psychology: Human Perception and Performance*, conducted by researchers Joshua Rubinstein, Ph.D.; David Meyer, Ph.D.; and Jeffrey Evans, Ph.D., found that the effects of multitasking can actually be counterproductive.

Coming to Terms

Time cost, or potential efficiency cost, is the time that you lose by switching from one task to another.

"People in a work setting, who are banging away on word processors at the same time they have to answer phones and talk to their coworkers or bosses—they're doing switches all the time," says Meyer. Not being able to concentrate for, say, tens of minutes at a time may mean that it's costing a company as much as 20 to 40 percent of its income. The researchers refer to this cost as *time cost*.

"In effect," Meyer says, "you've got writer's block briefly, as you go from one task to another. You've got to …

1. Make a decision to switch tasks,

2. Actually make the switch, and then,

3. Get warmed back up on what you were doing."

Detrimental in Many Venues

The effects of multitasking may be detrimental to more than just your job. You may be putting yourself—and others—in danger by performing too many tasks at once.

Pause!

Talking on a cell phone while driving, for instance, may seem safe enough, but you may not realize how much attention speaking on the phone requires.

For many years, I've been an avid reader of *Men's Health*, and I greatly look forward to each new issue. One article titled "Dining A La Cart" discussed clever ways to eat while driving. It was among the poorest ideas they've presented. As more "technology" finds its way into vehicles, the prospects for human tragedy increase. Eating in the car is equally dangerous; such articles that even hint at how to do so effectively and efficiently are a disservice to motorists and pedestrians everywhere.

Inner Eyes and Ears

Meyer also has this to say about driving while cell phoning:

> A lot of folks think, "Well, cell phoning while driving is really no big deal and I can get away with it." Even if you have a cell phone that's not held by hand and can be dialed by voice, you still have a really big conflict because when you're driving you need to be looking at various different places, you need to be reading signs, you need to be talking to yourself about those [things] in order to—through your mental speech—make decisions about where to go with your car. And there's no way to do that while on the cell phone because you have to use your "inner ears" and "inner speech" and even your "inner eyes" to imagine what the person on the phone is talking about.

Some states, New York, for one, have made it illegal to talk on cell phones while driving. Headsets or hands-free devices still are okay, for now.

The same study also shows that the costs of multitasking increase with more difficult tasks. "A very simple conversation on the phone while driving a car—maybe 'Honey, please pick up some bread on the way home'—might not draw too much concentration," Rubinstein says. "But if the conversation becomes difficult or emotionally charged or mentally taxing—like 'Honey, the house is burning down, what should I do?'—it draws more attention and more mental resources away from your primary task, which is driving the car: You're more likely to have an accident."

> **Pause!**
>
> Even children are using the inefficient process of multitasking, and its effects are the same. Kids are trying to do too many things while they do their homework, according to researcher Joshua Rubinstein Ph.D., and it's decreasing the quality of their work.

Curbing the Urge

As people become more available by phone, email, and other means of communication, they feel as if they're always on call, a situation that can become mentally exhausting. As such, I'm willing to bet that sometime in the last 48 hours, if not the last 4 hours, you actually engaged in some form of multitasking yourself—doing two or more things at the same time.

> **Reflect and Win**
>
> Computers are equipped to handle more than one task at a time. Humans, however, are not computers, no matter what analogies or metaphors you may have heard.

> CAUTION
>
> ### Pause!
>
> At the workplace and at home, attempting to multitask ensures that you'll miss your day, your week, and ultimately your life. I know people who are 40 years old who can't remember where their 30s went, and people who are 50 who can't remember where their 40s went.

> ### Reflect and Win
>
> When you undertake original or creative thinking—work with numbers, charts, or graphs, or write, copy-edit, or proofread—put aside all other tasks until you've finished. Diverting your attention results in less than your best effort; often it leads to costly errors.

It's likely that you've been working on a personal computer recently and that, while you were running the word-processing software, you may have been engaging the printer, a pop-up spreadsheet, and a calendar as well. You may have been on the phone to boot.

It's too easy to fall into a familiar trap: "So much is expected of me that I have to double and triple my activities."

Nearly every message in society says that it's okay—or necessary—to double or triple the number of activities that you perform at once. You see advertisements of people talking on the phone while they watch television, or eating while they read.

Bob W., age 41, works for a large brokerage firm in the International Square building in Washington, D.C. He is friendly, successful, and always in a rush. He talks fast, moves fast, eats fast, and never lets up. Bob is hooked on multitasking. Many executives and career-climbers suffer from a misdirected sense of urgency stemming from far too many tasks and responsibilities. Certainly, it's appropriate to work more quickly than normal at certain times. It's a problem, however, when it becomes a standard operating procedure.

Twice as Much

The psychic toll that you place on yourself in attempting multitasking (or in doing one stressful job for too long) can be harmful. Your brain can become overtaxed! Workers on the job ingest an estimated aggregate of 15 tons of aspirin daily just in the United States. Could multitasking be a contributing factor?

Job-related stress accounts for most of the absenteeism and illness that the typical professional today experiences. At least one in four professionals contends with anxiety-related illness. The Wellness Council of America reports that medical benefits per employee in 1992 averaged about $4,000 but by 2000 had risen alarmingly to $12,000. A three-time increase within a decade is a *phenomenal* rise. Another increase like that would put many companies out of business.

Consider air-traffic controllers who have been on duty too long, had too many planes landing at a given time, and are responsible for safekeeping hundreds by making the right decisions with split-second timing. It's no wonder that this is a high-stress, high-burnout position, one that professionals usually abandon at a young age.

Be Effective, Never Mind Busy

Researchers at the Medical College of Wisconsin have discovered that if you perform a task as simple as tapping your foot, you activate the primary motor cortex, a section of your brain. If your task is more involved, if it includes planning to tap your foot to a sequence (such as one-two, one-two-three, one-two, one-two-three), then two secondary motor areas in the front of the cortex are engaged. You are drawing upon more of your brain's functioning capacity.

Don't worry, your brain can handle it. The point is that when you engage in multitasking—such as attempting to watch TV while eating, or doodling while you talk on the telephone—your brain functioning changes to incorporate the extra activities.

If you want to do the best at whatever you're doing, allow your brain to concentrate on one activity—focus on one thing at a time. If it's a complex task, consider whether you're working on several parts of the same task or two different tasks. It sounds simple enough, but this advice contradicts social and cultural messages that imply that doing many things at once leads to greater efficiency.

> **Pause!**
>
> Research suggests that when you do two things at once, it's probably symptomatic of an ability (and burden) shared by the whole human species. That doesn't necessarily make it effective. The false economy of attempting to do two things at once is ingrained in a culture that rewards the workaholic, the 16-hour-a-day entrepreneur, the supermom, and the hyperenergetic student.

> **Reflect and Win**
>
> "Men give me some credit for genius. All the genius I have lies in this: When I have a subject at hand, I study it profoundly. Day and night it is before me. I explore it in all its bearings. My mind becomes pervaded with it. Then the effort which I have made is what people are pleased to call the fruit of genius. It is instead the fruit of labor and thought."
>
> —Alexander Hamilton

A One-Minute Measure

I sometimes conduct a brief exercise with my audiences when speaking at conventions and executive retreats. I ask audience members to take out their watches and do nothing but stare at them for a solid minute. Few can do it! In this society, you're fed a message that emphasizes the importance of motion and activity. Merely reading, thinking, or reflecting doesn't look busy enough.

When Doing Nothing Pays Off

Has the following happened to you? Somebody walks by your desk and, horror of horrors, you're reading! Maybe you get a funny look or guilty feelings because you're not "in motion." Yet studies show that informed people in executive positions read two to four hours each day. So, to be as productive as you need to be, you often act in ways that run counter to what society tells you is "productive activity."

To reach your full potential, you've got to break out of the mind-set imposed by others. Sometimes the best way to be productive is to sit at your desk doing nothing—at least, nothing that looks like anything to people walking by. Reading or looking out the window in contemplation could be the single most important and productive thing you do in a day.

Reflect and Win

Too often, you probably invest your time in tasks before you reflect on them.

What happens when you jump between different projects? It may feel "dynamic"—after all, you're exerting lots of energy. Yet there's a loss of productivity. You and a friend can test this easily at your desk or table.

Try This at Home

Decide on any three minor tasks in which the two of you can engage simultaneously. One task could be stacking pennies, another could be drawing 15 stars on a blank sheet of paper, and a third could be linking paper clips. You each have the same number of items.

You and your friend start these tasks at the same time. You stack a few pennies at a time, make a few stars on a blank piece of paper, and link some paper clips, indiscriminately alternating between the three tasks. Meanwhile, on the other side of the table, your friend stacks an equal number of pennies to completion until there are no more. Then (s)he turns to making stars on a page and reaches 15. Finally comes linking the paper clips until they're all linked.

Who do you think will finish faster and easier, and be in better shape mentally and emotionally? I'll bet on your friend who focused on the task at hand, took it to completion, then turned to the next one while you (ha, ha, ha) were bouncing back and forth between activities. You may have been more prone to errors, such as knocking over one of your stacks of pennies.

Even if you were quite an adept task-juggler, you wouldn't be able to keep pace, or the quality of your work would not be as good. Perhaps your paper clips would become tangled, or your 15 stars would lack artistic merit.

Multiply the effect of this test by how often you flip-flop between activities in a day or year, and it's easy to understand why you're losing productivity. Continually switching from task to task is not as productive as staying on one job until completion.

Dare to Focus

For today, give yourself the benefit of working on one thing at a time. You may have to switch gears when the boss comes in, when that important phone call comes through, or if you receive a fax that has to be acted on right away. When you switch gears, switch them entirely: Give your complete and undivided attention to the pressing issue at hand. Try it out. You might find that this is a happier, more effective way to work.

If you notice yourself falling into behavior patterns that resemble computerized multitasking, try these solutions:

- Take a 15-minute break once during the morning and once in the afternoon. That also means: Don't eat at your desk. Get away so that you can recharge your battery.

- Hold regular meetings with your team to discuss how everyone can be more efficient—without multitasking. Focus on the big picture of what you're all trying to accomplish. Often new solutions to old problems will emerge, and activities that seem urgent can be viewed from a broader prospective.

- For a more human workplace, furnish your office with plants, pictures, art, or decorations that inspire creativity.

Reflect and Win

The best way to handle several projects is to begin working on the most important one until its completion and then go on to the next project, and then the next, until you are finished.

When you're feeling overwhelmed or time-stressed, ask yourself who created this situation. Often you'll discover that you did. Of course, sometimes the boss lays a bombshell on your desk and you're asked to do more than usual. It's still your responsibility to head off this threat. Acquire resources that will equip you to handle tasks that come your way, whether it's learning new software, learning a new language, or acquiring more training.

Distraction Can Be Handled

In 1990, author Alvin Toffler told me that the workplace is a terrible location for getting things done these days. With the distractions in your office, it's often better to work at the library, in the conference room, or on a park bench. This is especially true when you're doing conceptual or breakthrough thinking, when you need to have quiet space.

I was once consulting for a supervisor in Minnesota with six employees; he wanted to use his time more efficiently. He said that his employees came to him with questions every couple of hours. That seemed harmless enough, but look at how it built up: If an employee asked a question every two hours, the supervisor received four from that person each day.

With six employees, that meant 24 questions a day, or 120 interruptions each week, resulting in disruptions of the manager's work three times each hour in a 40-hour week! I devised a system to help him cope with the interruptions and regain control of his time; I called it the "J-4 System." The J was for Jeff. You can use your own initial. The system works much the same way you fend off too many beeper messages (see Chapter 16, "Staying in Touch Too Much").

I had the supervisor put the questions into four categories of manageability. The first distraction, J-1, was already answered in print and did not need a personal reply (it was in the company policy manual). The supervisor was then able to tell his employees, "Please don't bother me with J-1 distractions."

The second distraction, J-2, was a question that a peer or bookkeeper could answer; the supervisor did not need to be bothered with this type of question either.

J-3s needed only a short answer, usually a yes or no. Such questions required interaction with the supervisor, but not much—a quick phone call or intercom buzz.

The final category, J-4 distractions, required the supervisor's response.

How many questions were at the J-4 level of importance? Even assuming that each person asked two J-4 questions per day—60 interruptions each week—this would cut the number of interruptions in half! Almost immediately, the supervisor was able to better use his time and reduce his level of stress.

With this system, you'll gain greater control over your work, find more time, and feel more relaxed. You'll even be able to do breakthrough creative thinking at your own desk.

You're likely to face more distractions in the future, not fewer. To regain control over your life, learn to cope with distractions in new ways.

Anxiety Tugs

I once heard anxiety defined as "the attempted unification of opposing forces." What majesty—this says it all! Anytime you're anxious, stop and figure out what opposing forces you're attempting to unite. Are you working on some low-level task when there's something far more important for you to give your attention to? You feel anxious. Your intuitive alarm system is ringing.

Your anxiety stems from your attempt to work on a low-level project (force number 1) when you know that there's something else more appropriate for you to be working on (force number 2).

If you've been multitasking for a long time and you suddenly attempt to switch to working on one thing at a time, guess what happens? You may feel a sudden increase in anxiety. It's like trying to kick an addiction to a chemical stimulant. The natural inclination is to get back into the addiction. So it is with multitasking.

It's important, therefore, to understand that at first it may feel awkward to not multi-task. Below is a system for overcoming the feelings of uneasiness.

Reflect and Win

Classify the types of interruptions that you receive; then you can cut them down and cope with them better.

Let's Play Concentration

To become a master of doing one thing at a time, pick an activity you enjoy, where there's a high probability that you can engage in it without doing anything else. It might be driving your car with the radio off, reading in your favorite armchair without snacking, or listening to music instead of banishing it to the background.

- ◆ Start with small segments. If you're reading in your favorite armchair, promise yourself that you'll go 10 minutes without any munchies the first night. The second night, go 15, and so forth. You may soon be able to read for an hour without having to resort to snacks.

- ◆ If you're involved in conceptual or breakthrough thinking, or creative problem solving, find as quiet and comfortable a place as possible.

- ◆ If you're confronted by many tasks competing for your attention, identify the one that's most important to tackle, and stay with it until completion (or for as long as you can). If you're temporarily pulled away by something else, return to the important task at hand; again, stay with it to completion or for as long as you can.

Suppose that it's your job to handle a multiplicity of items competing for your attention. Practice giving short bursts of full attention to the task at hand before turning to the next thing demanding your attention.

Look at an airline reservation attendant in the middle of a high-pressure situation. The approach is one person-and-ticket situation at a time; often the attendant doesn't even look up from the computer monitor. The same principle holds for a good bank teller, a good bus driver, or a construction worker five stories above the ground.

Here are some more tips to stay focused on the task at hand:

♦ Initiate personal balancing techniques: Take deep breaths, stare out the window, see yourself tackling the situation easily. Or, try closing your eyes for a few seconds before confronting the task again. (More on this in the forthcoming chapters.)

♦ Practice using the interruption-management system discussed earlier in this chapter.

♦ Observe the people in your organization who concentrate well. What do they do that's different from what everybody else does? Talk to them; learn from them.

♦ If it's necessary, bring earplugs to work. Use a sound screen, if it helps. (See Chapter 10, "Becoming a Snooze-Savvy Sleeper.")

♦ Let others in on your quest to increase your powers of concentration. Mutual reinforcement can help.

Some Combos Work

For the most part, leave the multitasking to the computers. However, there are a few times when it's perfectly permissible to do more than one thing at a time—and most of these occur away from work. Obviously, at dinner with a friend or a loved one, you'll be talking and eating simultaneously, but that can be seen as one event (in some parts of the South, they call it "visiting," and it claims a person's whole attention).

Generally, it's okay to drive and listen to the radio, cassettes, or CDs. The exception is when the decibel level is so high that your concentration is impaired (or you don't hear that ambulance).

Exercising with a Walkman isn't terrible, but it's not the greatest. At my health club recently, I was bemused to see a lady who was on the stair-climber with a Walkman, and she then opened a book and started to read. I almost asked if she wanted to chew some gum, to see whether she could do four things at once.

Physical exercise is ideally its own reward. Still, I know many people who use workout exercise tapes or get on a stationary bike while watching television. It seems to work well for them, so there's probably no real harm.

Other activities in which it's okay to double up include the following: walking and talking with a friend, taking notes as you listen to a lecture, and talking to your lover while you're having sex (depending on your partner, this can enhance the experience).

The Least You Need to Know

- ◆ The more often you can get into the habit of doing one thing at a time, the better you'll do.
- ◆ Practice doing one thing at a time. Promise yourself that you'll go for 10 minutes on a task the first day, 15 the second, and so forth.
- ◆ Devise an interruption management system so that you and your staff can remain productive.
- ◆ Most of the areas in which it's okay to double up on activities are outside the work-place.
- ◆ In general, leave multitasking to computers.

Chapter 23

Treading Lightly—And Loving It

In This Chapter

- Streamlining your life leads to great things
- Taking stock of your priorities in life, one at a time
- How to pare it all a little each day
- Make your personal systems simpler

Are you ready to learn about merging and purging—clearing out what you don't need so that you can have more of a "life" each day? To tread lighter in this life?

Merging and purging files (and other things that you're hanging on to) is more than good housekeeping; it's an emerging discipline among winners in society today. It's essential because, even with all the new high-tech tools, paper will continue to mushroom for the foreseeable future. Once you let go of all that stuff you're holding on to, you'll experience the same reward as a good garage cleaning or unblocking that backed-up plumbing will provide. Freedom!

The Benefits of Paring

Contemplate all that you encounter in the course of a day, week, month, and year: faxes, memos, reports, newspapers, newsletters, bulletins, magazines, bills, calendars, promotional items—and that's only the beginning. How would your life be if you merged and purged these items on a regular basis as they came into your life?

You'd have far more time. Why? Because accumulations, by nature, rob you of your time. First you acquire them, then you handle them, look at them, move them, attempt to arrange them, file some, discard others, try in vain to find the items you need, and then put up your hands and say, "I can't win."

You know that you're hanging on to too much stuff, and it's weighing you down. When are the best times to merge and purge what you've retained? Try these on for size:

♦ When you approach a birthday, particularly a zero-year birthday, this is one of the great times in life to get rid of the stuff that you no longer need. Ages 30, 40, 50, and 60 work well.

♦ New Year's is a good time, especially if it's the change of a decade.

♦ Spring cleaning is good time for clearing out the old and making room for the new. The arrival of fall (toward the end of the summer around Labor Day) works as well.

♦ Merge and purge when you move. There's no sense in paying movers to haul marginal "stuff" to your new location.

♦ When you change jobs or careers, you'll have to clean out your old desk at work. That's usually a given.

♦ Passing one of life's milestones—the birth of a child, the death of a parent, graduation, retirement, getting a major raise, and anything on that order—can often serve as a reminder to re-examine what you're retaining. Rearrange your affairs to accommodate the new you.

♦ Any time the spirit moves you is a good time to merge and purge.

♦ As you finish reading this particular paragraph, put down the book and actually go ahead and merge and purge in some area of your life. Make it an easy win, something that you can tackle and master in 10–15 minutes.

Merge and purge right after you've filed your taxes. If you procrastinate—and who doesn't?—fear not. After you've finished filing, there are benefits accruing. For one, you can get rid of most receipts and documents from the tax year three years prior to the one you've completed. You have to hang on to the forms filed, but not the nitty-gritty details. (If you've been audited, or if you anticipate problems with the IRS, that's a different story.)

Case by Case

When you don't feel in control of your time, everything in your life may seem as if it's running together in one big blur. Thus, the easiest way to approach merging and purging is to examine the most important compartments of your life one at a time.

Examine your desk and what needs to be there, then your entire office, and then where you live, your car, and other important areas of your life. Here are some suggestions:

- Do you have a file folder, a notebook, or a magazine box where you keep all travel-related materials? This might include booklets on hotel and air fares, frequent-flyer numbers, passports, numbers for taxis and other transportation, and vacation club folders. I keep such phone and membership numbers in one long file on my hard drive; a print-out in a small point size tucks into my portable appointment calendar. Wherever I am, day or night, I have the information that I need.

  I've maintained such a list for more than 15 years, and no one has ever gotten hold of it. The power and efficiency that it gives me is tremendous. Whether I'm at an airport, in a taxi, at a hotel, or in a phone booth, I have all the phone numbers, membership numbers, card numbers, codes, and everything else I need to stay efficiently in motion. You easily can do the same with a palmtop (palm-sized computer).

- You can undertake the same type of exercise in merging and purging items at your desk when it comes to key service providers, records related to your automobile, insurance forms and policies, banking information, and other areas where efficiency matters. In all cases, it takes a little time to merge and purge what you've retained and get it into a streamlined, highly useable form. Once you do, your efficiency level will soar.

- The same maneuvers can be undertaken around your office. What can be consolidated, reduced, eliminated, relocated, or donated? Is your office configuration serving you best? Do you now need to move things to improve your daily efficiency? Can hard-copy items be scanned to see if they're now on disk and you no longer need the hard copy? If you have four stacking trays, can you reduce the number to three? Do you even need an inbox anymore?

- At home, if you maintain a desk or any type of home office, reapply all these methods and go a step further. For example, could you use a 31-day tickler file in your home desk as well as the one you use in your office? If you use scheduling software at work, do you need to update your system at home?

2-4-6-8, What Can You Consolidate?

Can you consolidate family-related records so that you're in greater control? For example, all of Tommy's documents related to grade-school enrollment, immunization, early-school-dismissal policy, and summer camp could be kept in the same three-ring binder. All records related to your car (purchase documents, registration, tax information, inspections passed, repair records, special installations such as a CD player, and so on) could fit into one file.

Your car is also an important area of your life and, based on what may have accumulated, requires merging and purging as well:

Reflect and Win

It's better to keep your car records in your home office if that's where you make phone calls and payments concerning your car. You can always keep a backup of much of the documentation discussed here, stashed someplace deep in your car's trunk.

Pause!

If you're high on the prospect of streamlining your life, then you've got to think about paring a little at a time; there is no other way. You already have a full-time job and a raft of responsibilities.

◆ Can you get all your credit cards, library cards, and the like into a secondary wallet to be hidden someplace in the car? I do this rather than carrying a wallet with 25 different cards in it. Why? Because at any given moment, the only cards that I actually need are my driver's license, one ATM card, and one credit card.

Anytime I might use one of the other cards, I'm usually with my car. By safely stashing the cards that I would only use with my car someplace within the car, I free myself from carrying all of them. This has several time-saving advantages. One, you're less likely to lose a majority of your cards if you lose your wallet. Two, it's far easier to find your license, major credit card, and ATM card if they are the only ones that you carry in your wallet.

As a safeguard, you might want to copy all your credit cards and library cards on a copier, and keep a backup sheet at home and hidden in your car. (If cars disappear frequently in your neighborhood, skip this one!)

◆ I also find it a great time-saver to have all my maps in one place, within reach while driving. I use side pockets built into the driver's-side and passenger's-side front doors. You may use your glove compartment, a compartment between your two front seats, the trunk, or whatever space you have. Essentials such as car registration and proof of ownership stay snug at the bottom of my glove compartment.

Your Possessions and Your Time

Half the trouble of staying in control of your time is staying in control of your possessions. There's so much you have to keep tabs on that merging and purging could almost be a full-time job. If you're willing to occasionally consume one Saturday morning getting these systems into place, you'll find that the payoffs come back to you over and over again.

Reflect and Win

An easy way to organize many small items is to use individual envelopes, small plastic sandwich bags, or clear zip-lock baggies. This enables you to see what's inside and keeps the items dry and together.

Discarding over Time

Don't attempt to tackle all arenas of your life on the same Saturday morning. You won't finish, and the process itself may scare you away for a year or more.

Try these ways to cut down a little at a time without breaking your stride:

◆ Anytime you're waiting for someone at work, at home, or in your car, use the extra few minutes to pare something where you are. If you have to drive your children around town a lot, after a few days you ought to have your car's glove compartment and trunk whipped into shape.

◆ When you've finished a big project at work and you're not ready to tackle some other major, intellectual pursuit at the moment, pare your holdings as a form of transition. For example, if you've finished a big report, can you delete previous versions on your hard drive? Can you chuck rough drafts and notes that are no longer needed?

Retain What You'll Use: The Replacement Principle

Uncomplicating your own systems is synonymous with getting into a replacement mode. When you take in something new, something else has to go. The following table offers some everyday examples of nonreplacement policies (left column) contrasted with replacement policies (right column).

The Replacement Principle

Nonreplacement Policy	Replacement Policy
Your child's collection of videos grows to beyond 50 as you buy or copy the classics and latest hits.	You decide with your child in advance on a total number of videos (s)he can have. Each new one means replacing an old one.
Your file cabinet keeps growing until you need to buy another one.	Your files stay the same size; for each item that you add, you discard one.
You keep old equipment in closets or storage bins, thinking that it'll come in handy.	As soon as you buy new equipment, you donate the old equipment to a charity and get a tax deduction.
You've collected books for years and now now have no hope of reading what's on the overflowing shelves.	You retain only books of continuing sentimental value, scanning or copying key pages of most of the rest and then giving them away.
You have a 6.2-gigabyte hard disk and are considering getting more disk space.	You don't need more disk space because you prune your disk of outdated files at least once a month.
You have an unread collection of annual reports and other items from investment houses.	An investment firm sends you an annual report; right away you replace last year's.
Your clothes drawers and closets are filled with items that you haven't worn in years.	There's plenty of space in the house for clothes that you actually use; you give the rest to charities.
Your record collection spans many shelves and is covered with dust; you know you hardly ever play them.	You sell, trash, or donate those LPs and buy a few "greatest hits" CDs that you will play and enjoy.

If you're not constantly reducing what you hold on to, you're at the mercy of an era that keeps offering more than you can respond to. Seize control of your time—merge, purge, and then go splurge!

Traveling Light in Actual Traffic

The bad news about traffic in most urban and suburban areas is that it continues to get worse. There may be no meaningful solutions for another decade or more. All the prognostications about people telecommuting and using video phones and wall-size screens to conduct conferences with participants at remote locations simply haven't panned out to any significant degree.

In most metro areas, progression into the downtown centers is still essentially a one-way flow in at the beginning of the day and a one-way flow out at the end of the day. I have been self-employed since 1984, so I have been out of the traffic loop for a long time. When I was mired in it, I couldn't believe that anyone would ever endure it for the duration of his career. I knew I wouldn't.

In my last job before becoming self-employed, I literally moved across the street from my office. I lived in a high-rise building, and my balcony was literally in sight of most of the peer group with which I worked. However, no one actually figured out that my condo was at that location. So, even sitting out on the balcony at 5:00 or 6:00 P.M. for years never resulted in being spotted by a coworker. All the while, I had a four-minute commute to the office, and that was on a bad day.

Expect Delays

Delays are now the norm in our society, especially when it comes to travel. Delays are costly in numerous respects to you, the individual, being delayed; the carrier or transportation provider; and the environment because oil and gasoline are burned that aren't resulting in forward motion.

On any given day, you are likely to experience delays, frustrations, and confusion along with hundreds of your fellow passengers, so prepare yourself mentally and emotionally.

Commuting by Carrier

Conventional wisdom used to be that time spent commuting by bus, rail, or even plane essentially was lost time. You could do some light reading, but between passing cups down the aisles, trying to keep from bumping into other passengers, and simply having a pleasant journey, no heavy-duty assignments could be tackled. Increasingly, however, all commuting time is fair game for getting serious work done. Can you be effective and still travel light? You bet!

If you are boarding just a short flight, with your palmtop, you can dial up and download your email just before getting on the plane—no papers, no wires, very little weight. During the flight, you can answer all emails, sending them to the outbox. You can read correspondence, correct it, make notes, add to a database, calculate complex cash-flow analysis with spreadsheet software, listen to a lecture, you name it. The moment you step off the plane, you can send all your email, pick up any new email, and answer calls.

There is no need for lugging weighty workloads or incurring long bouts of lost time anymore; it's a traveler's choice. The key, of course, in every travel encounter, is desire and preparation. What do you want to get done, and will you take the time and energy to assemble the tools that will ensure your high productivity? For the seasoned traveling business executive, this is a no-brainer. If you're just starting to travel for business, a new world of efficiency awaits.

In any case, always line up your ducks—bring precisely what you need to be at your working best. I find checklists to be extremely handy. For example, before I leave for a speaking engagement, I use a checklist so that I don't have to reinvent the wheel each time, racking my brain to determine if I have brought everything I need.

The Ever Powerful Palmtop

As we proceed into the future, capabilities of your palmtop will likely expand unabated and hence will become even more useful while traveling. Increasing numbers of Internet sites will be available, and the speed and flexibility with which you can send and receive email will increase. Powerful palmtops can contain huge databases, scheduling software, spreadsheet software, and other key applications that will only become easier to use and more efficient. Therein lies the trap. If you are undisciplined, it is easy to fall prey to …

- Checking and rechecking for email all day long.
- Surfing sites when there is other important work to be done.
- Using other components and capabilities of wireless technology for something that does not support your career or long-term prosperity.

Hence, handheld devices can be the antithesis of effective time management—it all depends on how you use them.

The Least You Need to Know

- Merging and purging what you're retaining is an emerging discipline among winners in society today.
- The best times to pare are a birthday, a change of year or season, one of life's milestones, or anytime you have the spirit to do so.
- Pare a little at a time; biting off too much may tempt you to think that the situation is hopeless when it's not.
- Examine your work environment to determine what forms can be eliminated. It all counts.
- Uncomplicate your own systems by not volunteering to be inundated by junk mail and irrelevant stuff; rely on the replacement principle.

Part 6

Your Relationship, Your Time, and Your Sanity

You're making great progress! You're all the way up to Part 6, and this last part of the book is the clincher! Wouldn't it be nice to apply much of what you've learned thus far to the very personal aspects of your life? There is a wonderful assortment of chapters here. They'll focus on making time for each other—as in a partnership, having some kind of life when you're a parent, carving out real leisure in your life (would you believe it), considering a sabbatical, and keeping everything in perspective.

If you've been thinking, "It sure would be nice have some kind of home life," you'll probably want to get started immediately. Alternatively, if your first thought is "What's a home life?" you too, are an excellent candidate for gaining great insights from the chapters that follow. Either way, you're hooked.

Chapter 24

The Couple Corner: Finding (or Making) Time for Each Other

In This Chapter

◆ Being connected takes cooperation

◆ Exhaustion overrules vibrant relationships

◆ Men have needs, too

◆ Making your relationship Job 1

It's relatively easy to manage your time if you live alone with no significant other to converse with, make plans with, or accommodate. You'll face your work and domestic challenges, but, in comparison with those who have a meaningful relationship with someone else, managing your time is far less of an issue.

In this chapter, you'll learn how to make certain that you have the time you need to accommodate all aspects of your life. In particular, we'll address the dynamics of couples—married or not, with children or not—and discuss how they can carve out some time for each other. In the chapter that follows, we'll tackle the more involved notion of carving out time while maintaining effective parenting.

Routine and Regimen

Jacqueline Taylor believes the primary way to manage your time most efficiently is to stay completely focused on what you want to accomplish. At age 42, she is the new chief executive officer of a manufacturing company that produces home security devices. Her responsibilities include heading four divisions, managing six affiliates, maximizing shareholder value, reporting to the board of directors, and keeping the operations profitable.

Taylor begins soon after arising, which is 6:15 sharp every morning. She has already mapped out the night before what she'll tackle at the start of her day. She spends the first three hours at home and then proceeds into the office for a 9:15 arrival. She departs from work when she feels satisfied with what she has accomplished—usually between 7:00 and 10:00 P.M.

"I'm passionate about my work," she says, "and ruthless about how I allocate my time. If somebody wants to present a plan that is not in alignment with my objectives, I don't devote a second to it. I steer them in another direction, don't schedule a meeting with them, and don't give them any encouragement."

She goes on to say, "I can't remember the last time I had a business lunch; they take too huge a chunk out of the middle of your day. Most times, I have a salad and a slice of pizza, or a bowl of soup right in my office. There are important reasons for connecting with others. So I schedule to meet people occasionally for a light dinner after work, or for a light refreshment after that."

Ms. Taylor has never been married and has no children. By the standards of most, she also has no social life. She doesn't do errands, shop, or cook. There's practically no food in her kitchen, and if anybody ever dropped by—although nobody ever would—she'd have nothing to offer them.

She's got a routine worked out that maximizes her time—one that has become comfortable for her. (It wouldn't work for most of us.) For some of us, there are other people, other interests, and other demands beyond our jobs. Focusing on the traditional man-wife couple, let's first consider common elements of the woman's perspective.

Connectedness Takes Work

Couples who have a tight relationship continually put energy and effort into it. Their union doesn't happen by chance, although some blessed individuals have personal chemistry that seems to jibe with one another to the *n*th degree. Even among those lucky couples, however, it's likely that there's a high degree of listening, cooperation, and respect for one another's schedules.

Work Appeal

Most women today hold a job outside the home in addition to maintaining the brunt of household responsibilities. Sociologist Veronica Tichenor from the University of Michigan says that women are putting in longer hours at the office than ever "because they enjoy it." Yet, they're still doing most of the housework because they want to or feel that they have to. This includes even top female executives.

Part of the appeal of work is that there are indicators nearly every step of the way to let you know whether you're on track, meeting the quota, or turning a profit. You get evaluations, you get performance appraisals, you get raises, you get promotions. What corollary is there in your home life? How do you know when you're a good partner, spouse, or lover?

Get a Wife

Some working women come to the conclusion that they would have a wonderful life if they had the equivalent of a "traditional wife" who stayed at home, kept the house in order, took care of the kids, cooked the meals, and handled all the errands. This is only an alternative for the ultrarich; however, most women still do the housework, no matter how demanding or exhausting their work might be.

Many women confided to Tichenor that, regardless of their achievements in the workplace, they still feel a strange and strong need to be regarded as excellent homemakers. If you're a woman, you probably already know and feel this on many levels. If you're a man, keep reading this section because it's going to be the key to your carving out time for one another.

> A woman's responsibility for her family is a 24-hour task. Her time plan is a plan for living. There must be time allowance for the necessary work of the household, such as food preparation, serving, cleaning, and laundering. Family obligations, however, do not cease with the completion of the technical work of the home. There are children to be trained, supervised, and enjoyed; the interests and activities of other adults in the family group must be shared; time for civic interests as well as for social activities and obligations must enter into the larger concept of time management for the housewife. —Irma Gross and Mary Lewis, *Home Management* (1938)

Many women fall into this syndrome, but, as Irma Gross and Mary Lewis recounted in *Home Management*, "the wise homemaker still will not let the interests listed above make such inroads upon her time as to unbalance her living in terms of health and personal development." They recommend "time for rest, sleep, recreation, and hospitality, together with sufficient leisure to pursue some phase of living that will keep her emotionally stable and intellectually alert."

Pounded into Their Souls

This 1938 book admonished its female readers that if their housekeeping was too disorganized it could "interfere with the development of the various members of the family and their happiness of association."

From this—and a ton of other materials that you could assemble from 1938, earlier, and even later—it's easy to see why women have an ingrained notion of having sole responsibility for the complete management of the household. While they appreciate any help that others provide, regardless of what else is going on in their life, they often regard the state of their home as akin to the state of their being. (Guys, are you reading closely?)

Hired Help

Particularly among executive women, there has been movement toward maintaining outside services to help manage the household. When dollars permit, there's less reticence to bringing in a nanny, cleaning crew, gardener, window-washer, and delivery services. Women today buy prepared food for a dinner party, whereas in previous years they would not have.

My view on outside services is to use them to the max! Where is it written that your guests will leave unsatisfied because your food was catered rather than personally prepared by you? Is it somehow unholy to pay someone to take care of a task that you'd prefer not to do and to free up hours for you in which you could earn more per hour than the person you're paying?

> **Reflect and Win**
>
> If you're in a committed relationship, every time you accomplish something through delegation, through reliance upon the services and efforts of others, you potentially free yourself on both a physical and an emotional realm to be more of a partner to your partner. Got that, pardner?

Your Partner or the Rest of the World

When I was writing my eighteenth book, *Breathing Space: Living and Working at a Comfortable Pace in a Sped Up Society*, I made the strong suggestion that the crunch of too many things competing for one's time and attention was actually keeping couples apart from one another. Now, it's abundantly clear that this is so!

All the tasks, attention-diverters, and stimuli in your external environment nearly guarantee that you'll have nothing left for your partner. You can be physically there, talk the talk, and go through the motions, and even semideceive yourself that you're succeeding. To be there, however, in a physical, mental, and emotional sense, and to offer the complete essence of your being all but requires that you disengage from the mountains of minutia that are already overcomplicating and glutting the lives of most adults in society.

Pause! _____

Do you want to be with anyone when you're exhausted? Do you care to be with a partner who's exhausted? If you're both exhausted, will that be of value to either of you?

Physically and Emotionally Drained

The highest divorce rates occur in the more complex, technically sophisticated societies. It doesn't take some enchanted reasoning to understand that the nuances of what it takes to fan the flames of a relationship can't be given short shrift. It can't be afforded only the remnants of what's left of you after the overinformation society has buffeted you for yet another day.

In addition to potentially bringing people closer together, technology serves as an impediment to relationships. Are you any closer if you're able to beep, page, or dial your sweetie all day long? Are you less close if you do not?

Transcending Technology

The strongest relationships have a spiritual component that transcends technology. People in such relationships can be away from each other for hours, days, weeks, months, and, in some cases, years and still maintain a strong connection.

The time that people spend on the Internet can be a contributing factor to their being apart from one another. Do you know any families that have two or three computer screens in a row so that they can all sit down at a table and independently surf while being in proximity to each other? I thought not. For most of us, the majority of our surfing is done alone, at a desk or a table, without anyone else present. If there is a loved one in the room, we are certainly not giving our full attention to that person.

An hour of earnest conversation between two people will result in a higher level of connection or at least understanding of one another than simply sitting side by side and watching the boob tube. Unless, of course, you really have nothing to say to one another, and you would rather bask in the reflected, contrived glory of those on the screen, in which case, you might as well turn on another episode of *Survivor*.

Need a Deck Chair?

Engaging in only traditional and minuscule measures to free up some of your time and being, such as occasionally retaining outside help, is like rearranging deck chairs on the Titanic. If you feel the integrity of your relationship slowly starting to unravel—and if you value your relationship highly—to stay with the sea analogy, it's time to launch all ships.

- Delegate any task that you possibly can.
- Let go of perfectionistic standards that keep you mopping floors when you should be making love.
- Carve out a few minutes of uninterrupted time for each other every day—and several hours every weekend.
- Ask for help.
- Turn off the TV an hour earlier than normal, or don't turn it on to begin with.
- Schedule dates on your calendar.
- If both of your jobs allow for it, schedule unhurried lunches.
- Take 10-minute walks together after dinner.
- Leave nice notes around the house.
- Read a joke book together.

The Male Factor

In many ways, the 1990s was a decade of male-bashing. Males were seen as some unflattering things:

- Neanderthals
- Hot-blooded animals
- Uncouth detractors of society
- War-mongers
- Pumped-up athletes
- Exploiters of women
- Child-support deadbeats
- All of the above

In some circles, it is held that men aren't interested in relationships, raising children, or staying for the long haul. Men have a good time and then they leave. If you find one you can trust, you're among the lucky few.

The problem with this kind of banter, beyond the obvious, is that it presupposes that an entire sex is wrong! From a bioevolutionary and cosmic perspective, how can a sex be wrong? Men have needs, aspirations, and desires. A man in a relationship has needs, aspirations, and desires.

See in a Different Light

I counseled three couples as part of a feature story run on the front page of the *USA Today* lifestyle section. One of the couples was a minister and his wife. The wife lamented that, with his growing congregation, she had less and less time to spend with him. Even Friday and Saturday evenings, which traditionally had been date nights for them, were now consumed by the minister's visits to sick or hospitalized members of the congregation.

Most of the minister's visits lasted only 20 minutes, but by the time he got back, the magic of the evening was on the wane. I suggested a tactic to them that they felt was worth considering.

Reflect and Win

Whether you've been in your primary relationship for 10 years or 10 weeks, an essential activity in making the relationship work and carving out time for each other is to look anew at your partner, to see what it would take to connect with and be with your partner on the highest level.

Date Night

Hereafter, the wife would accompany her husband in the car on Friday and Saturday evenings whenever he called upon the sick. Because most of his visits lasted 18–20 minutes, she could sit in the car and read a magazine or listen to songs while he made his visit. When he was finished and got back into the car, they were both there, dressed and ready to go. The night was still young and held great potential.

I caught up with them several months after they put this plan into practice. It worked from the first Friday evening on.

Creative Thinking Works Wonders

By examining the responsibilities and activities of your partner, actually comparing calendars, and applying a high dose of creative thinking, you may surprise yourself with the amount and quality of time you can carve out for one another.

I had a girlfriend who was studying for the CPA exam. Her preferred method of studying was to go to a university library, with all of her books and paraphernalia and a few snacks.

She'd find a big table in the corner and camp out for hours. In the past, this was a lonely, if necessary, undertaking for her. Few of her previous boyfriends found this to be enticing. I thought that this was pretty close to heaven. I was always working on new outlines for speeches and researching for books and articles.

Oh, what fun to be able to go to the library with someone who was equally intent on getting a whale of a lot of work done while being together. We would work for 50 minutes and then take 10-minute breaks walking and talking. Then we'd get back to work and repeat the process. When it was done, we'd go out for pizza. I accomplished alot during those sessions. She passed her CPA exam on her first try!

What similar types of arrangements can you find in your relationship? Maybe you both can exercise, travel, or work together.

Your Relationship: Job 1

It seems that for a relationship to work in these harried times, it has to be the most important element in each partner's life. If the relationship comes in second to work, chances are good that the vibrancy of the relationship will dwindle.

It's Not Either/Or

If you're a career-climbing overachiever, this doesn't mean that you have to mute your goals or aspirations, or be something that you weren't intending to be. Plot your career strategy in the context of being in a committed relationship. This will work, and the most successful people on the planet routinely have strong and committed relationships. It's no coincidence. They draw strength and sustenance from this relationship. Many report that it actually gives them a sense of freedom.

From Heaven to Earth

What are the hallmarks of a relationship in which couples steadfastly make time for each other without ignoring the other aspects of their lives? Foremost is respect for each other. During the early part of a relationship, when you're in rapture with one another, it's easy to show respect. You're practically bending over backward to be on your best behavior.

Once the initial rush is past (or the honeymoon is over)—and for some people, this can be 18 to 24 months or longer,—many partners begin taking each other for granted. This is so even if they had sought the right relationship for years!

Here are some ideas on how respect is played out among couples who intend to make time for each other:

♦ When some time opens up for one partner, the other partner is immediately called to see if there's a match in terms of available time with each other. The relationship continues to come first.

♦ They go out of their way to ensure that they understand one another. They talk, debate, or argue until they've cleared up an issue. They don't broad-brush over differences, but they work toward an understanding. The longer they are together as a couple, the more adept they become at this.

♦ They continually validate each other, telling each other what they appreciate about one another, finding the good in one another, and positively reinforcing one another as often as they can.

♦ They acknowledge and recognize each other for the little things that each does. They also express their appreciation in no uncertain terms.

♦ They are reassuring to one another. They know that no partner comes without weaknesses, and while it's easy to love the facets about someone else that please us, accepting the whole person is a much more challenging task.

♦ They're devoted to one another. They don't allow other people to come between them; in fact, when approached by outside potential partners, they end that relationship and then report the occurrence to their mate.

♦ They convey a strong sense of caring. They leave notes for each other. They send email messages, leave phone messages, and leave unannounced, small gifts in odd locations so that their partner encounters them when it's least expected.

♦ They recognize that, no matter how busy they are with their careers and other activities, keeping the relationship alive takes work. Each is committed to devoting the time and energy to keep the relationship alive, and each partner knows it.

> **Reflect and Win**
>
> How about practicing some that other successful couples do at the close of the day: Each recaps what the other did that was particularly pleasing. "I greatly appreciated your coming to the office to drop off the package." Or, "I like the way you cheered me up when nothing seemed to be going right for me earlier today."

> **Pause!**
>
> Do you know anyone who professes to be in a committed relationship but gives it short shrift? Take a good, honest look at yourself—if this description fits you, it's time to reorganize your priorities before your relationship is damaged.

In this roster, notice how winning couples carve out time and attention for each other almost automatically as they proceed each day. So, when the relationship is foremost in each of the partner's lives, time for each other materializes in ways that don't happen for couples who knowingly or unknowingly assign secondary status to their relationship.

Ideas Galore

If you're ready for action, here's a potpourri of strategies and techniques to get your relationship back on to the high road.

Paging All Baby-Sitters

Call everyone in the local community shopper newspaper who advertises baby-sitting services. Also post your own ads. Your assignment is to develop a roster of 8–10 baby-sitters in the local area so that you're never at a loss for one when you need one. Also enlist grandparents, relatives, and anyone nearby who could possibly serve in the same capacity. You don't want your relationship and, indeed, social life to hinge upon your ability to get a baby-sitter on any given evening.

Pick a Date

Set aside one night per week as a mini date night. This could be having a light workout together, cooking on the grill, strolling through a mall, playing Scrabble or cards, or anything other than watching television or a movie (too much focus on the screen and not on each other).

Kids Want Attention

If you have children—the topic of the next chapter—plan to have time together while your kids are attending various classes or activities. Plan to drop them off together, spend the first few minutes seeing what they're doing, and then taking off for a walk or whatever and coming back to be with them for the last few minutes as well.

CAUTION

Pause!

Don't knock marriage encounter groups until you've tried them. Couples who attend say that the experience has been rejuvenating for their relationship or marriage.

Groups to Encounter

Investigate some of the local marriage encounter groups popping up in many areas. These are usually weekend affairs in which you're able to forge stronger marital bonds in a safe, relaxing, pensive atmosphere that enables couples to talk quietly and privately to each other about their lives and relationship.

Little Things with Large Meaning

Therapists agree that having mom and dad head off for a weekend to have some time together is actually healthy for children. Kids need to know that their mom and dad can have fun together, without them.

If you simply can't get away—or don't want to—make a big deal out of walking by the lake, playing some favorite songs, having a picnic in the backyard, thumbing through your photo albums, going to brunch at that four-star hotel, or even making something together.

Reflect and Win

Traditions between couples and within families are often underrated. By making the most out of recognizable dates on the calendar, you establish the potential to do it again and again.

Establish Nonholiday Family Traditions

Don't simply celebrate birthdays, *celebrate* birthdays! Also, do something very special for your anniversary, or the anniversary of the initiation of your relationship, the anniversaries of graduations, promotions, relocations, and special achievements in each of your lives. Mark these on both of your calendars far in advance.

The Time Master Says

Joe Jeff Goldblatt, Ph.D., is Dean of George Washington University's Graduate Program in Special Events. Goldblatt says, "Life is a special event." To truly have time for each other, celebrate all the special events that you can in your lives.

The Least You Need to Know

- If you're alone, it's relatively easy to manage your time.
- Most women today hold a job outside the home in addition to maintaining the brunt of household responsibilities. Many accept domestic help when offered but still want to stay in control.
- As a potentially successful partner to another person, are you willing to learn about your partner's needs, aspirations, and desires, and to help meet them?
- Hidden opportunities to be together exist no matter what workload one or both partners face.
- Celebrate the occasions in your lives, big and small, at every opportunity.

Chapter 25

Calling All Parents

In This Chapter

- ◆ The family in flux
- ◆ Good parenting means sacrifice
- ◆ How fathers can pick up some slack
- ◆ Planning for family events

Surveys conducted by some of the leading pollsters in America show that adults feel as if children today are far more spoiled than children of their own generations. They have more material objects, are more likely to be over-weight, are less likely to participate in household chores, and may have worse manners. These same adults probably fail to realize that they're the ones who have raised these kids and who continue to have the most influence over them.

Movie producers market their PG-13- and R-rated films to attract 11- and 12-year-olds.

Television commercials are increasingly zealous in their pursuit of the youth market. Advertisers seem to be boldly venturing forward without shame. Still, parental influence is a strong and viable force when applied appropriately.

In this chapter, you'll learn tips for managing your time with your kids despite the daily obstacles you may face.

Time and Effort: Payoff Forever

It takes time to raise a child effectively, but the rewards are self-apparent. Spending lots of time with your child during the formative years actually yields marvelous payoffs, particularly if your child grows up to be a fully functioning, balanced, happy, well-adjusted adult. And the time savings can be spectacular, like not having to take your children back and forth to counselors and therapists. Seriously, though, the erroneous time- and cost-saving notion of plopping your child down in front of the TV and having it serve as a quasi–baby-sitter, in the long run, can prove to be costly.

Fewer Kids, Great Needs

In the early 1900s, four out of five households included children. Today, only one in three households have children. Amazingly, half of all households are comprised of families that have no children under age 18, all of which means that fewer adults today are involved in parenting than any time in the past 100 years.

Concurrently, more than 50 percent of all children will spend some time during their upbringing in a single-parent home. One child out of three is born to an unmarried mother—and among African-American children, nearly two children out of three are born to an unmarried mother.

Married or not, most mothers are now employed. Most families require two incomes to reach their desired standard of living, putting single-parent families in financial straits.

Pause!

Parenting today is more challenging than in previous generations.

Divorce rates in America continue on at about 50 percent of all marriages, and the likelihood of divorce increases with each remarriage. With fewer adults involved in parenting comes an increased resistance to support services and programs designed to help children.

It's a Different World

If you're parents of a newborn, it's almost a given that for the first two or three years, you'll be sacrificing your time and body in devotion to your baby. Some couples have an arrangement in which one keeps working outside the home, while one becomes the primary caregiver—usually the woman, but in a growing number of cases, also the man.

The key to effective parenting and to maintaining control of your time is essentially to sacrifice yourself for roughly the first three years so that your child is reared in a wholesome, nurturing, reinforcing atmosphere. This affords you the greatest opportunity for raising a brighter, more alert, healthier child. Fortunately, the things that good parents traditionally have done to raise their children remain relatively the same:

- ◆ Read to your child.
- ◆ Hug, cradle, and comfort your child (especially important).
- ◆ Nurture your child in every way by talking, playing, or just noticing what he or she is doing.

Contradicting the Assumptions

One of the heartening developments of parenthood in the last decade or so is the trend among some yuppie-age fathers to become more involved in their children's lives. One St. Louis–based accountant commented, "It's a wonderful thing to be able to see your own children grow up." Starting in the early '90s fatherhood became visibly vogue. Many surveys indicated that young fathers value being fathers as much as anything else in their lives and careers.

What Men Want

84%	Being a good father
74%	Having a close spousal partnership
67%	Being healthy and fit
53%	Being socially responsible
52%	Achieving balance with work, family, and social life
47%	Having good friends
30%	Making good money
27%	Achieving career advancement

Source: Consumer Survey Center Poll, conducted for Slates/Levi Strauss August 1996

Why this movement arose is not abundantly clear. It may be because of the increases in divorce, the rise of dual-career marriages, or perhaps the fact that many fathers didn't have the kind of relationship with their own father that they had hoped for during their childhoods.

The women's movement may have had much to do with the expanded roles that some men now play in the lives of their children.

Focus on Your Children

Giving your complete attention to your child bolsters your child's ability to feel confident and at ease when you're not around. The child begins to learn that sometimes Mommy or Daddy has important things to do and can't give him any attention. But when Mommy or Daddy does give him attention, it's complete and undivided.

If you want to raise an insecure and unconfident child, stay preoccupied all the time whenever you're with your child. That'll do the trick in a hurry.

How are you when you're not playing with your kids but doing something else that sends them messages? How about the way you serve dinner?

- Do you start and stop?
- Do you talk on the phone?
- Do you go upstairs to do something?

Here's a more probing question. Would you act like that in front of company? If not, then why do you do so in front of your kids? The message that you're giving your children is that there's so much to do in life that you can't keep up if you simply sit there at the table with them. That, in turn, tells your children that such an existence will be theirs as well.

Pause!

> Not giving your child your complete and undivided attention when you're together sends negative messages on several levels—such as you can't manage your own affairs, you'll never have enough time to completely be together, the child isn't important, your loyalties are divided, and "I must work harder to get Mommy or Daddy's attention."

The Time Master Says

> If there's one part of the day when you want to be sure to give your children undivided attention, make it dinner. Serve them, and then sit with them for the whole time. Talk to them. Give them a strong, clear message that the pace of the world has little effect on your family's ability to have a complete, engaging dinner with one another.

The "Too Much" Trap

Amy takes tae kwan do lessons, starts on the soccer team, plays piano, and has a big part in the school play. Jason is on the tennis team, takes trombone lessons, serves as a traffic monitor at school, and sits on the student council.

I'm Always Busy, Therefore I Am

Increasingly, we transmit our predisposition toward overengaging in activities to our children. It's not enough to be a kid anymore, to do your homework, get good grades, have some friends, and leave it at that. Too many children of yuppie parents have become yuppie juniors. They're occupied every moment of the day.

A quick, but not easy, way to carve out more time for your children as well as for yourself (because you're usually the one schlepping them all over creation) is to help them decide which highly desirable, enjoyable, fun-filled activity they will not participate in for at least the current season. Is the quality of their life likely to diminish? If anything, it may improve.

Kids in Balance

I'm not knocking the value of engaging in activities that someone enjoys, that make a person more effective as a human being, and that serve others. I'm talking about the fine balance between engaging in some activities and being overbooked—and you know exactly what I mean!

> **The Time Master Says**
>
> A study at Cornell University found that with children, from birth to age 18, whether the mother works outside the home or not, the father's parenting responsibilities were nearly the same!

A Chip off the Old Block

Are you a little league coach, a scout master, and a fund-drive chair? Are you doing more for your community than for your kids? What's behind your overvolunteerism? Do you have the erroneous notion that others are keeping score?

As a parent you are always setting an example, so if you are overloaded with outside activities and volunteerism, as admirable as that may seem to some people, you're teaching your children to be overloaded as well.

The Kids Can Pitch In

A growing number of parents, particularly women, find that effective parenting today hinges on the ability to get their kids to pitch in with chores. At the least, kids need to be responsible for keeping their own rooms orderly. From about age six on, this should be an everyday habit. Until then, you'll probably have to help them.

Since my little girl, Valerie (now age eight), was three years old, we've practiced what I call the replacement principle, which I presented in Chapter 23, "Treading Lightly—And Loving It." In a nutshell, whatever you add to the room merits one other thing being removed. Add a new video? Sure. Which one do you want to give up?

Kids and Their Homework Habits

Harris Cooper, professor of psychology at the University of Missouri, says, "In addition to the whirlwind of social, cultural, and sports activities, many children aren't receiving the

The Time Master Says

As a rough guideline, about 15–20 minutes of homework per day is appropriate for children up to grade two, about 30–60 minutes a day for grades three through six, and up to two hours for junior high. In high school, assignments can vary widely, but beyond three hours may tax even the most ambitious students.

proper parental support when it comes to homework. Among those children of parents who both work, either the parents are too pooped to help, or feel guilty and give the child too much assistance—and end up doing most of the homework."

Your role as parent? To encourage your child to do his own homework in a timely manner as it's assigned, help out when needed, but don't do the homework.

A 1991 study conducted by the U.S. Department of Education of 13-year-olds indicated that American kids do less homework than their counterparts in other countries. Only 31 percent of kids in the United States have more than two hours of homework daily. This contrasts with other countries, as listed here.

Homework: U.S. Kids Versus the World

United States	31%
Taiwan	44%
Former Soviet Union	52%
France	55%
Spain	62%
Ireland	66%

The same study revealed that 22 percent of children in the United States watch five or more hours of television daily. This compares unfavorably to other countries.

Watching Television: U.S. Kids Versus the World

United States	22%
Former Soviet Union	19%
Spain	11%
Ireland	9%
France	4%

Helping with Homework

When it comes to helping your children with their homework, here are guidelines:

- ◆ Set a regular time for homework every day. Also establish ground rules for what takes place during this time, with no electronic/entertainment intrusions.

- ◆ Set aside a desk or table in one of the rooms in your home so that your children will have a regular place in which to do homework.

- ◆ Assemble appropriate supplies such as pens and pencils, magic markers, crayons, scissors, rulers, note pads, and dictionaries.

- ◆ Be available to offer helpful suggestions and guidance only. Offer clues so that your child proceeds down the right path without actually receiving the answer.

- ◆ Offer lavish praise when a child has completed a difficult math problem or has written a nifty book report.

Reflect and Win

Behavior that's rewarded is repeated. If you want to get your children to do homework and do it well, frequently reward them for the good behavior that they exhibit—directly after they exhibit it.

PCs and Their Limitations

Having a computer in your child's life does not enhance his ability to do homework or have a more rewarding childhood experience. Ensure that your child knows the basics first.

"Rather than take over kids' lives, computers should add a new dimension," says Barbara Bowman, president of the Erikson Institute for Advanced Study in Child Development based in Chicago, Illinois. A program on animals, for example, is much more meaningful if your children have already visited a zoo or a petting farm. Don't allow a virtual experience to be the substitute for a real experience.

If your child is old enough to be doing homework on a computer, that's a different story. Writing papers, doing research, and solving problems can all be enhanced by a computer. You run the risk of having the child use the computer for anything but homework, so provide periodic monitoring.

A Strong Connection with Your Kids

Homework or not, raising happy, well-rounded kids requires effective communication, much like having a rewarding marriage or primary relationship. In a survey conducted by

Roper Starch Worldwide, the following data was generated among parents of students ages 10 to 14:

◆ About 46 percent of kids and 27 percent of parents say that they spend less than a half-hour a day in conversation with each other.

◆ Most parents underestimate their child's maturity level and misconceive what's important to them. Parents believe that the top priorities for their children are having fun, being with their friends, and looking good. Children report that their top priorities are their future, their schoolwork, and family matters.

◆ Twenty percent of children say that it's easy to talk with their parents about things that matter; 26 percent say that it's somewhat to very difficult to talk about such things. All the rest report that it is somewhat easy to talk about such things.

Stay in Touch, or Lose Touch

Against such a backdrop, how do you stay in touch without spending oodles of time but nevertheless conveying to your kids that you care? Among a variety of options, try these:

◆ Convey trust at an early age. If your children know that you listen to them, they'll open up to you about everything in their life, even when confronting problems at school, with drugs, or with sex.

◆ Who in this world isn't pleased when asked for his opinions? Your children, among everyone else, will feel particularly pleased. You can ask them about big things or little things; it doesn't matter.

Reflect and Win

Listening doesn't have to be a formality. Often, your child will open up to you while you're walking along, driving the car, or raking leaves. As you develop a bond and rapport with your child, opening up to one another may happen spontaneously.

◆ Let them have their say. Don't anticipate what someone is going to say or finish a child's sentences. You wouldn't do this at work, so don't do it with your children. Give them sufficient time to explain themselves—more time than you would afford to an adult.

◆ While you're letting them explain, pay attention to their body language and emotions. Are they holding anything back? Is there something they'd like to say but are not saying well? Is there something that they want you to draw out of them?

Get Coordinated

Whether a mother and father, a mother alone, or a father alone take major responsibility for rearing and directing the affairs of the children, coordination is vital. One mother of three comments that she always reviews her week in advance on Sunday evening, even if it's only for 5–10 minutes.

In viewing the week as a whole, there are fewer surprises, fewer time crunches, and less anxiety. If you merely get up each day and try to determine what it will take to get you and your children through the day, it's likely that you're going to run into snags. Your time horizon wasn't broad enough. A peek at the next week affords you a better opportunity to manage the pace with grace.

Some family counselors believe that multiweek, month-long, or multimonth planning is even more desirable. As you plot out dates of birthdays, time off from school, other family celebrations, kids' lessons, and other events, you gain a broader picture of who needs to be where, when, and supplied with what.

One parent prefers to do family planning as much as two years in advance. He's frequently asking his children's teachers and school administrators the dates of events so that he can plot them on his calendar and ensure his attendance or participation. He laments that he has to force the dates out of others because they haven't mapped out their activities that far in advance!

Learn to Overestimate

The more accomplished, effective, and intelligent you are, the more likely you are to fall into a time trap. Your optimism combined with resourcefulness leads you to believe that certain tasks will take x amount of time. If it turns out that they take 1.2 or 1.3 times your estimate, you're frustrated because things rarely seem to be completed based on your own perceptions of how long they should have taken.

Overestimate the time that a task or activity will take, particularly when in relation to your children. If you finish on time or in advance, you'll feel far less frustrated and/or you might actually feel victorious.

If you've fallen into the trap of overscheduling your child and underestimating the time that both of you will expend on activities (least of which is chauffeuring!), you'll be perpetually frustrated. If you—and, by extension, your child—have the wherewithal to schedule less and be generous in your scheduling, you're apt to lead more serene, less hectic lives. You'll have a greater chance of enjoying the few activities that you choose.

> **Pause!**
>
> "People sometimes feel that everyone else is accomplishing more than they are, but that is usually because they overestimate what others do and underestimate what they themselves do," says Windy Dryden, professor of counseling at Goldsmiths' College, London.

Caring and Sharing

If you're fortunate enough to be in a true parenting partnership with your spouse, both you and your children stand to benefit. While there are no hard-and-fast rules as to what equal parenting caregivers are supposed to do, here are some ideas:

- Alternate who gets up earliest on selected mornings to take care of breakfast and help the kids get dressed and ready for school.

- Alternate who gets up first on the weekend.

- Divvy up household chores according to personal preference or inclination—or, to remain completely egalitarian, based on a rotating schedule.

- Alternate who reads or plays with the kids. Alternate who chauffeurs the kids. Schedule who will serve as baby-sitter when the other parent needs some time away.

- Maintain equal contact and address information, including with doctors, dentists, coaches, teachers, and so on.

- Log in equal hours when it comes to emergencies, when the children are sick, or when one of the parents needs to break out of work.

CAUTION

Pause!

Many psychologists agree that the mother's acceptance, or lack thereof, of a potentially care-giving father plays a dramatic role in whether the father is successful. Some mothers lament that they want to have the father play a more prominent role in raising the children, yet they don't understand the power that they have to make this happen.

Where Are You Now?

When you look at your household calendar and it appears as if it's practically filled to the brim with kids' activities, see how many of those activities you initiated of your own free will, how many you participate in, and how many you actually enjoy. There's no use playing the martyr or the perpetually sacrificing parent.

How do you create the win-win scenario? Here are a couple ideas.

Find a Buddy On-Site

Suppose your child plays in a little league. When you attend such functions, perhaps you meet with another parent whom you befriend. Sitting in the stands, you both watch the game and have enjoyable conversations. It's one way to maintain a friendship, be a parent, and have a life.

Doubling Up: The Exceptions

You've already discovered that I'm not a big fan of doubling up on activities. In some instances, you can take your child to an event and at the same time read or take care of some light paperwork.

In Durham, North Carolina, there is a play center called Amaze-N-Castles. My daughter wants to go there all the time; we average about one visit per quarter. During those visits, she darts into the maze, where she runs, jumps, climbs, swings, slides down tubes, throws balls, and exercises in every way. The 90 minutes or so that she's there, I sit at a table and handle paperwork.

I look up every time she calls, and I periodically monitor what she's doing when she doesn't call. Meanwhile, for 90 percent of the time I'm able to take care of my stuff. I am completely present in both the drive up and the drive back, in getting her started, and in playing together in the arcade section of the facility. Undoubtedly, you have corollaries in your life.

Stage a Miniworkout

My daughter likes many activities that don't interest me, such as attending the gymnastics meets at the University of North Carolina. There are four events at these meets, including the balance beam, the vault, the uneven parallel bars, and the floor exercise. The event is held in an 8,000-seat gym—and 7,600 of the seats are open—so we're able to sit wherever we choose.

She watches intently. I watch as well and, at the same time, stretch, do light calisthenics, and engage in isometrics.

Movies Worth Watching

If your child clamors to watch videos, choose videos that you would enjoy watching as well. There are enough G- and PG-rated videos around in which both of you could find interest. Among these are various categories: historical biographies, comedies, period pieces, sci-fi's, and musicals (largely from the 1930s).

As Your Child Learns ...

My daughter tried skating once and was thrilled by it. She decided that it was worth pursuing and wanted to take lessons. When her mother brought her to skating lessons, her mother decided to rediscover skating for herself and took private lessons while Valerie was in a group lesson elsewhere on the ice. It's rewarding to rediscover parts of your own childhood.

The Least You Need to Know

- Up to age three, complex changes occur in the brain that lay a foundation for the child's whole life.
- The common denominator to effective parenting is the ability to offer your complete attention to your child.
- Encourage your child to do homework in a timely manner, and help out when needed—but don't do the homework.
- Convey trust at an early age. If your children know that you listen to them, they'll begin to open up to you.
- You don't have to overschedule your child. Start overestimating the time that both of you will expend on activities.

Eye on Leisure

In This Chapter

◆ *Leisure* means more than "couch potato"
◆ Using transition time to maximize the benefits of leisure
◆ Scheduling low-level leisure when you need it most
◆ Little ways to sneak in some guilt-free leisure time

"Leisure" as a concept has been on the rocks since PCs became popular. In our "24 × 7" society (and I hate both that term and the concept), it may seem as if opportunities for leisure would become more plentiful. After all, if everything is open all the time, then you have an array of options as to what you will engage in and when. In actuality, the opposite is true.

Knowing that something is open and available all the time doesn't necessarily prompt you to take advantage of the extended hours.

Sure, if you work the second or third shift, many elements of a 24 × 7 society are highly welcomed. Professionals working the "first shift" who have been short-changing their leisure for extended periods won't experience a change in their patronage of leisure-related businesses and activities because the hours of operation have changed.

Most people have an odd relationship with leisure—Americans, in particular. Periodically throughout the twentieth century, Americans have questioned the central reality of work and struggled with this strange and frightening concept of leisure time; in fact, "it's not a place we're really comfortable with," says Benjamin Hunnicutt, a professor of leisure studies at the University of Iowa. Hunnicutt questions whether work will ever be anything but the number-1 activity in our cultural hierarchy. If anything, he believes that it's the closest thing to a modern religion.

There's no disputing the value of having sufficient leisure in your life. Still, you want leisure, you need leisure, and you may even crave leisure. You instinctively know when you haven't had enough, and you seek it out with the relentlessness of a sperm trying to fertilize an egg.

When Boundaries Blur

Coming to Terms

To define **leisure** as time away from work is to misunderstand the concept. One group of researchers defined it as that which is worth your time and attention, given that you otherwise face a minimum of limitations and responsibilities. It sounds a little clinical, but what it means is rewarding activity free from work and preoccupation with work.

Whether or not it is human destiny to socially evolve into a world increasingly difficult to inhabit, insights on finding *leisure* abound. You can chart a new course, one to which perhaps the masses will someday gravitate.

Executives and entrepreneurs in industrialized societies have been attempting to accomplish more in the same amount of time by engaging in activities at a fast pace, doubling up on activities (shazam!), or giving less focused attention to activities. On top of that, they're attempting to time what otherwise would be leisure activities with greater precision. This doesn't lead to the experience of true leisure—rest, relaxation, regeneration, and renewal. Rather, it makes leisure much like everything else—moving too quickly, having too many stimuli, and ending too soon.

Forced-Fit Leisure Feels Phony

When the boundaries between and personal time blur, it creates the perception that you have no leisure at all. As I wrote in *Breathing Space*, if you attempt to force-fit leisure between periods of otherwise frenzied activity, your leisure is bound to suffer.

Most people cannot start and stop on a dime—they can't one minute be working hard and the next moment be totally engaged in some relaxing, rewarding activity. Human nature being what it is, we all tend to need some transition time.

Here is small sampling of what people are missing because they don't "have time":

- Sitting down for dinner as a family
- Making homemade dinners, baking bread
- Baking traditional holiday cookies, even with prepared dough
- Making gifts (and handmade Victorian valentines)
- Spending holidays together
- Sitting around with the family when it's not a holiday
- Relaxing and feeling at ease during family reunions
- Taking excursions together
- Going to church or temple (maintaining one's spiritual life)
- Going for a leisurely Sunday drive
- Attending cultural events (the opera or an exhibit at the nearby gallery)
- Dressing differently for different occasions
- Letting children be children (such as playing ball and not being rushed from one experience or activity to another)
- Putting children to bed with storybooks
- Reading the Bible or other religious books with your children
- Teaching with natural subjects, such as pond water and wild flowers
- Learning Mother's recipes
- Learning to play a musical instrument
- Sewing one's own clothes
- Writing letters
- Planting a garden and then eating or canning the produce
- Exercising or taking leisurely, relaxing strolls
- Relaxing at a spa
- Reading a literary novel or epic
- Maintaining etiquette
- Starting a hope chest for a daughter
- Courting

The Time Master Says

In 1986, 33 percent of Americans polled called leisure "important," compared to the results of a similar poll in 1997 wherein 57 percent called it important. In the same 1986 survey, 28 percent of Americans polled said that society needed to put more value on free time and stop emphasizing work. Eleven years later, that figure rose to 49 percent.

Transition Can Be Crucial

When the U.S. troops began returning from World War II, they were assembled in large numbers, consigned to ships, and, over several months, slowly sailed home. The time on board enabled them to reflect with one another, decompress, and mentally and emotionally prepare themselves for reintegration into civilian society.

When they returned, many were greeted by parades and celebrations. Not everyone had a smooth transition, but the probability of reintegrating into a peacetime existence was heightened because of the nature and duration of the transition time.

Conversely, U.S. troops departing from the Vietnam War came home one at a time. They came via jet planes that transported them in less than 24 hours from a hellish environment back to the world they had left. There was little or no transition time, no camaraderie with people who had shared a similar experience, and no time to mentally and emotionally prepare for re-entry into the civilian world. Most were not greeted as heroes or given celebrations. Consequently, Vietnam-era veterans had the most difficult time reintegrating into society of any class of American veterans.

You Need Slack, Jack

You're not returning from war, but the principle remains. When you build a little leeway into your schedule, you gain some psychic satisfaction that can't often otherwise be generated. As you get to know yourself better and better, you recognize that allowing somewhat generous time allocations for certain tasks is not going to turn you into a laggard.

Any time savings that you create through this method can be applied to other things that you want to get done. In other words, you'll be as efficient as before, but mentally you'll have aligned your day in a manner that enables you to feel less frustrated, more content, more energized, and ready for what's next.

The Time Master Says

Building slack into your schedule allows you to get back in touch with your own natural timing.

Personally, building slack into my schedule is as critical as anything. Having some time when nothing is scheduled—some whole days where it's not critical for me to do anything—is essential for my overall health and well-being. It helps me renew myself so that when I return to more vigorous pursuits, I have more internal resources at my command.

Nonspeed Zone Ahead

To handle challenging tasks under stringent time lines, sometimes you need to slow down a moment or two to get back in sync with your own rhythm, your own nature, and your own way of being. Hence, leisure gives you the ability to speed up when you need to.

Build in pockets of leisure here and there throughout the day and week to keep yourself in balance. For example, if you're scheduled to meet a friend at a restaurant at 7:00 P.M., arrive 10 minutes early and let yourself relax for those 10 minutes.

Preparing for Leisure?

The notion of preparing for leisure may seem a little foreign to you at first, but it makes sense.

The last time you took a big vacation, you marked it down on your calendar. You may have reserved airline tickets or hotel reservations. Undoubtedly you discussed the event with others in your family or with friends. You made plans, wrote notes, and spent money, all in preparation for this time away. Mentally and emotionally, you geared yourself to the reality that it was coming. The same process is advantageous when it comes to experiencing leisure on a daily basis.

A Pleasant Commute

Following World War II—through the 1950s as suburbs started to spring up—and during much of the 1960s, the commute at the end of the day reasonably provided the mental and emotional transition time vital to enjoying one's time at home. The roads weren't so crowded. You could get a seat on passenger trains or subways.

Soon commuting became a chore, then highly burdensome, then stressful—and now, for some, a prompt for outbreaks of rage and even violence. Today the commute for most people does not serve as a valid transition time between work and leisure. For many, it represents a daily ordeal. See Chapter 7, "What Matters Most to You?" for commuting tips.

Transforming Rather Than Arduous

Suppose you're stuck in a daily arduous commute. You hate it—every morning you crawl along at a snail's pace down that interstate highway that is nothing more than a moving parking lot. However long it takes you to arrive, you perceive that it's three times as long. How do you turn such an experience into more productive time, one in which you're prepared to actually have a life the rest of the day?

Reflect and Win

In his book *Your Body Doesn't Lie*, Dr. John Diamond reveals how classical music offers the right syncopation to get your body back into a more natural alignment. If you don't like classical music, put on something else that relaxes you.

Make sure that you condition your car: Use the time to check that your air-conditioner works, close all the windows, and then put on a cassette or CD that you truly enjoy.

Make the interior of the car or, if you use mass transit, the personal space around you as supportive as you can. For some, that means simply closing your eyes; for others it means donning earphones connected to a Walkman, for others it's reading, and for yet others it's staring out the window.

Boost Your Fun Potential

If you're committed to having more leisure in your life, initially you're going to have to be vigilant about it. It takes guts to buck the norm in a society of frenzied, exhausted overachievers. It's all too easy when immersed in such an environment to believe that's normal and acceptable.

Here, then, is your miniplan to effectively take time out for leisure—leisure that you want, need, and deserve.

Mark It on the Calendar and Make It Come

When you go on a big vacation, you mark it on the calendar and go through all kinds of supporting behaviors to ensure that you take off as scheduled. I'm suggesting that you treat lower-level leisure episodes—the week-to-week and daily kind of stuff—with the same vehemence.

Put low-level leisure time on your calendar:

- Look forward to it.
- Dwell on it.
- Talk about it.
- Make plans around it.
- Revel in it.

Once you treat leisure as an important component of your health and welfare, you won't have to be as vigilant. For now, make a commotion about it.

Leisure Counts

Leisure activities do not represent built-in excuses for you to cancel or reschedule them. You need to treat them with the same reverence that you presently exhibit with key prospect appointments or, heck, trips to the IRS auditor's office.

Occasionally compelling reasons arise as to why you need to change your schedule. So, every now and then, you can shuffle some items around on your calendar.

Get into It

When it's time for the leisure activity to commence, be there, experience it, and become immersed. Allow for this activity to be as important as any other. Let go of any left-brain, eyes-on the-clock, my-career-is-everything predisposition. If you're shooting baskets, shoot baskets. If you're hiking, hike. If you're meeting with the stamp club, meet with the stamp club.

If you find yourself wishing that you were someplace else or attempting to do other things than the leisure time you've scheduled, change your leisure activity; perhaps you've picked the wrong one. Don't, however, shortchange how much time you devote to leisure.

Be Gone, Guilt

Some people feel guilty when they work long hours because they feel that they should be with their kids, their friends, or someplace else. Conversely, they feel guilty when they're with their kids, friends, or someplace else because they feel that they should be working more.

In 1998, the Duracell Company's Ultra Battery division conducted a study to determine what people take with them on vacation.

Sun, Sea, Sand, and Electronic Leash

Cameras, CD players, camcorders	94%
Cell phones and beepers	38% (and rising sharply)
A notebook PC, palmtops, and electronic organizers	18%

When they take a vacation, they're overly concerned with what's going on back at the office. When they take a walk, they're too concerned about the voice mail and emails that might have come in while they were out. Precious reader, you will never experience leisure and its intended benefits if you feel anxious about what else you could or should be doing or what you're missing.

Time to Be Friendly

It's unfortunate, particularly for men, that as we age, we tend to have fewer good friends in life. Women seem to understand the need to make time for close friends at all ages.

Reflect and Win _____

Long-distance friendships may be hard to sustain, but creativity can keep them going. Whenever you're traveling for work, see if it's possible to create circular routes that include areas where your friends reside. Perhaps on your way back, you can stop off and see a good friend. If your friends are close by, all the better.

Many men need to work on it. Unquestionably, maintaining and cultivating friendships requires work and effort. The investment pays big dividends, however, because friendships enrich life.

Friends give you a support system beyond your family. They take you to places you've never been before or share insights with you that you wouldn't have seen on your own. Having good friends can even strengthen your marriage. If you're counting on your spouse to serve as the be-all and end-all, you're likely to be disappointed. Besides, depending on your interests, it might make more sense to go to the ball game or the opera with a friend than with your spouse.

How can you easily keep up with your friends—that is, ensure that they're in your path?

- Look for events in which you can include your friends when you normally wouldn't think of it.
- Plan vacations at the same time and destination.
- Join the same local group, cause, or activity.
- Establish a designated encounter each month, such as the last Friday.
- Introduce your spouses so that they will get to know each other better, therefore increasing the probability that you will see your friend more often.

Working to keep up these friendships will pay off in the long run with years of companionship. Is that worth a little of your time?

Getting Creative About Leisure

If you're single, your options for getting sufficient leisure abound. Depending on your work situation, you can take off at a moment's notice. You can take advantage of holiday weekends or perhaps go whole hog and explore the possibility of going on sabbatical (the topic of the next chapter). If you're married—and particularly with children—having leisure for yourself and having leisure for your family can be much more of a challenge.

The trend in America has been toward more frequent but shorter vacations, often boxed around holiday weekends. If you use the contrarian approach and take your time off when the rest of the world isn't, then holiday weekends are a good time to stay at home and let everybody else compete for highway lanes and parking spaces.

In my book _The Complete Idiot's Guide to Reaching Your Goals_, I list a wide variety of possible goals in various categories such as social, leisure, and lifetime goals. Here are some ideas on how to make the most of your leisure:

◆ Start a policy of receiving only magazines that either make your life simpler or amuse you.

◆ Book only one-flight, nonstop flights for vacation. Anything else taxes you in ways that you don't need to be taxed.

◆ Buy bubble bath today, even if you're not sure exactly when you'll use it.

◆ Install a hammock in your backyard. (See the advice about bubble bath.)

◆ Take on new friends who engage in leisure activities that you find very alluring and who will teach, guide, train, and include you in their activities.

◆ Open your home more frequently to others via parties, receptions, meetings, and brief visits.

◆ Find others in your town who like to play in ways that you like to play.

◆ Take frequent walks in shopping malls, along city sidewalks, down nature trails, and anyplace else you feel safe.

◆ Visit the library one evening a week, and read whatever magazines appeal to you. Join a monthly book review discussion group.

◆ Buy a joke book, learn some card tricks, practice impersonating others, or learn to juggle.

◆ Take an impromptu weekend trip to someplace you haven't visited.

◆ Consider taking up a sport that you've never attempted, such as golf, archery, hiking, or snorkeling. Or, take a class on crafts, be it wood, pottery, metals, ceramics, leather, stained glass, jewelry, or woodworking.

◆ Become an amateur geologist, going on your own "fossil" hunts. This could be as simple as finding rocks and breaking them open, or looking for petrified shark's teeth, troglodytes, or minerals embedded in stone.

◆ Buy a telescope and start watching the sky.

◆ Train a hamster, a gerbil, a cat, or a dog.

◆ Get on the committee that sponsors a festival, holiday parade, street fair, or exposition.

◆ Take a course in handwriting, calligraphy, or sketching.

◆ Visit one new restaurant a month—or, if the spirit moves you, once a week.

With your spouse or significant other, go to a restaurant much earlier than usual some evening, linger over drinks, linger over appetizers, linger over the entree, linger over dessert, and take your sweet time leaving as well. By the time you're out of there, the world will have changed. So will your attitude.

The Least You Need to Know

- Leisure means enjoying rewarding activity free from work and preoccupation with work.

- Recognize the value that transition time plays in improving the quality of your leisure.

- Do something bold (for you) to rediscover leisure, such as meditating or teaching a course in which you are already a master.

- Educational travel can change your perspective about the world; check it out.

- Linger long at dinner when you feel like it.

27

Sabbaticals: Why You Might Want to Take One

In This Chapter

◆ Taking some major time off now and then

◆ Making your vacation your employer's idea

◆ Surviving a sabbatical's early days

◆ How others handle it

Taking a sabbatical from work is not for everyone, nor is it practical for many people, although everyone could probably benefit. If every cell in your body rebels at the notion of taking a sabbatical—"Where could I ever find the time?" or "Who can afford it?"—then all the more reason for you to peruse this chapter.

A Time and a Purpose

The universe is governed by laws. Some laws are readily apparent, such as laws of cause and effect, laws of gravity, and the laws of motion. Somewhere in the big book of karmic order, it surely says that ever so rarely you need major time off. Forget all the logical explanations as to why this is all but impossible, and stay with me.

Live Long and Renew

Earlier chapters have discussed the likelihood of your living and working longer. The longer you work, the greater the odds are that you need time away from work. If the need for income, to watch over Michael and Michelle, or simply to feed Rover, were not issues, could you mentally and emotionally acknowledge that your inner and outer beings desperately crave a month or three months away from work?

One man from Sacramento remarked that it was about 15 days into his trip to the Andes Mountains before he actually realized how long he was going to be away. His 90-day sabbatical started with one week in a cabin in Wyoming with no TV and no phone. He promised himself at the outset that he wouldn't bring his notebook computer, so email was not available.

> **Reflect and Win**
>
> Even if you can't foresee the possibility now, hold on to your hat—there may be a sabbatical in your future.

> **Coming to Terms**
>
> **Restoration**, in the personal sense, is a conversion or return of something that was missing.

He did phone home every couple days to make sure that the place was still standing. Otherwise, this was to be a time of deep reflection, renewal, and *restoration* of the parts of him that he feared were all but lost.

Faculty members at colleges and universities have long been privy to the benefits of taking a semester-long sabbatical, with pay, every six to seven years. With a little planning and forethought, many university professionals extend their sabbaticals by taking a second semester off, usually without pay, hence racking up 8 to 12 months away from the ivory tower.

Programs Vary Widely

Corporate sabbaticals, the kind in which you're much more likely to be interested, vary widely. Most tend to be short. Three months would be a long time; two months or one month is more like it. They're also likely to be unpaid.

Examples of Programs

Sabbatical programs in companies certainly make for interesting reading. For example, Microsoft allows its vice presidents to award high-achieving employees with what is called the "Microsoft Achievement Award." This allows for up to eight weeks of paid vacation. Employees with seven years of tenure who are consistently high performers are eligible. One such Microsoft employee spent his time away behind a telescope and learned about astronomy. He also began hand drawing and took his father on a golfing trip.

Farther down the West coast, the Intel Corporation, an international computer chip producer, also allows full-time employees eight weeks of fully paid vacation every seven years.

Sticking with high-tech firms, Adobe systems offers a three-week paid sabbatical to employees after five years of tenure. The departing employee must give his or her manager 60 days' notice. This bonus is added to the employee's annual personal days of vacation.

Everyone Returns

One nationally renowned law firm grants its partners a whopping six-month paid sabbatical after five years as a partner, and again every six to seven years afterward. So far, all partners taking sabbaticals have returned—no one has taken a sabbatical and changed firms, changed his line of work, or, for that matter, retired.

For nonpartners, three months of paid time off are granted after 10 years of service and then every 7 years thereafter. So, stick around for 24 years and you get a total of nine months off. (I'm not sure if that's the world's greatest trade-off, though!)

Here are other examples of programs:

- Another law firm of high esteem offers its partners three months of paid time off every eight years.

- Goldman Sachs Group, investment bankers, has no formal sabbatical program, but employees are granted leave on a case-by-case basis.

- Morningstar, Inc., the renowned mutual-fund–tracking firm, offers a six-week paid sabbatical every four years for all employees. The driving notion is that the sabbatical regenerates and renews employees and is a viable antidote against burnout.

Some Compelling Reasons

Why would a company offer sabbaticals at all? Isn't it a hardship to have a key employee leave for months at a time? What if he is a member of a team?

Sabbaticals are provided as a recruiting tool to attract top talent, or as a reward to keep valued employees. Competition for talented employees in some industries is vigorous, and companies will do what they can to retain the best.

Easier Than Downsizing

Some companies use sabbaticals as a way to facilitate their downsizing plans. A senior public relations manager at AT&T commented that "AT&T expects that a number of

The Time Master Says

Some companies offer paid sabbaticals with the provision that the time off be used for some specific purpose, such as community service, learning, or travel.

The Time Master Says

Sabbaticals are an international phenomenon. In the United Kingdom, the number of organizations offering sabbaticals increased from 18 percent in 1990 to 25 percent in 1997, according to a survey by Hay Management Consultants. A study by the Institute of Personnel and Development found that 13 percent of employees are entitled to sabbatical leave, although much fewer take a sabbatical.

people will not return, a situation that would ease the need to downsize."

At AT&T, more than 1,500 employees have taken unpaid sabbaticals in the last six years—while still retaining other job benefits such as healthcare insurance—and leave with the promise of having their job when they return. A few don't return, but the vast majority do.

Bring New Skills Back to Workplace

Many companies believe that sabbaticals offer key employees a way to learn, grow, and ultimately be more valuable to the firm. Indeed, the probability of most people bettering themselves and bringing new skills and perspectives back to the workplace has proven to be a bonanza.

Endless Options

Often companies grant sabbaticals to employees who will be engaged in job-related study or research. A lesser number of companies grant them for employees simply seeking rest or vacation, and still a slightly lesser number grant them for non–job-related study.

Some firms maintain a policy of one week's extra leave for each year of service. So, if you've been working for someone for six years, you're entitled to a six-week sabbatical. More organizations realize that as the nature of work intensifies, and as the number of hours logged in by management staff increases, taking a break beyond annual vacation time benefits both employer and employee.

One worker returning from a sabbatical said that he hadn't previously taken a break during his professional career. When he returned to work, he had more confidence and energy, thus benefiting his company. Being away was refreshing and rejuvenating. "The sabbatical gave me a chance to take stock, put things in perspective, and be clearer about what I wanted out of life," he says.

Tempting the Techies

If you're a techie, your odds of taking a sabbatical are high. Silicon Valley companies such as Apple Computers and Intel—which compete fiercely for top talent, and where many employees devote their minds and bodies to the job effort—increasingly are offering sabbaticals as part of their bait.

Genentech, a biotechnology company in San Francisco, California, offers full-time employees a sabbatical of six continuous weeks with full pay and benefits beyond their annual vacation time, starting in their seventh year of employment. The head of human resources at Genentech observed, "The sabbatical program is one of several awards given to employees in acknowledgment of the high level of intensive work and commitment required at Genentech." In essence, in exchange for a high level of commitment, Genentech bestows the incentive of a more significant break than is typically offered.

> **Pause!**
>
> Most experts agree that sabbaticals should not be seen merely as time off to recover from a variety of stress-related maladies.

Your Mind in a Different Gear

One of the biggest benefits of a sabbatical is the basic acknowledgment that you're going to experience a long time away from the job. That, in itself, can result in favorable physiological and psychological benefits. If you know that six months from now you'll have three months off, you can plan your affairs accordingly and perhaps pace yourself for the six months as well.

You want to approach your time off on an even keel. Remember, the sabbatical is not for attempting to overcome extremely stressful job-related maladies. That needs to be taken care of while on the job.

> **Reflect and Win**
>
> Some employers fear having employees go on sabbaticals because they believe that employees will use that time to look for new jobs. Data doesn't bear this out. And if you and your employer always have the opportunity to engage in long-term thinking regarding what you'll do when you return, you can increase the probability of a smooth reconnection.

Eliminating Obstacles

On your way to believing that you, too, can take a sabbatical, you may need to overcome some mental obstacles. The common ones are having enough money, caring for kids, and making a smooth transition back. Let's mow 'em down in order.

Money Concerns?

The more time you have before a sabbatical, the more time you have to plan your finances accordingly. Your daily expenses when not working are actually far less than when working. You don't have the commute, the corporate lunch, the dry-cleaning costs, and a variety of other nickel-and-dime items that add up to many dollars in the course of a week.

You can wear more comfortable clothing—and wear it more often—eat less expensively (and probably eat more healthfully), and forego expenditures related to keeping up with the corporate Joneses. You can walk and bike instead of taking a car.

If you opt to travel during your sabbatical, consult a few traveler's guides from your local library and find inexpensive lodging all over the world. You can also join vacation club or home-swapping programs, and essentially pay nothing for long-distance lodging.

If you're going on a paid sabbatical, then you've got it made in the shade.

What to Do with the Kids?

If you have young children and you're their primary care provider, chances are good you can't take a traditional sabbatical. Or, maybe you can bring them along.

A sabbatical can be at home, although for most people the full benefits of "time away" would be missed.

If your children are a little older, perhaps there's a neighbor, relative, grandparent, or semiwilling spouse who'll grant you the month or two months that you need to get away from it all. Perhaps they'll do it in exchange for you doing the same for them some time. Maybe they'll do it for you out of the goodness of their hearts.

If you have no children, you have no excuse.

> **The Time Master Says**
>
> While it might be emotionally difficult to spend one month away from your children, it could be an enriching experience for everyone. You can stay in touch by phone and email. Your children will gain a different perspective on life without you around for the time you're taking off. They may actually appreciate, respect, and love you more upon your return! Wouldn't that be a triple bonus?

Will I Fall Behind My Colleagues?

Will a few months away put you behind when you finally step back into the office? In today's overinformation society, no one has a long-term lock on what's coming down the pike next. In many respects, the two months or so that you're away will be an advantage because of the newfound perspectives that you'll gain.

You can quickly catch up on the corporate memos and scuttlebutt. That'll take maybe half a day. A coworker can bring you up to speed on any new programs or procedures in a couple hours here and there, and this type of learning is likely to be more efficient than learning things on your own, had you been there all along.

Within one week of your being back, you likely won't feel as if you've missed out on anything. You're more likely to feel as if your time away was too brief, like a distant dream.

Go for It!

Here's a brief action plan to help you make leaving a reality. Review Chapter 1, "The Overtime Epidemic: How to Nip It in the Bud," where you learned the vital steps for ending work at a reasonable time at least one day per week and then escalating it to more than one day. Much of the same philosophy applies here.

Make It So

Adopt the notion that it can be done; you can take a month or two or longer away from work. Having done that, now pick the actual time. It's no good to have a vague date: "Someday" never comes. If you keep postponing the time when you'll take a sabbatical, chances are good that it will never happen. One obligation after another will creep up, and any windows of opportunity will shut.

Visit Internet sites offering insights and reflections on sabbaticals. Major search engines such as Yahoo!, Google, HotBot, and NLSearch offer many websites at your disposal. Visit Deja News to see what people are saying in the newsgroups about sabbaticals. You'll quickly gain insights that may improve the quality and nature of your sabbatical.

> **CAUTION**
>
> **Pause!**
>
> The likelihood of your taking a sabbatical is directly related to your ability to set a firm departure date, amass a tidy sum (if it's an unpaid sabbatical), and announce to all of significance in your life that it's going to happen. Otherwise, you're fooling yourself.

I'm Going to Do It!

Once you're firmly committed, here are the steps to make it happen:

1. When you've picked the date, mark it on your calendar. Then circulate a memo, email, or what have you to coworkers, staff, peers, and anyone else. Break the news to your family as well, if applicable.

2. Set up a savings plan with your employer, bank, or other financial institution so that a specific (and sufficient) amount will be extracted from your paycheck each week, in anticipation of building to a sum that will see you through.

Reflect and Win

Set up a system so that you can stay as informed as you need to be without diminishing the impact of what you want to accomplish during your sabbatical.

3. Secure with your employer that all benefits still accrue.

4. Talk with your boss about the plans that he has for you upon your return. Build in some slack time so that you can get up to speed without feeling overwhelmed on the day you come back. Print an actual memo in writing as to what your tasks and responsibilities will be that first week, for the second week, and thereafter. Then file it away in a place where it will be secure.

5. As the magic time approaches, send a reminder of your time away to all correspondents. Some require only an email. Some require an email and a postcard or a call. Some require everything.

6. Arrange with staff support, your family, and all others how you want messages to be fielded, mail to be allocated, and other correspondence to be handled in case you will not be directly privy to these communiqués on your sabbatical.

7. Plan a minicelebration, both at work and at home, on the day of or a few days before your actual sabbatical begins. This will give everyone a vivid message that you're departing for a while. Have everyone attend, and whoop it up so that everyone has the message clearly stamped in their brains that you are departing for the next two months.

8. Put your other affairs in order, in case something out of the ordinary happens to you during your time away. Update your will, pay bills in advance, and ensure that certain minimum sums are in various checking and savings accounts.

9. Install appropriate messages on your voice mail, answering machines, and email so that uninformed people who try to contact you aren't left thinking that you're ignoring them.

10. Identify what you need in terms of clothing and implements. If you'll be traveling, consolidate as much as you can. Use the smallest containers and lightest objects. If

you have a specific mission for your sabbatical, such as doing research or volunteering in some capacity, identify in advance as many of the supplies and other tools you'll need to facilitate your efforts. Make checklists, checking them once and checking them twice.

11. Get a complete health checkup so that you leave with a clean bill of health, or at least the cleanest bill of health that you can. Visit your eye doctor, your dentist, and any other doctor with whom it makes sense to have an appointment.

12. If you'll be traveling by car, take your car in for a complete tune-up.

The Sabbatical Begins

On that first day, when you don't head into work and your routine is different, you'll probably feel good. Over the next couple days, if you're at home, you may feel rested. You get to clean out the freezer, take care of the minor inconveniences that you let slide during the interim, and feel in command of your home.

If it's not a stay-at-home sabbatical—that is, if you're on the road—almost from the opening day, you'll experience what the stay-at-home types experience by about the sixth or seventh day: "My goodness, this really is different."

Here's a list of do's and don'ts to help you along during these first few impressionable days.

Do:

♦ Allow yourself to get extra sleep. Everyone needs some, so there's no use pretending that you don't. However, after a couple days, your need for extra sleep should diminish.

♦ Allow yourself to try new foods.

♦ Take a multivitamin every day.

♦ Be open and responsive to new viewpoints, ways of thinking, and ways of accomplishing things.

♦ Allow yourself to explore, wander, or simply do nothing.

♦ Feel free to keep a pen and pad or a pocket dictator nearby to capture whatever thoughts strike you.

♦ Allow yourself the opportunity to just be.

Don't:

♦ Fall into the trap of trying to make every day and every moment "productive."

♦ Let your exercise routine slide.

◆ Be concerned if you feel out of sorts, out of sync, or just plain out of it.

◆ Feel guilty about the work and people that you've left behind.

◆ Second-guess yourself about whether you should have taken the sabbatical. The benefits may not appear for a while, perhaps not until the sabbatical ends.

The Time Master Says

A survey conducted by the International Foundation of Employee Benefit Plans found that a third of all American companies will soon have sabbatical policies in place. The larger your organization is, the greater the probability is that some sabbatical policy is already in place. The terms may differ greatly from one organization to another, from as much as six months off with full pay in some organizations to an indefinite time off without pay in other organizations, so you won't know until you investigate.

How about you? Are you inspired to take control of your time in a way that a small but growing number of others is beginning to discover? Happy time off!

The Least You Need to Know

◆ You may live longer and work longer than you currently envision, hence the greater need for time away from work.

◆ Some companies offer sabbaticals as inducements when hiring top talent.

◆ Approach your time off on an even keel: The sabbatical isn't for overcoming stressful job-related illnesses.

◆ Sabbaticals come in many varieties, from educational travel, to working in another profession, to pursuing your hobbies, to doing nothing in particular.

◆ You may feel disoriented the first few days—and even weeks—once the sabbatical begins.

28

Keeping It All in Perspective

In This Chapter

- ◆ Twelve measures to help you live in real time
- ◆ Staying off the perpetually overwhelmed list
- ◆ What the gurus say
- ◆ Older and wiser and more in control of your time

How would your life be if you could tackle problems and challenges as they arise? What would it feel like to engage in conceptual thinking whenever you wanted or needed to? What would you feel like if you had a sense of control and ease about each day? The short answer: You would be living in real time. Handling phone calls as they come in and finishing the task at hand are small but worthwhile achievements, and these acts of living in real time are within your reach.

Examine the following 12 components of living in real time, with the realization that each of these is within your grasp:

1. Leave home in the morning with grace and ease. As you know from Chapter 14, "Becoming a Filing Wizard," you can manage the details beforehand. Take care of as many things as possible the night before so that in the morning you only have to get bodies out the door.

2. Focus on the important issues facing your organization, your department or division, and your job or career. As you learned in Chapter 7, "What Matters Most to You?" when you take care of the important things, the others fall into place.

3. Handle and deal with the day's mail upon arrival, keep piles from forming on your desk, and handle phone calls within 24 hours. No need to be inundated by the mail, and no piles accumulate on your desk; there's no snarl of phone calls to get back to.

4. Enjoy a leisurely lunch. You know the importance of completing tasks so that when you go to lunch, you're at lunch. You actually enjoy your lunch, digest your food better, do better back on the job, and have a vastly improved gastrointestinal outlook. Can you beat it?

5. Complete work at a reasonable time, and feel good about what you accomplish each day. This is straight from Chapter 1, "The Overtime Epidemic: How to Nip It in the Bud"; leaving the workday on time and feeling complete is the single most important step you can take toward permanently winning back your time.

6. Maintain sufficient and up-to-date health, life, disability, and automobile insurance coverage. If you want to live in real time, this is part of the overall picture.

7. File your annual (and any quarterly) income taxes on time. Recognize that taxes are a necessary evil and will always be levied. Set up a tax log at the start of each year with room for each legitimate deduction, where you can file receipts and documentation. Buy and use tax return software.

8. Take time to be with friends and relatives. People, not things, count most in this life.

9. Stay in shape and at your desired weight. Health and fitness experts say that working out for as little as 30 minutes a day four times a week can keep you comfortably fit. If you're too busy to stay in shape, you're too busy!

10. Make time for hobbies. Revisit that stamp collection, garden, hiking club, or whatever you let slide. Living in real time means enjoying your most rewarding hobbies and pastimes regularly.

11. Participate monthly in a worthy cause. When you pick the one or two that matter most to you and take action, you feel good about yourself and about how you're spending your time.

12. Drop back at any time, take a long deep breath, collect your thoughts, and renew your spirit.

Once you realize what it means to live in real time—and how far you've strayed from the mark—there are several things you can do today to begin to catch up (or at least this week). Many are deceptively simple, but don't let that obscure the powerful results that they offer.

Do You Have the Whip?

As I travel around the country speaking to organizations, I am struck by the number of people in my audiences who seem perpetually overwhelmed. The irony is that these people could take breaks throughout their days and weeks, but they don't. The biggest obstacle to winning back your time is the unwillingness to allow yourself a break.

I spoke to one group of executives and their spouses, and learned from many spouses that their executive husbands or wives simply do not allow themselves to take a break.

The Miracle Minute

Paradoxically, increasing evidence indicates that executives will be more effective if they pause for an extra minute a couple of times each day. This can be done every morning and afternoon—when returning from the water cooler or restroom, before leaving for lunch, or when returning from lunch. And that's just the short list.

To insist on proceeding full-speed through the day without allowing yourself 10 minutes to clear your mind all but guarantees that you'll be less effective than those who do. Even the people who already perceive this need do not let themselves meet it.

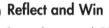

Reflect and Win

Seven hours and 50 minutes of work plus 10 one-minute intervals of rest or reflection in a workday make you more productive than do eight solid hours of work.

Clarity in Idle Moments

You'd think that entrepreneurs, running their own businesses and managing themselves, would be more inclined to take strategic pauses throughout the day—after all, they're in charge of their own schedules. Too often, it isn't necessarily so; the temptation to overwork can be ferocious. Conversely, if you work for others, perhaps a large organization, you may erroneously believe that pausing for the total of 10 strategic minutes throughout a workday could somehow jeopardize your standing. This misconception is unfounded.

Chuckling at Life

How many times do you actually let out a good laugh during the day, especially during the workday? Five-year-olds reportedly laugh 113 times a day, on average. However, 44-year-olds laugh only 11 times per day. Something happens between the ages of 5 and 44 to reduce the chuckle factor.

Once you reach retirement, fortunately, you tend to laugh again. The trick is to live and work at a comfortable pace and have a lot of laughs along the way—at every age. When you proceed through the workday without humor, the days tend to be long and difficult. Part of taking control of your life is being able to step back and look at the big picture, being able to see the lighter side of things. Some of your worst gaffes eventually evolve into the things that you pleasantly recall—or your best ideas! Pros who survive, laugh.

Reclaiming Your Time, Now and Later

The "Winning Back Your Time at Work" worksheet that follows includes nine activities: four at work, three after work, and two during vacation time. Each of these activities has a Lately, a Short-Term Goal, and a Long-Term Goal category. In the Lately column, enter how many times in the past month you have actually done each activity. In each Goal column, enter how many times you would like to, say, take a slow and leisurely lunch. In the Short-Term Goal category, for example, you could indicate two times per week.

Be realistic when recording what you have been doing. Be reflective in the short-term goal column, marking down what you can realistically achieve. Be visionary in the long-term goal column, marking down what you would ideally like to achieve.

Worksheet for Winning Back Your Time at Work: Today and Tomorrow

	Lately	Short-Term Goal	Long-Term Goal
Extra minute taken daily			
Leisurely lunches per week			
Hours per week in nonrush mode			
Full weekends you take off per month			
Days per month using alternate way home			
Days per month you have fun on the way home			
Days per month telecommuting from home			
3- or 4- day vacations you take annually			
Week-long vacations you take annually			

In the weeks and months ahead, review your chart weekly for reinforcement. You need to be taking breaks such as these throughout the day, week, and year. I don't know who else is going to tell you this, and I don't know how you're going to make yourself do it unless you systemize the procedure.

The Unproductive 80

You can pause more often when your day is not jam-packed. The Pareto Principle (the 80/20 rule) states that 80 percent of your activities contributes to only 20 percent of your results. The remaining 20 percent of your activities contributes to the other 80 percent of your results. Take a hardware store, for example: About 20 percent of its stock accounts for 80 percent of the revenues; the remaining 80 percent of the stock accounts for only 20 percent of the revenues.

The key to successful retailing is identifying the 20 percent producing the bulk of the revenues. A smart store manager knows to place that 20 percent where it's most accessible and to put the rest where it won't get in the way. As you learned in Chapter 7, you need to identify which activities at work (and in your personal life) support you and bring you the best results. Have the strength to abandon activities that don't benefit you—get rid of that unproductive 80 percent.

What the Gurus Say

Having made it this far in the book, you may wish to know what some authors have said about managing your time. Here is a brief summary of some of the longer-term surviving texts.

How to Get Control of Your Time and Your Life

This book by Alan Lakein is considered the classic in the field of time management. The information presented in this 1970 book is sound in that, even to this day, many can benefit from reading it. Lakein offers masterful tips for overcoming procrastination, and there is much worth knowing in this text. Lakein wrote his book, however, when the world population was a little more than half of what it is today. Understandably, he didn't address the changing structure of the family, including the problems of the two-career family and rearing children. Also, there is little coverage of the impact of technology on the use of time.

Acknowledging that today's readers require new approaches to managing more, Lakein recently came out with another book called *Give Me a Moment and I'll Change Your Life: Tools for Moment Management.* This book was designed to update the results-oriented approach of his earlier book and explains how to pay attention to moments as they come along and treat time as a limited resource.

First Things First: To Live, to Love, to Learn, to Leave a Legacy

First Things First, by Stephen R. Covey, Roger Merrill, and Rebecca Merrill, shows readers how to analyze their use of time and create a balance between their personal and professional responsibilities. This large book encourages readers to "put first things first" and act upon them. The authors teach an effective organizing process that helps the reader categorize tasks and focus on what is important, not merely what is urgent. The book presents profound insights, such as, "Doing more things faster is no substitute for doing the right things," and the real human needs are "to live, to love, to learn, to leave a legacy."

The quintessential advice is to first categorize your life in four quadrants labeled Urgent, Not Urgent, Important, and Unimportant. A task may have a deadline but not much importance, or a task may be important but may require preparation and planning. The authors say that you should stop doing what's unimportant and what lacks urgency. Instead, expend the majority of your energies where the important and the urgent intersect. Assuming that urgency announces itself, the real question is knowing what's important. The authors draw from a variety of sources to guide you toward determining the relative importance of tasks.

The Time Trap

This book by R. Alec MacKenzie was first published decades ago. It offers time tactics, interviews, and traditional time-management tools. Based on the theory that self-management is the key to handling time crunch, it focuses on the author's 20 biggest time wasters, such as telephone interruptions, the inability to say "no," and personal disorganization.

The sometimes laborious book offers instructions on how to combat such unnecessary distractions. It also includes information on time problems caused by technology, downsizing, and self-employment. The book's underlying premise is that readers can be taught "how to squeeze the optimal efficiency—and satisfaction—out of their workday."

Time Tactics of Very Successful People

Author Eugene Griessman presents often-cited time-management tips but then reaches beyond that and adds personal insights from well-known and successful people, including business leaders, Nobel laureates, and peak performers. This is a solid book on time strategies, although many cannot emulate some of the practices cited herein. If Ted Turner saves time by flying his own private aircraft, are you going to buy an airplane?

The time-management tactics from those who have achieved successful, balanced lives are presented in short "bites." These tips are designed to inspire today's time-starved readers—whether they're overworked managers, working moms, entrepreneurs on the go, or anyone in need of more time.

Take a Cue from Other Cultures

Some customs in societies throughout the world are well worth emulating when it comes to finding the time to relax:

- In France, it is the legendary two-hour lunch.
- In Latin countries, it is the midday siesta.
- In England, it is tea and crumpets at 4 P.M.
- In Japan, it is wearing only slippers once you come home.
- In the Aleutian Islands, it is carving ice sculptures.
- In Italy, it is having a candlelight dinner and being serenaded by musicians.
- In Australia, it is putting another shrimp on the "barbie."

And what about you? Can you withdraw from the maddening crowd? I'm talking having a life during your life, going whole weekends without doing anything, taking true vacations, and spending evenings sitting on the porch, as the late John Lennon said, "watching the wheels go round and round." These are not lost arts.

Here are suggestions for periodically abandoning the rat race, starting with small steps:

1. Give yourself permission to go a whole weekend without reading anything.

2. Put your home phone answering machine on Answer, flip the ringer off, and don't play back any messages until the next day.

3. Collect all the magazines piling up around your house, and give them away to a retirement community, library, or school.

4. Schedule that spa treatment you've been meaning to take.

5. Exchange photos with a friend you haven't seen in years.

6. Banish the beeper.

7. Get schedules of your favorite professional or amateur teams, and mark on your calendar the appropriate dates to sit back and enjoy the games.

8. Visit a botanical garden to enjoy the variety of flowers; let your sense of smell rather than your eyes and ears dominate.

> **CAUTION**
>
> **Pause!**
> Remember, when you force-fit leisure between barrages of constant frenzy, the quality of your leisure is going to suffer. For that matter, so are you.

9. Attend the graduation ceremonies of your local high school. Recapture the spirit of what it's like to complete an important passage in life.

10. Pick up a bouquet of fresh flowers at the grocery store or flower shop, and display it somewhere in your home.

11. Walk around your yard barefoot. Feel the grass between your toes. Stick your feet in dirt or in a puddle.

12. Visit a historical monument and let yourself become immersed in the challenges that people of that era faced.

13. Attend a free lecture some evening about a topic outside your professional interests.

14. Sleep late.

Hey, Now Is a Good Time

Marlee Matlin won the Academy Award for Best Actress at age 21; the late Jessica Tandy won it at age 80. The U.S. Constitution was written by men who were, on average, 40 years of age—when the life expectancy was barely 40. Sure, there were some old-timers like Ben Franklin, but most of the founding fathers were young by today's standards. Regardless of your age or how much time you have left in this life, anytime is a good time to practice measures for winning back your time. You may even find it rewarding to revel in your current age—it holds so much potential.

Reflect and Win

The key to accepting your age and your life is to realize that people shift into high gear at different times. It's hard to predict who's going to take off when.

James Michener didn't write his first novel until age 42. He produced one best-seller after another until his death at age 90.

Disappointed or Glad?

Alice Cornyn-Selby, a prolific author and speaker from Portland, Oregon, uses two powerful key phrases with her audiences:

1. "I have now come to the end of my life, and I'm disappointed that I didn't …."

   How did you finish that sentence? Whatever came up first is probably something that you want to do right away. No use putting it off any longer because it bubbled up to the surface immediately.

2. "I have now come to the end of my life, and I'm glad that I …." What did you derive this time? Was it the same issue that you addressed in the first statement? Was it something that you've already accomplished? When you begin to look at the

opportunities that await and those you can create, all the rushing about that came before and the times that you felt you were missing your life can begin to melt away as you head in the direction that will give you deep satisfaction.

The Rest Could Be the Best

Whether you're 20 or 80, or somewhere in between, start looking at your life as if the best years are yet to come, for indeed they can be. Sure, you'll get a little slower with each advancing year, but you have the ability to draw upon the wisdom that you've learned in each decade. Perhaps you'll be even more prudent with your time.

The Least You Need to Know

- Take time to be with and enjoy friends and relatives, and to re-engage in your hobbies.
- Devise a realistic action plan that ensures that you will master one of the important measures of living in real time. Then take on the rest.
- To reinforce your quest to maintain control of your time, peruse the works of others, or (least expensive and my favorite) keep rereading this book!
- You can choose to see the totality and completion of your life up to this minute, anytime you want.
- While you'll get older and slower, the best is yet to come because you'll be able to draw upon your wisdom to steer your life faithfully in the desired direction.

Glossary

contrarian   Somebody who opts to engage in activities at times and places when and where everybody else is not engaging in them.

cookie   An electronic marker that a website places on your hard drive so that if and when you revisit the website, your PC is electronically recognized and you may be directed toward website features that presumably lie within your area of interest.

dynamic bargain   An agreement you make with yourself to assess what you've accomplished (and what more you want to accomplish) from time to time throughout the day, adjusting to new conditions as they emerge.

ergonomics   The science that examines how devices should most smoothly blend with the human body and human activity.

Faustian bargains   Shady deals, named after the lead character in *Dr. Faustus*, by Christopher Marlow, who sold his eternal soul to the devil for a better time on Earth.

formulating   In the context of answering email, ensuring to the best of one's ability that the message is clear and accurate, and that it conveys precisely what the senders wishes to communicate.

hydration   When your body's tissues are sufficiently filled with water. To be dehydrated is to be parched.

insidious   Something that is treacherous.

leisure   Something that is worth your time and attention, or something that is worth doing. Enjoying rewarding activity free from work and preoccupation with work.

microsleep   A 5-to-10-second episode during which your brain is effectively asleep while you are otherwise up and about. Microsleep can occur while you are working at your PC or driving a car.

midnight   Originally halfway through the night because people went to sleep when it got dark around 7:00 or 8:00 P.M. and got up when it became light around 5:00 A.M.

netiquette   The combination of the words *net* and *etiquette*, to form a new word that means online etiquette.

opt-out capability   The ability of someone hit by spam to easily select to be removed from the spammer's list.

overchoice   The stress that comes from too many options, especially the "so-what?" variety.

piddling   Something that it is paltry, trivial, or inconsequential.

rapid eye movements (REM)   When sleeping, your eyes actually shift all over although your eyelids are closed; these movements and various levels of brain activity are essential to sound sleep.

restoration   A conversion or return of something that was missing, or to make whole again.

schlepping   A Yiddish word that means traveling or carrying a lot, as in "I had to schlep all the way to the store," and "He made me schlep all of his stuff."

seed work   Tasks that you can easily assign to someone else because the downside risk if that person botches the task is negligible.

self-storage unit   A for-rent, garage-like space that you can fill with any items that you don't need too often.

sound screen   An electronic device that creates a sound "barrier" that masks or mutes the effects of louder sound from beyond the barrier.

spate   A large number or amount.

stock message   A prepared email reply that you park in your templates, draft, or signature folder to reuse as the situation applies.

telecommuting   Working outside the office (away from your employer's base of operations) and staying in touch with coworkers via electronics, such as a computer, a fax, and a phone.

tickler files   A file system designed to give you a place to chronologically park items related to forthcoming issues and to remind you when you need to deal with such issues.

time cost   Also known as potential efficiency cost, this is the time that you lose by switching from one task to another.

triage   The practice of quickly examining a variety of items and allocating them based on what needs to be handled immediately, what can be handled later, and what can be ignored altogether.

white noise   A noninvasive, nondisruptive sound (much like that of rushing water, a fan, or distant motor noise).

Appendix **B**

Bibliography

Arnold, David, Ph.D., and Gail Rutman. *Business on the Internet: The Concise Handbook*. Eugene, OR: DA & Associates, 1999.

Bates, Jefferson D. *Dictating Effectively: A Time Saving Manual*. Washington, D.C.: Acropolis, 1981.

Biggs, Dick. *If Life Is a Balancing Act, Why Am I So Darn Clumsy?* Atlanta: Chattahoochee Press, 1993.

Cameron, Julia. *The Artist's Way*. Los Angeles: Tarcher, 1992.

Carr, David. *Time Narrative in History*. Bloomington, IN: Indiana University Press, 1986.

Cathcart, Jim. *The Acorn Principle*. New York: St. Martin's, 1999.

Choate, Pat. *Agents of Influence*. New York: Knopf, 1990.

Coleman, Dr. Paul W. *The Forgiving Marriage*. Chicago: Contemporary Books, 1990.

Connor, Richard, and Jeff Davidson. *Marketing Your Consulting & Professional Services, 3rd edition*. New York: John Wiley, 1997.

Covey, Stephen, et. al. *First Things First*. New York: Simon & Schuster, 1992.

Covey, Stephen. *The Seven Habits of Highly Effective Families*. Provo, UT: Franklin/Covey, 1997.

Csikszentmihalyi, Mihaly. *Flow: The Psychology of Optimal Experience.* New York: Harper, 1990.

Davidson, Jeff. *Breathing Space: Living and Working at a Comfortable Pace in a Sped-Up Society.* New York: MasterMedia, 1991.

———. *Marketing for the Home-Based Business, 2nd edition.* Avon, MA: Adams Media, 1999.

———. *Marketing Your Career and Yourself.* Avon, MA: Adams Media, 1999.

———. *The Complete Idiot's Guide to Assertiveness.* Indianapolis: Alpha Books, 1997.

———. *The Complete Idiot's Guide to Managing Stress, 2nd edition.* Indianapolis: Alpha Books, 1999.

———. *The Complete Idiot's Guide to Reaching Your Goals.* Indianapolis: Alpha Books, 1997.

———. *The Joy of Simple Living.* Emmaus, PA: Rodale, 1999.

Diamond, Dr. John. *Your Body Doesn't Lie: How to Increase Your Life Energy Through Behavioral Kinesiology.* New York: Warner, 1994.

Dement, William. *The Promise of Sleep.* New York: Delacort, 1999.

Dominguez, Joe, and Vicki Robin. *Your Money or Your Life.* New York: Viking, 1992.

Drucker, Peter. *The Effective Executive.* New York: Harper & Row, 1967.

Dychtwald, Ken, Ph.D. *Age Wave.* Los Angeles: Tarcher, 1989.

Faludi, Dr. Susan. *Backlash, The Undeclared War Against American Women.* New York: Anchor, 1992.

Farrell, Dr. Warren. *Why Men Are the Way They Are.* New York: McGraw-Hill, 1986.

Fisher, Jeffrey A., M.D. *RX 2000: Breakthroughs in Health, Medicine, and Longevity by the Year 2000 and Beyond.* New York: Simon & Schuster, 1994.

Friedan, Betty. *The Fountain of Age.* New York: Simon & Schuster, 1993.

Fritz, Robert. *The Path of Least Resistance.* New York: Fawcett Columbine, 1989.

Godfrey, N. *Money Doesn't Grow on Trees.* New York: Fireside Books, 1994.

Grant, Lindsey, ed. *Elephants in the Volkswagen.* New York: W. H. Freeman, 1991.

Griessman, Eugene. *Time Tactics of Very Successful People.* New York: McGraw-Hill, 1994.

Gross, Irma, and Mary Lewis. *Home Management.* 1938 (out of print).

Hampton Inns. *On the Road with Hampton.* Orlando, FL: Hampton Inns, 2000.

Jeffers, Susan. *Feel the Fear and Do It Anyway.* San Diego, CA: Harcourt, Brace & Jovanovich, 1987.

Johnson, Magic. *My Life*. New York: Random House, 1992.

Kanter, Rosabeth Moss. *The Change Masters*. New York: Simon & Schuster, 1983.

Kawasaki, Guy. *How to Drive the Competition Crazy*. New York: Hyperion, 1995.

Kobliner, B. *Get a Financial Life*. New York: Fireside Books, 1996.

Kostner, Dr. Jaclyn. *Virtual Leadership*. New York: Warner, 1996.

Kutner, Lawrence. *Your School-Age Child*. New York: Morrow, 1996.

Lakein, Alan. *Give Me a Moment and I'll Change Your Life: Tools for Moment Management*. Kansas City, MO: Andrews McMeel, 1997.

———. *How to Get Control of Your Time and Your Life*. New York: New American Library, 1973.

Lasn, Kalle. *Culture Jam: How to Reverse America's Suicidal Consumer Binge-And Why We Must*. New York: Morrow, 2000.

MacKenzie, R. Alec. *The Time Trap*. New York: AMACOM, 1997.

Moore-Ede, Martin, M.D., Ph.D. *The 24-Hour Society*. Reading, MA: Addison-Wesley, 1993.

Osborn, Carol. *Enough Is Enough*. New York: Putnam, 1986.

Peel, Kathy. *The Family Manager's Guide for Working Moms*. New York: Ballantine, 1997.

Peters, K. Joan. *When Mothers Work: Loving Our Children Without Sacrificing Our Selves*. Reading, MA: Addison-Wesley, 1997.

Postman, Neil, Ph.D. *Amusing Ourselves to Death*. New York: Viking, 1985.

———. *Technopoly*. New York: Knopf, 1992.

Proat, Frieda. *Creative Procrastination*. New York: Harper & Row, 1980.

Rifkin, Jeremy. *Time Wars*. New York: Henry Holt, 1987.

Rose, Kenneth. *The Organic Clock*. New York: Wiley, 1988.

Schor, Judith. *Consumerism*. New York: Basic Books, 1993.

Scott, Dru. *How to Put More Time in Your Life*. New York: Signet, 1980.

Sharp, Clifford. *The Economies of Time*. New York: Oxford, 1981.

Shenkman, Richard. *Legends, Lies, and Cherished Myths of American History*. New York: Morrow, 1989.

Smith, Marian. *In Today, Out Today*. Englewood Cliffs, NJ: Prentice Hall, 1982.

Stautberg, Susan S., and Marcia L. Worthing. *Balancing Act.* New York: Avon, 1992.

Swenson, Richard A. *Margin: Restoring Emotional, Physical, Financial, and Time Reserves to Overloaded Lives.* Colorado Springs, CO: Navpress, 1992.

Talley, Linda. *Business Finesse: Dealing with Sticky Situations in the Work Place for Managers.* Houston, TX: Leadership University Press, 1998.

Taylor, Frederic. *The Principles of Scientific Management.* New York: Harper & Row, 1911.

Thomas, Stanley. *The Millionaire Next Door.* Chicago: Dearborn, 1999.

Toffler, Alvin. *Future Shock.* New York: Random House, 1970.

Twitchell, James. *Carnival Culture.* New York: Columbia University Press, 1992.

Wagner, Ronald L., and Eric Engelmann. *The McGraw-Hill Internet Training Guide.* New York: McGraw-Hill, 1996.

Waitely, Denis. *Timing Is Everything.* New York: Pocket Books, 1993.

Wills, Christopher. *The Run Away Brain: The Evolution of Human Uniqueness.* New York: HarperCollins, 1993.

Index

Y-Z